From Love@AOL's Love Doctor

Dr. Kate's Love Secrets

Solving the mysteries of The Love Cycle

Dr. Kate Wachs

**PAPER
CHASE
PRESS**

New Orleans, LA

DR. KATE'S LOVE SECRETS
Solving the Mysteries of the Love Cycle
Copyright © 2000 Kate Wachs.

FIRST EDITION
ISBN: 1-879706-87-3
LC:99 080002

Cover Design: multifresh.com © 2000

This book is intended solely for educational information and not as medical advice. Please consult medical/health/mental health professional if you have questions or concerns about your health or psychological well being.

For my parents,

Charles and RoseAnn Wachs,

who taught me how to love and gave me their all, and in loving memory of

John M. Roraback, Ph.D.,

a magnificent thinker, innovator and dearest friend who, for 27 years, was always there for me at any hour of the day or night whenever I needed help with my relationship stages.
Thanks for passing through my life.

Acknowledgements

I have a lot of people to thank, and at the risk of sounding like the Academy Awards speeches, I'm going to get as many of them in here as possible! ;)

First, thanks to my clients and patients at The Relationship Center™, my *Love@AOL* Dr. Kate site readers, and my patients at Bay Medical Center, who have allowed me to learn through them and pass that knowledge on to you through this book. Thank you for trusting me with your problems and believing in my ability to help you. I have enjoyed you all and hope that I have given you something useful that you have used to enrich your lives. And thanks to all of you who encouraged me to write this information down, too!

To my loyal staff at The Relationship Center™ and especially Claude and Ed, thank you so much for working really hard so I could find the time to write this book. Your efforts and support are very much appreciated. Thanks also to my coworkers at *Love@AOL*, especially Bill Schreiner, its CEO of Love, who has been an absolute joy to work with for the past 3 years. Thanks also to Miguel Monteverde, who first hooked me up with *Love@AOL,* and to Matthew Meyers, Makis McDonald and Maria Monteverde for encouraging me both in my work for AOL and in the creation of this book. Thanks also to Diane, Sally, Heather and Kelly for assisting me with the Dr. Kate site on *Love@AOL,* which contributed the advice letters for this book, and to Diane Caesar for helping me catalogue the older letters. I've enjoyed being part of both of these teams, and a finer group of coworkers could never be found. I also thank *Love@AOL,* Steve Case and the upper management of America Online for allowing the advice and questionnaires I wrote for *Love@AOL* to be included.

Thanks also to the staff at Paper Chase Press, including Werner Reifling, for having the foresight to publish this book and for taking such a personal interest. Thanks also to Kristen, Jennifer, Kathleen and Bill for your editing and clerical help. Thanks also to Walter Perschke in Chicago, for reading the text, making suggestions and discussing everything with me at length on numerous occasions. I really appreciate all your time and effort.

It has been my privilege to know many special people over the past decades, including the professors who believed in me, encouraged me and went out of their way to make me feel special, including Dr. Carl Sipprelle, Dr. Joe Rook, Dr. Bill Cammin, Dr. Rulon Gibson, Dr. John Stumpf, Dr. Ted Balsam, Dr. Frank Leavitt, Dr. Maristella Goebel and all the selfless nuns who raised me academically. Too often, the people who inspire us are not properly thanked. So I want to tell you now that your example, wisdom and love have been exceptionally valuable and you are very much appreciated. Thank you.

I thank all my extended family, friends and supportive colleagues, including my friends at the American Psychological Association. Thanks especially to Dr. Fred Koenig, Dr. Lawrence Balter, Dr. Stuart Fischoff, Dr. Michael Broder and all the others in APA Division 46—Media Psychology, who taught me how to give psychology away through all forms of the media—including books, and enriched my life so much in the process.

Thanks especially to the hard-working members of the Public Affairs Department of APA, especially Pam Willenz and Doug Fizel. Thanks for encouraging me, for all your press efforts over the years and for our special camaraderie. Doug, I really miss you; your life was way too short. Thanks also to astute thinkers Margaret Durante and Lisa Wyatt for your enthusiasm, encouragement and valuable media advice and support.

I'd also like to thank my friends in the press, radio and TV media who regularly provide me with opportunities to give psychology away and help me see psychology through a different set of eyes.

I'd like to particularly thank my parents, Charles and RoseAnn Wachs, for showing me how to love, and for working so hard so that I could have the best in life. Thanks also for teaching me integrity and how to work my butt off for a good cause.

I'd like to thank my ex-husband, Donald, for showing me that marriage is even more wonderful than I had hoped and for giving me some of the very best days of my life so far. And finally, I'd like to thank my colleagues and very old and dear friends, Dr. John M. Roraback, Walter Perchske, Dr. Robert Beiter, Sigalit Zetouni, Sandra Otaka, Dr. Mythili Sundaresan, Judi Stein, Rick Karr, Dr. Tiffany Field, US Representative Jim Barcia, Pat Henaghan Inendino and Dr. Tom Burk for being there for me over the years through the various stages of my relationships. It has occurred to me that I have been exceptionally blessed with wonderful family and friends, and I thank you all from the bottom of my heart.

Kate M. Wachs, Ph.D.
Chicago, January, 2000

Contents

Stage 1 of The Love Cycle—
Finding love

Stage 2 of The Love Cycle—
*Making the
relationship work*

Stage 3 of The Love Cycle—
Letting go

Stage 4 of The Love Cycle—
Starting over

Appendices

Introduction

*A*riana was a young, successful, professional woman making her way in the world. Single and currently living with her boyfriend, she complained to her doctor about pain in her arm and fingers. He ran a series of tests, which all came back negative. Two days after he informed Ariana of the results, her pain suddenly disappeared.

Reviewing her history, the physician noted that she had previously experienced a number of strange symptoms, including problems swallowing, headaches, stomachaches, pain and numbness in other parts of her body and symptoms of a bladder infection. In each case, after a very comprehensive and complete workup, no pathology was found.

He ruled out medical problems and disease processes with appropriate testing and examination, and concluded that Ariana's problem must be due to some kind of psychological stress. So he sent her to me.

I conducted a thorough interview with the client, and found that each time she developed a symptom, she was upset about something in her relationship with her live-in boyfriend.

One day she reported to me that her arm went numb earlier that day. "And what else happened today?" I asked. "I had a fight with my boyfriend," she replied. This happened on several occasions, except that the physical symptoms would vary. As time went on, Ariana learned to acknowledge her psychological stresses—to bring them out in the open and resolve them. As she did, she experienced a corresponding decrease in physical symptoms.

Cases like this are not at all unusual. In my years at the medical center, I saw many people who developed psychophysiological symptoms because they simply had no one to talk to. Some people were single and living alone. Others were married or coupled, but living alone from an emotional standpoint. When they shared their feelings with their partner, they didn't receive emotional support, so they held their feelings in instead until they became physically ill.

Relationships are vitally important in human life

And that's how I learned how important relationships really are in human life. Most of us dump a lot of stress by talking with our friends and family about our problems. If you don't have someone to talk to—because you're single and living alone or because you're fighting with your spouse or significant other, you are much more likely to feel stressed out, keep it bottled up inside, and develop some kind of stress-related problem.

A matchmaker-psychologist is born

So how did I help these people? I did a lot of hypnosis to help patients leave the hospital sooner. But once they were discharged, I started to tackle the main problem: their relationships and/or lack thereof. I saw the couples for marital and family therapy, to help them communicate and resolve their differences, so they could once again be good companions to each other. And for the singles who had no one to talk to because they were single, I helped them look for ways they could meet a significant other.

At that time, there was really nothing available in the area except a singles dance held every other Sunday night in a church basement. There were no personal ads, no introduction services, no activities for singles—nothing.

So I sent my single clients to the dance, and decided that as a single person, I had to get out of town. I moved back to Chicago and looked around, and was surprised that while there were some introduction services then, none were run by a psychologist. Pretty amazing, I thought. In order to do this well, you would have to do a thorough interview, rule out people with serious psychopathology, provide backup when needed, and certainly a background in marital therapy would be helpful for matching people. And what about the matching? I knew that predicting the behavior of one person was extremely difficult, so predicting the behavior of two people and an interaction—which is what it would be if you matched them together—would be more like a guess than a prediction. But I decided that I could probably do it a whole lot better than someone without my training in psychology. And so I became the first psychologist-matchmaker in the US. To my knowledge, I remain the only psychologist-matchmaker in the US to this day.

The Relationship Center™ helps people find and fix relationships

My practice became The Relationship Center™ in Chicago. As part of the center, we have an introduction service, where I match people for the purpose of finding someone compatible and getting married. I also write personal ads for people and help them meet others that way, and the center sponsors parties, socials, book signings and other activities for singles. I also see singles and marrieds for psychological testing and counseling.

A client might be tested to learn more about her personality, then review her relationships in therapy, identify her problem behaviors and learn how to change them, then join the introduction service, find a spouse and get married. Years later, when they had stress in their relationship, the couple might both come in for a few sessions to learn how to be better partners to one another. In short, The Relationship Center™ is a place where someone can come to find help for all their relationship needs.

Over the past decades, I have consulted with thousands of singles, introducing them to other people and helping them develop healthy relationships. I have coached clients through relationships, guiding them through flirting, dating and commitment to happy marriages. I have also helped hundreds of couples fix their relationships to make them more fulfilling.

Love@AOL

In 1994, I approached AOL about an idea I had to collaborate with them. After many meetings and discussions, I ended up becoming the Psychologist/Relationship Expert for *Love@AOL*, the popular romance area on America Online. There, on my site (AOL Keyword: Dr. Kate), members can write me letters, take the compatibility and communication quizzes, and use a search engine to access thousands of responses I have written on dating, sex, marriage, online relationships, cheating, breaking up, divorce, surviving the death of a spouse and starting all over again.

I was amazed at the quality and quantity of the letters I received at AOL. I have received several hundred thousand letters to date, almost all of them from really nice, sincere people asking me to help them with their relationships. I was very impressed, both with the genuine, sincere and appreciative people who wrote, as well as AOL's ability to reach them with such amazing efficiency. I had found an avenue for giving psychology away at lightning speed! I was able to help many people, and I loved and still love every minute of it. I am very proud of my association with AOL.

Psychologists' view of relationships

Most people get their ideas about life and love by reviewing their life and the lives of their friends. They're also influenced by what they read, what they see on TV and film, and what they hear in music. But that's a very limited database.

When someone consults a psychologist for therapy, the psychologist accesses his database—which includes the relationships of anywhere from a few to hundreds of clients. The psychologist has a bigger database in his head, and can better advise the client from a broader, wiser view.

My unique view of relationships: creating and fixing them

When I advise a client, I pull from the database of the hundreds of couples I have seen for couples therapy, just as other psychologists do. However, I also draw on the thousands of people I have worked with in the introduction service, as well as the hundreds of thousands who have now written to me at *Love@AOL*. I literally have a database of several hundred thousand relationships in my head.

Most psychologists learn a great deal from their therapy clients, developing a feel for what works in relationships and what doesn't. However, I feel I've had a distinct advantage. I've not only worked on the fix it end, helping people repair their relationships; I've also been intimately involved in the creating end, helping people find and create the love they want. When I advise clients, I'm drawing on this unique view of relationships, the big picture perspective I've gained by helping people actually make relationships, as well as helping them fix them.

Along the way, I've passed on what I've learned through the media. I've written several magazine columns and hosted my own Dr. Kate radio show for WGN, answering questions on a wide variety of relationship issues. Now I pass the knowledge on through the *Love@AOL* Dr. Kate site.

How this book was born

As the number of letters in the Dr. Kate database mounted rapidly, it occurred to me that: 1) There are a lot of people out there who are confused about relationships and need help fast; 2) Many of those people probably don't have computers, and those who do could still use a way to learn about relationships when they're away from their computer.

It reminded me of the clients who used to say, "This is great stuff, Dr. Kate. Have you written it down anywhere? Do you have a book?" And so, this book was born. I had seen how important relationships were to people, and how sick they could become without someone to talk with to share their joys and everyday problems. I had noticed how little people knew about relationships—even though they are so important to human life. I had experienced how much people really want to learn.

It's important to grasp the big picture

In addition, I had also noticed a strange phenomenon—that many people became very upset when they reached a crinkle in their life that they didn't like. It might be a 26-year-old breaking up with her live-in boyfriend, someone getting divorced or someone whose spouse had just died. Or it might be a single person who was beginning to lose hope because she couldn't find anyone compatible.

People tended to be very nearsighted, as though there would be no tomorrow. They didn't grasp the big picture. They lost hope. They mourned and grieved, which was natural, but they also seemed to act as though the situation would never improve.

And that's when I realized that because of my unique work, I had gained a big picture perspective of life and relationships that most people never get. Having worked the creating and fixing end with so many people in various stages of their lives had given me a much broader, and I believed, clearer perspective, of how relationships really work. I had seen that everyone goes in and out of relationship stages during their lifetime.

First, we try to find love; then we try to make it last. Then if things go badly, we have to let go—experiencing a breakup, divorce or the death of a spouse. And then eventually, we heal and start all over again. We traverse relationship stages at different speeds, and how many times we cycle through varies from person to person, but the fact remains that anyone who ever starts dating goes through relationship stages. Even someone who is happily married all her life started out as a single person, and if her spouse dies first, will be single again in the future.

Everyone goes in and out of relationship stages during their lifetime. It's important to see the big picture.

Knowing that life is basically a **Love Cycle**—a series of relationship stages that we go in and out of—can make all the difference in the world in how you view any stage you're in when you're there. If you like the stage you're in—let's say you're happily married, then you'd better make it a priority and work on it, so it will last as long as possible. And if you don't like the stage you're in, knowing that it's time-limited can help. You'll see the light at the end of the tunnel and feel hopeful and more energetic. And that will help you think better, so you can do the work to get out of this stage and move on to the stage you'd prefer to be in.

And that, in a nutshell, is how this book came to be.

The goal of this book

The goal of this book is to help you be happy in whatever relationship stage you find yourself. If you like that stage, this book will help you get the most out of it and make it last as long as possible. And if you don't like that stage, this book will help you progress to a different stage when you feel ready.

I'll take you inside The Relationship Center™ and teach you the secrets I've learned over the years about dating, mating, marriage and how to survive cheating, breaking up, divorce and death, while remaining happy through it all. I will also teach you how to move from one relationship stage to the next with the least pain and the greatest happiness.

I'll share with you my perspective of how people behave in relationships, drawing on my dating and therapy population, as well as the letters I have received at **Love@AOL**, and my various other columns and radio and TV shows.

No one has ever written about the stages of relationships over The Love Cycle before. Yet from dating to mating to marriage through difficulties like infidelity, breaking up, divorce and death, The Love Cycle continues, and we are always in a relationship stage that is part of it. And understanding that simple principle can mean the difference between being happy and content with where you are in life to being miserable, depressed and unable to take constructive action.

The Love Cycle

This book is divided into sections that follow the relationship stages of The Love Cycle. For example, *Stage 1 of The Love Cycle—Finding Love* is covered in Chapters 1-5. In that section, we'll talk about the relationship stages you go through when trying to find love and make a permanent, committed relationship with someone, and I'll share with you the secrets to finding love. In Chapter 1, you'll Get Grounded and learn more about The Love Cycle and its relationship stages. We'll clear up some common myths about soulmates and love. In Chapter 2, you'll learn about Flirting and Dating, and how to take the first step toward making a relationship. Chapter 3 is all about Compatibility; we'll discuss common misperceptions about compatibility, and I'll share with you the important things to look for when seeking a compatible life partner. In Chapter 4, we'll talk about Sex In The Early Stages Of A Relationship, and how to avoid common mistakes.

Stage 2 of The Love Cycle—Making The Relationship Work includes Chapters 5-9. In this section, I'll share with you my secrets for nurturing your relationship. For example, *Chapter 5* explores *Making A Commitment* to someone, and when it's good to live with someone versus when it's not. In *Chapter 6*, I'll share the secrets of *Happiness & Relationships* with you, and teach you how to be happy, no matter what relationship stage you're in. In *Chapter 7—Communication*, we'll discuss the differences in how men and women communicate, and secrets of effective communication. I'll teach you some wonderful techniques you can use to make your communication the best it can be. In *Chapter 8,* we'll talk about *Sex In A Long-Term Relationship*—how to keep the fires burning your entire life. In *Chapter 9,* we'll talk about *Marriage—Taking The Big Step.* We'll talk about when you're ready for marriage and when you're not. We'll shed some light on common myths that make people unhappy in marriage, and show you how to make your marriage the best it can be. I'll also give you tips on how to put the spark back into your relationship.

Stage 3 of The Love Cycle—Letting Go includes Chapters 10 and 11. In that section, I'll share with you the secrets for letting go with the least amount of pain possible. For example, in *Chapter 10,* we'll discuss how to know when you're on rocky ground, and *What To Do When Your Relationship Is In Trouble.* In *Chapter 11,* we'll talk about *Loss & Letting Go*—when and how to let go. We'll discuss how to handle a breakup, divorce or the death of a spouse, and I'll teach you some valuable techniques you can use to shorten the time you spend in this painful stage.

Stage 4 of The Love Cycle—Starting Over includes *Chapter 12,* where we'll discuss how to get ready to move on, and how to tell when you're ready to begin looking for love again. I'll share the secrets of starting over with you, and teach you how to find hope to live and love again.

In the **Appendix,** you'll find a handy group of questionnaires, including the *Rate Your Date IQ Quiz, The Dr. Kate Compatibility Quiz* and *The Dr. Kate Communication Quiz.* As you read various chapters of the book, you'll be asked to use these questionnaires and the information you glean from them in different ways to learn about your relationship patterns and make improvements when needed.

For your convenience, I've also included in the Appendix several very important techniques which are mentioned throughout the book: *Thought-Stopping, The Dr. Kate Quick & Dirty Grieving Technique, How To Invite Your Mate To Counseling* and *Counseling Options.* That way, whenever I mention these techniques in the book or AOL Letters, you'll be able to find them easily.

In addition, the Appendix includes short articles about *How To Choose A Dating Service* and *How To Date Through The Personal Ads.* In the back of the book, there's a coupon that you can redeem on my next book, *Sex Secrets! Dr. Kate's Guide to Sumptuous Sex.* There's also another coupon you can use to obtain a discount on a Dr. Kate Relationship Seminar when I come to your area. To inquire about upcoming seminars in your area, call 1-800-460-8604.

Get the most out of this book

You can sit down and read this entire book cover to cover, and you might want to do that to get a broad overview. But then return to the chapter that corresponds to where you are in The Love Cycle and really concentrate on learning that material. Take the appropriate quiz, and learn how your behavior and thoughts are helping or not helping you progress; read the **Love@AOL** letters and do the exercises. If you're not happy with the stage you're in, read the chapter that corresponds to where you'd like to be. Take the quizzes, read the letters and do the exercises for that chapter, too.

Keep a Relationship Notebook, where you'll write all your responses to the exercises, as well as any other thoughts and ideas you have about relationships in general and yours in particular. That way, the information will be organized on paper, making it easier for you to organize your thoughts and feelings about relationships as well.

I am reminded of a client who came to my office for therapy. He was very excited that he had just read an amazing self-help book. "Great!" I said. "What did you learn?" Long pause. "Well, I learned...I mean, I learned...Well, it was just a really good book."

"NOT!," I say. If you can't tell me what you've learned from a book, then you are highly unlikely to use it to make your life better. In order to change something you're doing to make your life happier and more productive, you essentially have to do three things:

1. Remember what it is that you want to change;
2. Remember what you're going to do to change it; and
3. Do it.

If you can't remember what you're supposed to do to change your life, how can you possibly DO it?

And now the fine print

This book is for people who are ready and able to move on with their lives—to put ideas into action and try to make their life more fulfilling and happy. It is not a substitute for therapy and should not be used in that fashion. In fact, as you read on, you'll see that I often recommend therapy when people need more intense, focused care.

If you read this book and find that you are simply unable to get up the energy to fix your life in the ways I have recommended, even though it badly needs fixing, then please, by all means, see a psychologist for therapy. You may be able to use this book as an adjunct to therapy—to help you organize your thoughts and feelings to better discuss them with your psychologist. If you're not sure if this book is for you, ask your psychologist.

One quick word about style: Being a big believer in equal rights, I understand the idea that literature should be genderblind. However this presents a problem when trying to write straightforward, direct prose that is easy to read and remember. After enough "s/he's" and "him/her's," even I find material difficult to digest! For this reason, I will use "he" and "she" whenever I feel a scenario is more likely to apply to a man or woman respectively. When there is no specific gender that is more likely to occur than another, I will use the word "she." Why? Because my guess is that more women than men are going to read this book. And that those men who do read this book will be enlightened enough to enjoy the change of pace of "she" rather than "he!"

I hope that you will find this book entertaining and informative, useful and pragmatic. I have tried to give you down-to-earth, practical methods you can use to look at your relationships and make them better, techniques you can immediately apply to your life to help you live more joyously. This book contains my observations and opinions. If you should find that anything really doesn't fit you, it's OK not to follow it. However, before you cast it aside, make sure that it really doesn't fit. Remember that we all try not to look at our behaviors sometimes, but sometimes looking at them is actually better for us.

If you find that my words and techniques have benefited you, I'd love to hear your story. You can write to me care of my publisher, Paper Chase Press, or email me at ***relationshipctr@aol.com.*** I regret that due to all my responsibilities, I probably can't reply to you personally. However, if I think others might benefit from your experience, I might just publish your letter in an upcoming book! Now, let the journey begin!

Kate M. Wachs, Ph.D.
Chicago, January, 2000

Stage 1 of The Love Cycle—

Finding love

Chapter 1

Getting grounded
The Love Cycle—understanding life's relationship stages

Nicole is a 32-year-old professional woman. She put off serious dating until after she completed her medical degree and settled in Chicago. She is now happily dating and hopes to meet a compatible partner, fall in love, marry and start a family.

Chris and Dennis have been happily married for 10 years. They met, fell in love, married, had three children and are still very much in love. Chris and Dennis both work, but life is centered around family, friends and church.

Suzanne is a 68-year-old woman who has been married for 50 years. Her husband starting cheating on her shortly after they were first married, and has had many mistresses over the years. Suzanne and her husband have been separated for 10 years. Now that her children are grown, with children of their own, Suzanne is finally coming to terms with the fact that her husband is never coming back to a married life with her. She will have to file for divorce, then work on starting over as a single woman at age 68.

Caryn and Scott were married to each other, the second marriage for both. Both have two children, but Scott's are grown and living on their own, while Caryn's are young and still living at home. Caryn and Scott love each other very much and have a passionate sex life. But they have trouble communicating when they disagree. They fight with as much passion as they make love. Life together has been a series of chaotic ups and downs. After divorcing their first spouses for one another, they married, but they fought so much, they ended up getting divorced. Yet they still love one another, so they got back together and are now trying to work out their problems.

What do all of these people have in common? They are all in different relationship stages. They are also all past or present clients of The Relationship Center™ in Chicago.

Nicole is single, never married and dating; she's in the introduction service. She's looking forward to moving from the Finding Love Stage to the Married Stage.

Chris and Dennis are previous clients of the introduction service. They happily traversed the Finding Love Stage and entered the Married Stage. They have worked out their problems and continue to do so, every day of their relationship. They have careers, but they appreciate what they have together, and focus most of their energy on each other and their kids.

Suzanne is in the Letting Go stage. She's completed the therapy to be sure that she is making a healthy decision by divorcing her husband. She has explored her marriage in depth and learned what she could from it. She is now in the process of divorce. Eventually, when she feels ready, she will begin to start over and date, perhaps eventually finding a more compatible mate. In the meantime, she surrounds herself with positive friends and family, work and outside interests. Realizing that she will probably have more feelings about her life as the divorce moves forward, she takes it a day at a time, and tries to keep herself centered and balanced.

Caryn and Scott have been through many relationship stages together, from Dating to Marriage to Divorce and Starting Over. They are in therapy, learning to communicate better, so that they can traverse back to a happily married life together.

Nicole, Chris, Dennis, Suzanne, Caryn and Scott have all been through various relationship stages before. They are currently in a certain relationship stage, but how they handle it and what they do in this stage will determine how long the stage lasts, and whether or not they end up living most of their life in the relationship stage of their choice. They have put a lot of effort into learning about their relationships, how they got to this point, and how to make their relationships work so their future will be the best it can be.

The Love Cycle—understanding life's relationship stages

Do you understand the role of relationships in your life? A lot of people don't, and their misperceptions lead to unhealthy habits and overall unhappiness. So let's first get grounded with one of the most important love secrets:

> *Most of us go through a series of relationship stages during our lifetime.*

Does that surprise you? "Wait a minute," you may be saying, "I've gone through one relationship after the other, and my experiences don't have anything to do with *stages*, just rotten choices and bad luck."

That's what relationships look like to most people, but until you begin to see the patterns, you can't see the whole quilt.

Just like Nicole, Chris, Dennis, Suzanne, Caryn and Scott, most of us go through a series of stages, from dating, sex and commitment/marriage, to divorce and starting over. Along the way, we suffer through cheating, breaking up and making up. Even if you are fortunate enough to stay happily married to one person your entire life, you were still single once—and you may be single again if you outlive your spouse.

So it's absolutely imperative to see life as a series of relationship stages. No matter what relationship stage you find yourself in at the moment, you've got to look at the big picture.

> *It's important to see life as a series of relationship stages. Always look at the big picture.*

Why is it important to view life this way?

Because if you don't like the stage you're in now (alone, breaking up, cheating, divorcing), you'll feel better knowing that it is time-limited. The stage you're in doesn't have to last forever, and knowing that can help you tolerate the discomfort. If you can focus on the big picture and understand that it's normal to go through relationship stages, you're also less likely to feel stigmatized or desperate when you find yourself in the midst of a breakup or divorce.

Instead, you'll be able to act wisely to shorten your discomfort and move on quickly to a better stage. You'll understand that when you are ready, you can start over and find someone more compatible—someone you will love who will also love you back.

What if you're happy with your love life? Then realizing that you are in a relationship stage should help you value it more, cherish it and use the techniques and methods in this book to help it last as long as possible.

The goal of this book is to help you be happy in whatever relationship stage you find yourself—and if you don't want to stay in that stage, to help you progress when you feel ready.

Life doesn't always work out according to plan

Although you can control the way you look at relationships, you can't always control relationship stages. Popular, high-profile NBC broadcaster Katie Couric, 42, knows all about that. In January, 1998, Couric lost her 42-year-old husband to colon cancer. By all accounts, she and her husband had been close and loving. They expected to grow old together.

Ekaterina Gordeeva was only 24 years old when she lost her husband and fellow Olympic gold medal ice skating partner, Sergei Grinkov, in November, 1995. Grinkov was 28 when he suddenly died of heart failure while skating during a practice session. He was Gordeeva's teenage love, husband, skating partner and father of their daughter Daria.

Sudden tragedy strikes not only the famous, but the rest of us as well. John, a 51-year-old psychologist, died suddenly of a heart attack while telling his wife a funny story over breakfast. While John knew he had asthma, he never considered himself to be seriously ill. John and Nancy had just married each other 3 months earlier. They were elated that they had found one another and expected to stay happy and together for many decades to come. They certainly never expected to have it all end so soon over coffee and bagels on what started out as a normal day.

Danny had never been seriously ill in his life. He was trim and although he smoked a little, thought he was in great shape. One hot summer day, he suddenly keeled over from a massive heart attack while mowing his lawn. His wife, Shari, could not revive him. He was 44.

So even if you have a good marriage, you can't guarantee how long it will last. As in all these cases, your marriage may end due to circumstances beyond your control. Then you will be in another relationship stage—Starting Over—whether you like it or not.

But sudden death isn't the only external force that can split up a happy, committed relationship. Sometimes couples make unfortunate choices that lead to divorce. One very common scenario is the married couple who works hard to achieve a mutual goal, only to lose the marriage in the process. Couples set some kind of material goal—a bigger house, sending the children to college—and then put all their effort into achieving the goal. Caught up in the process, they don't realize that the time they're spending away from home is taking a toll on their marriage in the present. Eventually, either one spouse tires of being lonely and wants a divorce or the couple grows apart until they just don't know each other very well. They didn't take time to work on the marriage itself, so it disintegrated; they were too busy working on their material goals for the future. They took their marriage for granted, and lost it as a result.

When a relationship ends due to death or divorce, it is very stressful. Stress accompanies any major life change, but if you didn't see the divorce or death coming, the emotional shock just intensifies your distress. You didn't expect this. You thought this marriage would be forever. You thought your life was stable. You expected to grow old together with your favorite companion. All of a sudden, nothing is the way you thought it would be. Besides losing your best friend and partner, you have lost your dreams and expectations. Shock is worse than stress. It makes the situation even more difficult to bear, and it can be emotionally and physically debilitating. It can cause your immune system, which protects you from serious disease, to malfunction, causing serious medical problems.

Understanding life as a series of relationship stages can minimize or totally eliminate the shock you feel when life doesn't work out the way you had envisioned. It can help reduce the stress you feel when you move to a new stage. If you are aware that your life is a series of relationship stages, you can appreciate what you have while you have it and work to keep it that way. But when life doesn't go the way you'd like, you're also better equipped to handle it. You knew you would be single again after your marriage; you just didn't know when that point would come.

If you look at life as a series of relationship stages, you'll appreciate what you have while you have it and handle it better when life doesn't work out the way you want.

Where did your attitudes come from?

Before you can truly understand life as a series of relationship stages, it's important to understand how you developed your ideas about relationships, including any misperceptions you might hold about life and love.

None of us was born with an owner's manual, and for thousands of years we have tried to figure out what makes us tick and how to live more productively. We've come a long way from the days when people felt bumps on the skull and drilled holes to let the evil spirits out, but we still have a long way to go.

Unfortunately, most people aren't taught anything about relationships in grammar school—or any school for that matter. Instead, they develop their early ideas about relationships from watching their parents. Since most of us come from "dysfunctional" families, we also pick up a lot of bad habits along the way. Compounding that problem are the ideas we develop about romance from movies, TV, novels and songs. Because those stories and lyrics are written to sell, not necessarily to reflect reality, we learn many erroneous myths and generally strange ideas about how life and love are supposed to work.

We learn to play house when we're little, and our parents read us fairy tales—Sleeping Beauty, Snow White and Cinderella. Most women have been raised on the fairy tale myth of Prince Charming. He comes to save us, to take us away on a big white horse, and somehow we end up in a beautiful house, complete with loving spouse and angelic kids, living happily ever after. Because these fairy tales end at the marriage altar, we learn that love is supposed to work like magic.

We also talk to our friends about our relationships and compare notes. As a result, our ideas about love are likely to reflect some combination of parent and family influence, pop culture, our own relationships and those of our friends. But that's a very limited, and often erroneous, database to pull from, and we can end up believing in unfortunate myths and unrealistic expectations.

The being in love myth

Because of this hodgepodge of erroneous input, many people feel that *being in love* is preferable to *loving someone*. In truth, what many people think of "being in love" is usually a stage in a relationship–the infatuation/excitement phase, where you feel very excited about your partner.

> *What many people think of as "being in love" is actually the infatuation stage in a relationship— a time when you feel very excited about your partner.*

You actually experience a physiological change—your adrenaline is surging and your endorphins are firing. Endorphins are neurotransmitters in the brain that give off opiate-like substances that make you feel happy, excited, on top of the world. You are energized, but may have trouble concentrating. This **excitement or infatuation stage** occurs when you first meet someone and are powerfully attracted. If you are also doing some heavy-duty lusting, you are sexually stimulated as well, and can find yourself consumed by romantic and sexual fantasies about this person.

Physiologically, excitement and anxiety are both the same. Your adrenaline rushes, your muscles tighten, and your blood goes to your brain and internal organs—it's the fight-or-flight response. Subjectively, it feels different to us, but physiologically, it is the same.

Part of what keeps the relationship so exciting in the early days is that it's new. Anything new is usually more exciting than something you're accustomed to. You don't know your partner yet and every meeting leads to new discoveries—some positive, some negative. You don't know if you can trust your partner yet. You don't know if you'll end up loving one another or if the whole thing will suddenly end. You could lose the relationship at any point; the more you get involved, the more you risk.

As time goes on, if your relationship lasts, you begin to trust that your partner will be there for you tomorrow. As you begin to feel more comfortable, the anxiety of the early days tapers off. So the relationship gets a little more stable, a little less nerve-wracking, and a little less exciting at the same time. It's a normal, healthy trade-off.

The nesting stage

Eventually, if the relationship lasts, you enter the next stage, where your brain produces a "nesting" chemical called oxytocin. This stage is cuddly, comfortable and more gentle, and although it's a very pleasant feeling, it's much less exciting than the infatuation/excitement phase. It's how people feel when they "love" someone.

> *Just as life is a series of relationships, relationships themselves have stages. Both the infatuation ("in love") stage and the nesting ("loving") stage are important.*

So just as life is a series of relationships, relationships themselves have stages. Both the infatuation stage and the nesting stage are important. But many people confuse the being-in-love/infatuation stage with real love. Infatuation is certainly a wonderful feeling. It may lead to love and often does. But problems arise when you can't settle into the next stage and enjoy its unique qualities, or when you view the loss of that heady excitement as evidence that you have fallen out of love.

Moving to a more comfortable, less exciting stage is the natural evolution of a relationship—not the death of it. The only kind of relationship that sustains that early excitement is one in which you don't trust your partner and can't depend on him to be there. In this type of unhealthy coupling, you essentially stay in the excitement stage for an extended period, but at a terrible personal cost.

So understanding the *stages of individual relationships* is just as important as understanding the *relationship stages* that you will experience throughout your life. Erin had to learn both.

Erin's Story

Erin, 26, found herself in a precarious situation one weekend. She had attended the World's Largest Office Party in Chicago, traditionally a drunken fest held in the weeks preceding Christmas, with the proceeds going to charity. Many young single professionals flock to the party right after work and spend several hours drinking, dancing and meeting comely members of the opposite sex. Erin had attended the party before. But this time, Erin had more than usual to drink. The next morning, she woke up next to a guy she had never met before and did not recognize. She realized that she did not remember much that had happened the night before.

Concerned, Erin came to see me to talk about her behavior and her romantic relationships. As we reviewed her relationships, Erin realized that she had a pattern of being attracted to someone for about three months. Then the glow would fade, and she would find enough wrong with him that she would not want to continue the relationship. Before long, she'd find someone else she would become enamored with and repeated the same pattern.

Erin was addicted to the infatuation stage of the relationship—the first three months when her endorphins were firing, her adrenaline was surging and she was in the excitement mode of the relationship. Part of what made that stage so exciting for her was not knowing when it would end. She liked what she saw about her current lover and hoped that what she didn't see would also be good. But as time went on and Erin got to know her lover in different situations, dating him three to four times a week for three to four months, she picked up other information little by little.

Some of that information was what she wanted, but some wasn't. When enough information she didn't like finally crossed threshold into her awareness, Erin would suddenly pop out of her dreamlike state and realize that she was in love with someone, but it wasn't this man. It was the man she had hoped he would be.

Erin was too eager to put someone into the lover role in her life. She unconsciously overlooked problems and warning signs that this man might not work out, and instead threw herself into every relationship that initially seemed attractive. Then three months into the relationship, when she finally let herself see some of his less-attractive qualities, she just lost interest and moved on. She wasn't willing to go into the oxytocin stage—the nesting stage. She wanted the incredible excitement phase and the high it brought with it. She was addicted to infatuation.

To break this unhealthy pattern, Erin needed to explore why she was so addicted to the rush of infatuation. She needed to realize that unless she changed her behavior, every relationship she entered would eventually fail, because no healthy relationship can sustain that rush. Rather than moving from one relationship to another in search of eternal infatuation, Erin needed to learn to appreciate the cuddly warmth and security of the nesting stage of the relationship.

The soulmate myth

How many times have you heard that there is one right person out there for you, your soulmate? Perhaps you've found yourself thinking, "If I can just find him, everything will be perfect!"

This myth causes people a lot of grief. After all, if you actually believe this myth, you may as well give up! If there's only one person out there for you in the entire world, how can you ever find him? What if he's not in your town, not even in your country, but in some place you'd never even think of visiting?

I have talked to many lonely and confused people who can't make up their minds about marrying a particular person. What holds them back from experiencing the happiness of a committed relationship? The fear that the next person they meet might happen to be their soulmate. Not only does this destructive myth prevent marriages, it also breaks them up.

I receive hundreds of letters from people who decide within days of meeting someone new that they have finally found their true soulmate. On occasion, infatuated people desert their current mate and loved ones and travel halfway across the country to be with their soulmate—someone they've only met online!

In fact, there's no such thing as your one, intended soulmate. You're not limited to one specific person who's out there somewhere waiting to be found. The bottom line is that there are many compatible partners for you and for everyone—people you can love, live with and be happy with. The story will just be a little different with each person. One partner might be more fun, but less responsible. Another partner might be very responsible, but need help loosening up. You can connect in many different ways with many different people.

So if you're hanging onto the soulmate myth, now's the time to let it go. There are many people out there that you can be happy with, and you should be able to locate one of them. Then with hard work and a lot of sustained effort, the two of you can create a happy, healthy relationship together.

Why are we attracted to certain types of people?

Even though each of us has many potentially compatible partners out there, finding one can be difficult if you routinely choose people who are bad for you. We human beings are comfortable with what we're used to, even if it's not good for us.

If you have a pattern of choosing unsuitable partners, don't trust your feelings or your heart alone. Your head has to tell you that the relationship is good for you, and you can see that from looking at the effect it's having on your life.

In my private practice, I have treated many women who are chronically attracted to abusive men. I have received even more *Love@AOL* letters on this topic. Women are surprised to find that they break up with one abusive man only to go right back into another abusive relationship. "Why am I attracted to these men?" these women ask me. "And how am I attracting them?"

When you are chronically attracted to a type of person who isn't good for you, look at your family history. In particular, take a close look at your relationship with your opposite-sex parent. For women, does this man remind you of your father? For men, does this woman remind you of your mother?

We are comfortable with what we grew up with, even if it's not good for us. If you feel a strong hook to someone who isn't good for you, chances are you are reliving events from your past. Matt is a good example.

Matt's Story

Matt's mother was a professional woman and socialite. She was well-respected in the community, but never did much with her son. She got her strokes from the outside world, so she focused most of her attention there. She never wanted to be a housewife or mother and resented being put into that role. As a result, Matt always felt he had to compete for her attention with strangers. He was never very successful at it.

When he grew up, Matt became enormously attracted to Bianca, a woman who never gave him what he consciously wanted—a secure, stable relationship. She would manipulate him, get him coming to her, give him some positive reinforcement, then cut him off and accuse him of being too clingy. Their relationship went on like this for years. At times, Bianca would frustrate Matt by being involved with other men, but he still hung on, feeling complimented that she kept in touch with him even while she was carrying on with another lover. When those relationships ended and Matt and Bianca tried to renew their relationship, the woman would invite him places, then ignore him while she socialized with her friends.

Matt and Bianca were locked in an extremely unhealthy relationship. Matt worked desperately hard for Bianca's attention and approval, and she let him think he was going to get it. She gave him some minimal attention and approval to keep him interested, then yanked it back, leaving him desperate, but even more addicted to her.

Matt was attracted to Bianca because she reminded him of his mother. He wanted to have a close relationship with Bianca because he could never have one with his mother. But the Catch 22 was that the reason Matt was so hooked into Bianca and wanted the relationship so much was because Bianca, like his mother, would never let him have it. So once again, Matt repeated his unhealthy, but well-known and comfortable-in-a-sick-sort-of-way, lifelong behavioral pattern—never getting what he wanted from a woman.

Matt needed to work through his addiction and get off his relationship hamster wheel. He needed to avoid women like Bianca, who would only frustrate him. Instead, Matt needed to learn to appreciate a woman who would give him a healthy, satisfying relationship—a woman who would give him the companionship and love he was seeking.

If you find yourself caught in a destructive relationship pattern like Matt, then you, too, should consider therapy. A psychologist can help you identify your unhealthy relationship pattern and teach you how to stop making the same relationship mistakes over and over and over again.

Set your goal—make The Love Cycle work for you

Now that you know about The Love Cycle and its relationship stages, the stages of loving within a particular relationship, and the problems caused by unhealthy patterns and expectations, it's time to learn another secret:

> *The happiest people are those involved in happy relationships.*

Although this secret may seem more like common sense than any big mystery, it's important to remember it and use it for motivation when you need it. If you've been dating without success for a long time and are ready to give up, reminding yourself of this secret can help you stay focused and motivated. Studies show that happily married people are the happiest. Next in line are happy singles. And the most unhappy people of all are the unhappily married.

> *The happiest people of all are the happily married, followed by happy singles. The most unhappy people of all are the unhappily married.*

Are you in the relationship stage you want to be in? If so, learn how to stay in that stage. Don't take it for granted. Realize that you are in a relationship stage, and it can end sooner than later. Appreciate where you are and what you have and do the work to help it last as long as possible. Learn the techniques in this book and use them to maximize your opportunities.

> *If you like your current relationship stage, do the work to stay in it.*
> *If you don't like it, do the work to get to another stage of your choice.*

If you're not happy with your current relationship stage, learn how to progress. Start by doing the following exercise to learn about your past relationships. Be sure to read *Chapter 3—Compatibility*, as well as the chapter that corresponds to the relationship stage you'd like to be in. Apply the relationship secrets you learn from this book, and before long, you should be able to move into the relationship stage of your choice. Bon Voyage!

Exercise: Plot your relationship history

As you work through his book, I'm going to ask you to do a number of exercises. Start by getting a sturdy notebook or setting up a file in your computer that will become your Relationship Notebook. If you have thoughts or questions about anything you read, write them down in the notebook. Whenever you do an exercise, write it in your notebook. Some of the exercises will build on each other, including exercises from previous chapters. So writing everything in your notebook will help you stay organized and maximize what you learn. You'll be able to remember ideas better because they will be organized better on paper and in your head.

You can learn a lot from your past relationships. For each relationship you've had, ask yourself the following questions:

- 💜 How old were you when you started dating this person?
- 💜 How did you meet?
- 💜 What did you like about the relationship?
- 💜 What did you like about your partner?
- 💜 What didn't you like about your partner?
- 💜 How long were you together?
- 💜 Why did you break up?
- 💜 Did your partner remind you of anyone in your family?
- 💜 Did your partner remind you of anyone else you have dated?
- 💜 How long were you alone between that partner and the next one?

Write down your responses to each question. Review the answers when you're finished. Do you notice any patterns? What are they? What steps will you take to change your relationship pattern?

For example, let's say you learn that your relationships frequently break up because you date men you meet in bars, who then end up being alcoholics. An obvious place to start changing your life would be to stop going to bars to meet men! Instead, read **Chapter 2—Flirting & Dating**, to discover better ways to meet compatible partners.

Or perhaps you find that you always fall in love with people, only to have them leave you. And you're not really sure what happens. Then read **Chapter 3—Compatibility** and **Chapter 7—Communication**. Were you really compatible with those partners, or did you just think you were because you wanted so desperately to be? Was your communication faulty such that the two of you could not get along, no matter how much you cared for one another? Be sure to take the quizzes for those chapters and follow the suggestions at the end to help you break your pattern.

For each unhealthy pattern you find, brainstorm ways that you can change it. Write those ideas down in your notebook. Remember to start by reading any relevant chapters in this book. Take the quizzes in the Appendix and follow the recommendations listed at the end. In addition, check out my site on AOL (AOL Keyword: Dr. Kate). Use the search function to find more articles I have written about your problem. You can also read the books listed in the Recommended Reading section in the Appendix for more help. If your problem is serious and needs professional care, and especially, if you try to fix your own pattern and can't, then consult a psychologist for more in-depth exploration and treatment.

Remember, it's your life. If you don't want to be in the relationship stage you're in, do the work to get into another, more satisfying relationship stage. If you like where you're at, do the work to stay there for as long as possible.

Chapter 2

Flirting & dating
Taking the first step

Shortly after I opened The Relationship Center™, a woman offered me $5,000 if I could get her married—provided she didn't have to date beforehand. "I'll give you $5,000—heck, I'd be willing to give you $10,000—if you can just get me married without me having to date!"

Most people are not THAT opposed to dating, but you could say that dating is a bit of an acquired skill.

No matter what your views on dating, help is here. Whether you're a novice at dating, someone learning to date again after a long marriage or time off, or a veteran just looking to spruce up your dating skills, you'll find information you can use in this chapter. First, take the **Discover Your Date IQ Quiz** in the Appendix. After you take this objective look at your dating skills, return to this chapter for some dating secrets and tested methods for making your dates enjoyable and productive.

Let go of your misconceptions
There are several dating myths circulating today that cause people grief. Let's start by questioning those misconceptions and changing them for more positive and realistic ideas.

Dates don't magically appear
Some people think that they shouldn't really look for anyone, because when the time is right, they'll just meet the right person. This myth says that the fabulous person you've been dreaming about will show up when you least expect it and aren't looking. Closely related to the prince-on-white-horse and white house/picket fence fairy tales, this fantasy has been problematic for a lot of people. If you believe this myth, chances are good that you will stay single forever.

People who tell you this myth are either: A) Well-meaning mothers and fathers who met their mates in high school or college; B) People who are suspicious of change in general; C) Hopeless romantics who don't have much grasp on reality; or D) People who don't want you to find someone because they haven't and misery loves company. (Keep in mind that people in category D have followed their own advice, so if anything, you might consider doing the opposite!)

In general, be wary of any advice you get from well-meaning relatives and friends. Their opinions may be based on their dating experiences of 50 years ago and their own myths and daydreams, seasoned by sensationalized stories they've read or seen on TV about people victimizing others through various dating methods. Besides, these people are very different from you. What worked well for them—or didn't work at all—may be totally different from what would or would not work for you.

So in general, don't believe anyone when they tell you not to really look for someone because he's just going to appear when the time is right. On the other hand, if you tend to be too intense about dating, or if you've been looking too hard and are feeling discouraged, then repeating this myth to yourself at times may be useful. But never use this myth to justify dropping out and waiting for life to happen to you. It is far better to be proactive in your dating life, not *reactive*.

What about dating friends?

The same people who tell you that a dreamboat will drop out of the sky may also tell you that you should never ask a good friend out or it will ruin the relationship. This statement is too exaggerated to be true.

If you and your friend are both reasonably healthy and mature, with good self-esteem, and especially if you have known each other at least a year or more, dating should not hurt your relationship. If you ask your friend out and the romantic relationship doesn't work, there isn't any reason why you can't go back to being good friends again. You care a great deal about each other, and just because you don't find each other compatible in the romance/sexual arena doesn't mean that those other areas of compatibility have disappeared.

On the other hand, if one of you is easily embarrassed, self-conscious, has low self-esteem or is otherwise ill-equipped to deal with a possible romantic rejection, even though your friend accepts you on so many other levels, then you should not date each other.

What about dating people at work?

There are plenty of places to look for compatible people, but work isn't one of them.

Work relationships involve too many potential complications. Changes in any large company or institution are largely outside your control, so even if you choose someone who is equal in status to you now, a promotion or company reorganization could suddenly make that person your boss or vice versa. You should never date a student or someone you are supervising in any capacity, as people will assume that you can't be objective when evaluating that person's performance.

Then there's the problem of gossip. Even if you're careful to choose dates from different departments, you may be chagrined later to find that two of your former or present dates are now working together and possibly chatting about you! People in the workplace love to gossip, so it's difficult to mix your new love with the office staff at Christmas parties, company picnics and other gatherings. To have any privacy, you would basically have to hide your relationship, which makes it rather like dating a married person, doesn't it? Not much fun for either party.

But the biggest potential complication of all is that if the relationship doesn't work out, it can be very difficult to get over someone you have to work with every day. If that person isn't a good sport and just happens to become your boss, your professional life can become seriously problematic.

And just in case those reasons aren't enough to keep you from dating at work, consider this: When you date a coworker, you will probably end up talking shop on your date. And what's fun about that?

What about meeting people through "natural ways?"

The same people who tell you that Prince Charming will suddenly turn up on your front porch are likely to emphasize the importance of meeting people through "natural" methods.

But think about it—what does meeting someone "naturally" really mean? If the Romeo of your dreams rings your doorbell out of the blue, call *Sightings*. If he's wearing armor and riding a big white horse, call the psych unit of the nearest hospital and report him missing. If he bumps into you on the street, be careful. He could be a good guy, or he could be a psychopathic maniac. Are you sure he hasn't just been standing there all day, trying to pick people up? After all, if you ask enough women passing by, one of them will eventually say, "OK."

I recall a married man asking me why people needed introduction services. Why couldn't they just meet each other the "natural way?" I asked him how he had met his wife. He told me that he used to hang around the Emergency Room of the local hospital and talk to the nurses and other hospital personnel. Of course, he had done this 30 years ago! I reassured him that his tried and true method of 30 years ago would be a bomb today. Instead of meeting comely nurses, he would probably get thrown out by security!

The fact remains that after high school and college, there is really **NO** good way of just bumping into people who are mostly all single and have time to talk. Even in graduate school, students are often married and far too busy to interact with other students. While you can certainly be open to meeting people spontaneously in a safe neighborhood or environment, it is hardly a method to be relied upon.

How to meet people

So if your perfect date isn't going to drop out of the sky, may not be one of your good friends, can't be a coworker and probably won't *naturally* end up on your front porch, how *are* you supposed to find a date?

There are many different ways to meet people. The method you use should depend on how old you are, what relationship stage you are in, which stage you'd like to be in and when you'd like to get there.

For example, if you are single, never-married, age 28+, emotionally mature and ready to settle down, then you're in the Dating Stage, and trying to get to the Married Stage as soon as possible. It's best if you use a method that can find you potential marriage candidates in the most efficient manner possible, e.g., a quality introduction service or online or offline personal ads.

On the other hand, if you are just recently divorced and in the Starting Over Stage, those methods would probably be too intense for you. You need to just get out and socialize a bit, so developing a new hobby or joining a new group might be just what you need. It isn't important for you to meet people of the opposite sex just yet, as you are not ready for a new relationship. As you heal, you can change what you do to meet people, choosing activities that are more likely to include compatible members of the opposite sex who are also single. When you are finally finished healing and are ready to handle more active dating, then you, too, can use the most efficient methods—a quality introduction service or the online or offline personal ads.

Similarly, if you are not emotionally mature, not ready to settle down or too young for a dating service, then singles dances, community and university activities or sports might be just your ticket.

Here's an overview of the various methods available, and who might best use them.

Introduction/dating services

Introduction services have been around for many years now, and in my opinion, reputable introduction services are the most efficient methods for meeting a compatible mate. When you use an introduction service, you can target the kind of person you want to meet. In particular, you should tell the interviewer that you want someone who also desires your relationship goal (marriage or marriage and children). You can also describe the personality qualities and other characteristics of people you would like to meet. Depending on the procedures of the service, the interviewer then tries to select matches for you based on those criteria, or in a library-type service, you look through profiles of available candidates and select your own based on your criteria. If possible, choose a service that offers feedback after the dates. That way, if something doesn't work out, you gain some kind of insight into the reason. You may then be able to use that information to make future dates more successful.

Unfortunately, some people have heard the myth that dating services are for losers. In reality, nothing could be further from the truth. People who use quality introduction services are often more goal-oriented and proactive. They see a need to change their personal lives, to find more compatible people to date, so they take action.

Usually, people who take such a practical, goal-oriented and organized approach to their social lives are just as practical, goal-oriented and organized about the rest of their lives as well. So on the whole, members tend to be very successful. They tend to have more money than time. It makes sense for them to have someone else interview potential candidates and act as an intermediary, to save time and effort in finding compatible partners. That way, they can devote what time they do have to meeting the person and developing a relationship.

Services vary in their methods, stated goal and price. Introduction services that cater to people who would like to find a marriage partner tend to attract women over 27. So if you are a younger male, you might want to try online or offline personal ads instead. However, if you are a younger female (23+), you should have no problem finding a compatible partner at a reputable introduction service. Dating services that emphasize dating for the sake of dating and feature organized activities for their members would be more appropriate for younger people or those who are not ready to marry yet, but who want to meet quality people who have passed some kind of screening interview.

Conversely, marriage-minded men over the age of 40 tend to be in high demand at most introduction services. Women over 40 (and especially women over 50) do need to be careful, however. It's important to select a service that has enough members of an appropriate age for you. Before you join, ask how many men they have in your age range who would also like to meet you. Then of those who can accommodate you, pick the one that feels most comfortable.

One quick word about price: The most expensive services are not necessarily the best, but the cheapest services are usually not worth much.

For more information, as well as questions to ask before joining a service, see **How To Choose A Dating Service** in the Appendix.

Personal ads, online and off

Personal ads have also proliferated over the past 20 years. You can find them everywhere—on the Internet or offline in daily and weekly newspapers, and in special newspapers printed just for people looking for people. My site on AOL (Keyword: Dr. Kate) is located within **Love@AOL** (Keyword: **Love@AOL**), which hosts the largest collection of online personal ads placed by people all over the country. Called the **Love@AOL** Photo Personals, they allow you to browse or search for certain keywords to find someone who shares certain qualities, goals or interests. You can use *Keyword: Personals* if you subscribe to AOL, or you can find them on the web at http://www.love.com.

If you are in the Dating Stage and hoping to move into the Marriage Stage soon, I highly recommend that you limit your interactions to people who are single, emotionally available, living in your geographic area (no more than an hour drive), and who also desire marriage or marriage and children. Avoid those asking for a casual relationship. The **Love@AOL** Photo Personals allow you to search for these characteristics, along with others. Offline ads usually make some kind of reference to relationship goals. Use your head, and if you want marriage, avoid ads that talk about "looking for summer fun!"

But are personal ads dangerous? The answer is not usually—no more dangerous than dating someone you meet at a singles dance. In reality, most people who use online or offline personal ads are actually quite pleasant. The myth that the personals are dangerous is too exaggerated to be true. While there have been occasional news stories about a misfit using the personals or the online experience to hurt someone, you wouldn't call a car or plane dangerous and advocate a return to covered wagons just because there are occasional car or plane wrecks. In contrast, just as the recent movie *You've Got Mail* portrayed, many interesting, well-adjusted, attractive and successful people use the personals and chat online to meet others for healthy relationships.

But just as you need to learn automobile rules of the road to make driving a healthy experience, following certain guidelines can greatly enhance your enjoyment and safety when using personal ads. See **How To Date Through The Personal Ads,** located in the Appendix. In addition, I recommend using a community service like AOL rather than other online or offline ads. You can spend more time chatting with someone before talking on the phone or meeting them, and if you have a problem with a member harassing you online, you can report it to AOL's Member Services. Plus AOL has records of its members (a paper trail), whereas the Internet does not.

If you are a poor judge of people, you should not use personal ads of any kind, online or off. On the other hand, if you are pretty good at reading people, personal ads can be a good adjunct or an alternative to a dating/introduction service, particularly if you have more time than money. Just remember to limit yourself to people who are single, emotionally available, living in your geographic area (preferably within one hour of driving time), who also share your relationship goal (marriage or marriage and children).

In today's day and age, personal ads and introduction services constitute the easiest, most cost-effective and efficient methods of meeting someone.

Meeting through friends

Meeting through friends is fine, **if** you have a lot of friends with great people judgment, who also have large quantities of single, emotionally available and emotionally healthy people of the opposite sex.

Most of the time, meeting potential dates through friends isn't an option because your friends are married, teach grade-school kids or just don't have an appropriate pool of compatible matches for you. And even if you do score the occasional date through a friend, you may run into problems. If you and your date don't work out, you may bump into him again at parties thrown by your matchmaker friend. In addition, sometimes well-meaning friends feel hurt when you don't like their romantic choices for you.

There's certainly nothing wrong with trying an occasional date through your friends. But relying on this as a method of meeting people would prove highly frustrating for most people.

Singles groups, dances and other activities specifically for singles

In most cities, there are many singles groups, singles dances and other activities organized specifically for single people. You can certainly meet appropriate mates this way; it just takes longer, since the method is much less direct. At any event, you may meet three to five people, and you have no way of knowing that those are the most compatible three to five people attending the event. In all probability, they aren't. In addition, once you have dated someone from the group, you may find it awkward to return to the group to look for someone else. Nevertheless, if you are not ready to move into the Married Stage, but are sufficiently healed from divorce to be able to mix with more of the opposite sex, or if you just like mingling with groups sometimes, you may find it fun to meet people through activities specifically organized for singles.

Groups and their activities tend to come and go as their usually single leaders become attached and move on to other interests. So if you are going to pursue this method, you'll need to become an expert on what is happening in your community. Check for notices in the Friday or weekend sections of your city and neighborhood newspapers. If your city has a singles magazine or newspaper or a city magazine, you can also check there. Sometimes clubs are listed in the Yellow Pages under *Clubs*. You can also use the Internet to find various groups and activities in your community. Ask your friends for their recommendations. Be organized and keep a file with your findings, so you can remember everything you've learned and pick and choose the singles events you like.

Hobbies, fun classes, volunteering, church, community events and activities for mixed groups

In any community, there are many classes, church functions, community events and activities hosted by various organizations that are open to the general public, regardless of their age or marital status. It is possible to find a compatible mate by attending these events, but it will usually take longer because this is a much less direct method than meeting people through an introduction service, personal ads or even singles events. The people you meet who are interesting may be married and off-limits to you, for example.

However, if you are not ready to move into the Married Stage now and will not be for the next two to three years, and in particular, if you are just recently divorced or too young to get married at this time, then you may want to socialize with others by developing new interests and hobbies and attending events open to the general public. You can also develop platonic friends this way, and that can be particularly helpful if you have just lost many of your friends and your social life in a divorce. When you meet people this way, it's fairly easy to start talking, since presumably you are all interested in the topic of the event at hand.

Activities available in most areas include city cultural events, festivals, parades and fairs, and church choirs, groups and activities (potluck suppers, carnivals, bingo games and raffles). In the surrounding area (don't forget the suburbs!), you should be able to find art shows, auctions, bird shows, dog shows, cat shows, coin and stamp shows and flea markets. There may also be occasional car shows or air and water shows. Call the mayor's office and the local Chamber of Commerce and check the *Chase's Calendar of Events* for upcoming activities and events nearby.

If you're young or active, you could join a tennis, skiing, running, biking or hiking club, take a fun class in these sports, or join a gym.

To increase your knowledge and have fun at the same time, check out the just-for-fun classes hosted by your YMCA or YWCA, community colleges, park districts, recreational facilities, clubs or private organizations. If you're ready to meet opposite sex people in your age range, look for an activity that tends to pull those people. Younger men might try ballet class or jewelry-making, for example. Women might take a class in computers, cars, coins, wine-tasting, trains or historical events.

Volunteering can also be rewarding. Use the Internet to locate volunteer groups in your area, and ask your friends and acquaintances for suggestions. If you are ready to meet the opposite sex, choose an activity that appeals to single people who might someday be marriage candidates for you. Women might choose to build houses with Habitat for Humanity, for example. Men might prefer to hold AIDS babies in the hospital (a legitimate way to meet nurses and other warm-hearted females). Don't be shy. Ask the volunteer coordinator what sex, age and marital status the volunteers tend to be.

If you're near a university, check out classes, art shows and cultural events open to the public. This would be particularly good if you are under 25 and single. If you are over 60, be sure to check your local seniors groups as well. They often host a variety of fun activities and events at a discounted price.

If you are in the Starting Over Stage, be sure to read **Chapter 12—Starting Over,** for more ideas.

Bars and dance clubs

Singles bars were the rage in the late 70's—early 80's and many a person went home with a stranger for a one-night stand. *Looking For Mr. Goodbar,* a movie with Dianne Keaton, was an excellent portrayal of this lifestyle. While bars catering to singles still exist in Chicago and other cities, going to a bar to meet someone is generally not a good idea. It's difficult to have a decent conversation in a bar, and many men tend to treat a woman differently when they meet her in a bar. I know it's a new millennium, but some things never change—at least not while we're alive.

In my opinion, it's best if you only go to dance clubs or bars because you want to engage in an activity—dancing, singing karaoke, shooting pool or throwing darts. That way, you'll be happy, because you will be successful at engaging in that activity. You won't be disappointed that you didn't meet the love of your life before last call. If you do meet someone new in the process, just give yourself a little more time to make sure he's sincerely interested in you—no one-night stands!

Chance encounters

It does happen, but not often. Complete strangers can meet, like each other, and end up dating. You may meet at the L station, on the bus, in an elevator or at your local grocery store. If you are an excellent judge of people and have a lot of street smarts, you can meet someone to date this way. However, please do not rely on this as a method to meet people. The number of sincere people out there trying to meet people like you is pretty slim, and if you use this as a method, you're more likely to experience more unfortunate encounters than magnificent ones. And if you have anything less than impeccable judgment in people, or if you tend to have bad luck with people who try to use you or abuse you, please don't try this at all.

Whatever method of meeting people you use, it's important to be friendly and give signals that tell your date you're interested. That brings us to a discussion of flirting—a commonly overlooked, often misunderstood, but very important art form.

The secrets of flirting

Flirting is showing interest in someone in a playful way. It's trying to connect with a person of the opposite sex in order to get that first date. It's engaging someone you barely know in order to peak his interest and get him interested in learning more about you. Good flirting is respectful, slightly irreverent, classy, playful, warm, affectionate, spontaneous, charismatic, lively and joyous. It involves teasing in a way that is supportive to the other person. Flirting is different from seduction; it is playful and fun and doesn't presuppose that it will lead to anything else.

To flirt well, you have to have a sense of humor and like people in general or at least the person you're flirting with. You also need to be relaxed and not take life or yourself too seriously. When people have trouble flirting, it's often because they're too anxious. It's hard to think **FUN** when you're feeling stressed. So, let's talk about the secrets of effective flirting.

Attitude

You have to think positively and slightly irreverently to flirt. Find the fun in the situation. Allow yourself to reflect on it; be amused and laugh. Then spread that infectious good humor to others through flirting.

Facial expressions

The most important part of flirting is SMILING—a big, 1000-megawatt smile. Your smile cues the other person that you are playing, not making jokes at his or her expense. No matter what the words say, the smile tells the person that you are friendly, warm and affectionate.

Eye contact

When you lock eyes with a person, it says that you're interested—at least for a short time. It is personal, natural, open and refreshing. Shy, self-conscious people often have difficulty making eye contact. If you have trouble looking directly at someone, try staring at the bridge of his nose. He won't be able to tell the difference. And you'll be able to flirt!

Body position

Leaning forward toward the person and standing closer—slightly closing the interpersonal space—tells the other person that you're very interested in what he has to say. Keep your arms open, not crossed in front of you, to show your openness and interest.

Gestures

Light, non-sexual touching of the person's hand while telling a story, a soft touch on the shoulder when you return to your seat, touching the rim of a wine glass while gazing into the other person's eyes—all are flirtatious gestures. Women can also tilt your chin down and then look up and smile. If you have long hair, play with a strand of it or swing your hair around every so often (don't overdo it!) for extra flirting mileage.

Verbal content

Flirtatious statements are positive, upbeat, warm, friendly and playful. This is not the time to solve the problems of the world, so steer clear of discussions about religion, politics or controversial topics. It's time to relax and talk about the lighter side of life. Be personal. Talk about something that has to do with the flirtee. Be supportive and complimentary.

Personalizing the experience

Use expressions that suggest that your interactions are personal and special, e.g., *"I'm so glad you told me about that." "Are you saving that chair for me? How nice!" "I'm so glad you wanted to share that with me"* (said while lightly touching the person's hand or arm).

Crossing a small boundary to act more familiar

This takes a bit of confidence, intuition and skill, but when used well, can be very effective. Let's say a woman is passing two men who look interesting. She hears one man ask the other a light-hearted question. She could spontaneously answer the question and smile as she walks by. If the men are interested, they will laugh and begin talking to her.

Similarly, if a man is passing a woman who is having trouble getting her coat on, he can stop and politely help her on with her coat. The woman may initially look startled, but then relax and start talking to the man if she is interested.

In order to flirt in this manner, it's very important to accurately assess the mood of the other people involved. Only use this method if they seem to be in an open, playful mood and looking for company.

A WORD OF CAUTION (OR WHEN NOT TO CROSS SOCIETAL BOUNDARIES)

When people flirt, they sometimes joke about things they would never seriously discuss with someone they hardly know, e.g., sex (or lack thereof), someone else's sex life and marriage. Be very careful with this. If you do occasionally joke on this level, be sure to cross back into less dangerous territory in short order. Otherwise, women come off as being too "loose" and looking for sex, while men will appear to have a one-track mind. In general, talking about sex or some aspect of sex that is not normally a part of polite conversation, or making suggestive comments about yourself or the other person crosses the bridge between *flirting* and *seducing*.

Looks

You don't have to have sensational looks to flirt well. Anyone who can smile can flirt. In fact, when you're frozen and don't know what to say, say nothing. Just give great eye contact and smile!

The stages of dating & relationship making

Just as life is a series of relationship stages, dating also has stages. To help you understand the process, picture six circles, one inside another.

Circle 1—Strangers

When you first meet someone, you are *strangers*, so you start on the outermost circle. At this stage, you basically use "press release talk"—making only positive comments you wouldn't mind seeing in 4-inch high letters on the front cover of the local newspaper the next day. You don't really know one another, so you keep it light, do a little harmless flirting and set up a date.

Circle 2—Acquaintances/casual dating

Once you begin to date, you move one circle in and progress from being strangers to being *acquaintances*. At this stage, you share predominantly positive feelings about non-controversial topics and experiences. The experience should be upbeat and fun. After all, that's what you're there for—to have fun with each other on the date. If you talk about what you don't like about life, it becomes more negative and stressful, and who needs that, especially on a date?

At this stage, talk about what you **like** about your job, family and hobbies. Don't share your negative feelings or discuss controversial topics like abortion, religion or hot-button political issues. Don't share any confidential information about yourself, particularly details of your past relationships. For all you know, your date will not get any closer, and it's none of his business whom you have dated in the past.

Here's another secret to consider: When a man asks about your past loves at this stage, all he's really asking is, "Are you normal? Do I want to get involved with you?" So don't answer the question literally by giving a discourse on all your past sexual encounters, or you won't hear from him again. You start at zero and lose points if he doesn't like what happened in any one relationship. You also encourage him to make broad overgeneralizations about you if you present this information too soon.

Instead, answer the real question: *"I've had some relationships"* (Good—he doesn't want you to be completely inexperienced), *"and I've learned a lot."* (Great—she's not bitter!). *"Now I'm hoping to find a compatible partner and settle down in the not-so-distant future."* (Oh good, her goals are the same as mine.) Then change the subject.

Circle 3—Romantic friends

As you get to know and trust one another more, you move into the third circle, the **Romantic Friends Stage.** This means you have become somewhat physically intimate. You are kissing, holding hands and may very well be infatuated at this point. Here you can begin talking about semi-negative topics. For example, if you've had a difficult day, you can talk about your frustration. You can also discuss more controversial issues. However, keep in mind that your conversations should still be primarily positive, and your dates should still end on an upbeat note. It makes you feel better to leave your troubles at home, and it certainly makes for a more enjoyable time together.

Circle 4—Intimate romantic lovers

As your trust deepens and you spend more and more time together, you move into the fourth circle, the **Intimate Romance Stage.** At this level, you become more sexually intimate with one another. You share confidential information, including whether either of you has ever had any sexually-transmitted diseases (STDs). You need to know about his sexual history, and he has a right to that information from you. It's important to know what risks you are taking before you take them. Even if neither of you believes you have ever had an STD, you should still use latex condoms to help prevent disease, as well as another form of birth control to further help prevent pregnancy.

At this level, you talk a bit more about your previous relationships, but neither of you wants or needs to know every little detail. The best approach is to summarize your experiences with as positive a spin as possible, and talk about what you've learned.

Most dates and pre-relationships don't make it past Circle 2, the Acquaintances/Casual Dating Stage. Special, compatible people get to Circle 4, the Intimate Romance stage. If that intimacy grows, you move to Circle 5.

Circle 5—Deep intimacy

Circle 5, **Deep Intimacy,** is the stage you share with your spouse or truly significant other, the person with whom you share all the better and worse. You share thoughts that you wouldn't tell others, and you share intimate feelings only with each other. You trust each other completely. This is the most intimate stage you can share with another person.

Circle 6—Self intimacy

The last circle is the tiniest one. It's not a dating stage, but rather, a state of being. In this circle, there's only one inhabitant—you. Circle 6, all the way in, is **Your Self.** This innermost circle is that part of you that you share with no one—not your spouse, your platonic friends or your psychologist. It's healthy to have some things you keep all to yourself.

To develop a healthy relationship, try to pace your relationship in a relaxed, comfortable and fun way. There's no rush; take your time. Don't jump from being Stage 1 Strangers to being Stage 4 Sex Partners before your relationship warrants it. Otherwise, the incongruity between your emotions and your actions is likely to make the relationship fall apart. Instead, start in the outermost circle and work your way in as the trust deepens and the relationship between you grows. Also, be careful to have the relationship before you start analyzing it, fantasizing about it or making plans that assume it will continue.

Who does what?

Now that you know where to meet people, how to meet people, and what to expect in the dating cycle, it's time to talk about dating protocol. This can be confusing, particularly if you haven't dated in a long time or have never dated much.

Women asking men out

While women still prefer to be asked out, rather than do the asking, societal restrictions have relaxed on this issue. So whoever is interested in the other person should ask that person out. But there is a limit. If you're female and ask him out first, wait for him to ask you out the next time. That way, you won't start a pattern where you're doing all the asking.

Women calling

It's a practical reality that women generally want relationships more than men do, and if you come on too strong or too fast, he may run in the opposite direction. For that reason, women should generally allow men to take the lead; keep him approaching you. It's OK if you call him between dates, particularly after you know him better. It's even OK to ask him out first. But it's better to let the man take the lead as soon as possible and let him call more often. If he's busy chasing you, he doesn't have time to obsess about his relationship insecurities and whether or not you're the right woman for him. All he knows is that you are exciting and enticing, and he wants *more.*

Who pays?

On the first date, the man should pick up the check, and the woman pays for incidentals such as parking and the tip. That's provided the man asked the woman out. If the woman asked the man out, he should still find a way to contribute a substantial amount to the date. It's more romantic, and women love romance. For example, if the woman invited him to dinner, he can take her to a movie or the theatre afterward.

On subsequent dates, whoever asks the other person out should pay the lion's share of the date, but you should never split the check. Splitting implies separateness, whereas treating someone evokes a feeling of coming together, of being a couple, of sharing—which is, of course, much more conducive to romance and the development of a healthy relationship.

If you're treating, don't let your date see the check and spend only a few seconds making sure the tab is correct. If you're being treated, you should pay for parking or leave the tip—without looking at the bill. Just guess at the approximate amount and leave more rather than less, so that the amount comes out in the approximate range. Bring enough money with you and be sure to visit the ATM *before* the date, not during it.

On future dates, how much each contributes financially to the dates should depend on how much money they make. If they are about equal in the financial assets department, they can take turns picking up the majority of the tab. If the man makes more money, it's fine if he picks up most of the tabs. The woman can do thoughtful things that take more time than money, like cooking dinner for him or baking something every now and then. If the woman makes more money, she should pick up every other tab and suggest less expensive activities, so that the man can afford to alternate with her. He can also contribute by helping her—doing some simple car maintenance or shoveling her driveway. Or the woman can do the car maintenance and the man can do the baking—whatever their particular skills might be!

The idea is to act like a contributing, caring person, not a prince/princess, at the same time that you promote the feeling of togetherness and romance.

By the way, there's nothing inherently wrong with a woman picking up more of the tabs if she makes a lot more money. However, society is generally very critical of this kind of arrangement, and it often puts too much pressure on the couple. The man may feel intimidated and emasculated and lose interest in the woman. So it's better if the woman chooses activities the man can afford every other date, or allows him to contribute to their relationship by doing things for her.

Secrets for great dates

Everyone has individual likes and dislikes, but most of us appreciate attention from the opposite sex, a fun time on a date and a partner who has good social skills. At The Relationship Center™, people who practice my dating secrets tend to be extremely popular in the introduction service (age range of 23 to 84), while people who don't follow my tips frequently get negative feedback from their dates.

So I urge you to consider using my secrets. If you decide not to follow them, watch how your next several dates go. Then you can decide what works best for you and your dates.

Set the mood

Saturday night dinner with drinks and music afterward is usually a good choice for a first or early-stage date. Another choice might be Sunday brunch, with some activity (e.g., visiting an art fair, catching a matinee) afterward. Pick a place that's datelike and appropriate to how long you have known each other. Don't take a first date to a family restaurant or any busy or loud place where you can't talk privately and easily. A restaurant with soft music is fine, but if you have to shout or strain to hear one another, it's not a first-date kind of place.

Dress appropriately

Wear clothes that are clean, in good condition and fit whatever you are doing on the date. Don't wear a silk suit and high heels to a picnic. It's always a good idea to briefly discuss what you each will be wearing before the date, since women often dress up more than men do. Keep your date's style—preppie, conservative, casual, grunge, biker, artsy, classic—in mind when you dress. If you dress like a biker chick for a businessman who wears suits and takes you to classy restaurants, don't expect the relationship to progress very far.

Be sure your grooming is impeccable. Present yourself in a tasteful, classy way. Wear cologne, but not so much that he can smell you across the room, and don't wear clothes that are too seductive or revealing.

Time your arrival

If possible, the man should pick the woman up. Don't make arrangements to show up separately unless you're meeting through a personal ad and this is your first or second meeting. Do your best to arrive on time. If you're early, wait until the proper time before ringing her doorbell. If you're going to be more than 5 minutes late, call and let her know.

If you are meeting in a public place, make sure that you can get a message to your date if you're running late. For example, you might tell your date to meet you at the hostess stand in the restaurant rather than the piano under the tree in the hotel lounge. When you first meet, gently squeeze (don't shake) your date's hand, smile and say, *"Hi! I'm _____. It's good to meet you."*

Practice your social skills

Social skills are behaviors you do that show consideration and respect for the other person. They set the mood for romance and make the other person feel cared for. Based on the comments of people who meet through The Relationship Center™, social skills go a long way toward making your date feel special and regarding you as special as well. A good first impression also paves the way for you to move to the next stage of dating. With that in mind, here are some tips.

A man should always go to the door to pick up the woman and walk her to her door at the end of the evening. Open doors to cars and buildings and let her go first. Be aware of where she is and stay with her. Don't run into the restaurant to avoid the cold while she's still struggling to get out of her seat belt.

On the sidewalk, stay close, but don't crowd her. Walk on the side closest to the street and stay with her when you're crossing a street instead of racing ahead. Don't hold your date's hand or try to put your arm around her on the first date, unless you're crossing a busy street or in a crowd and might otherwise lose her. If she's carrying packages, offer to take the load or share it. Help her with her coat before attending to your own. Pull out her chair, push it in under her and see that she is comfortable. If you're in a restaurant, ask her if she wants to order a drink or appetizer, and let her order dinner first. Pay attention to any subtle cues she might give that something is not going well, and make an attempt to fix it. For example, if she doesn't like the table, offer to summon the waiter and change tables.

It's not usually appropriate to bring flowers or a gift to the first date, and it's never appropriate to try to enter her apartment unless you're invited. If your date lives in an apartment building, be friendly with the doorman, but don't reveal any personal details about you or your date.

Women should allow their dates to show them these courtesies and graciously say, "*Thank you,*" whenever appropriate, such as when he helps you with your coat or opens the car door for you. Never laugh nervously at his attempts. Instead, show your appreciation by smiling and being warm, friendly and gracious.

In the early dating stages, women should not introduce their dates to their children or family members. And never make your date wait while you finish dressing—it's much too intimate and rude.

Show your interest

During your date, it's appropriate to make friendly hand and eye contact. In fact, sit perpendicular to one another at dinner so you can "accidentally" touch when talking and gesturing. Don't decide to eat dinner at the bar because it's faster. If the table you are offered is not conducive to conversation, politely ask for another one.

Give your date your undivided attention. That means no ogling of other women or men as they pass by, no prolonged trips to the restroom, and no cell phone conversations. Speak softly enough that only you and your date can hear the conversation. Think as positively as possible about your date and avoid mental comparisons with your last love.

Treat the waiter with courtesy. Never be rude if you don't like your dinner or are displeased with any other aspect of the restaurant.

Keep the conversation going

Ask questions to show interest and really listen to the answers. Make eye contact as much as possible. Also, show that you're paying attention by making reflective statements *("It sounds like you had a great time")* and supportive statements *("I'm glad it worked out for you"),* and by sharing information about yourself. Try to achieve a balance. Don't talk too much about yourself or conversely, ask so many questions that your date feels interviewed. Be careful that nervousness doesn't cause you to talk too much or too little. It's OK if there are some silences; that's normal and goes unnoticed when people are comfortable with each another.

Don't lie, but also, don't share too much about yourself too soon. Don't reveal all your rotten qualities on your first date. Your date will believe you, but will also assume there are more, since everyone usually talks about their good qualities and holds the negative stuff back for later. So listen to your conversation as you're having it, and do your best to put your best foot forward. Otherwise your attempt at honesty will backfire, and your date will come away with a negative misimpression of you.

Keep the conversation focused on positive topics. Totally inappropriate subjects are other men and women; how much you hate your ex, your mother, your job or anything else; your bad experiences with personal ads and dating services; and how awful it is to be single.

On the flip side, don't ask your date questions about personal or off-limits topics such as money, ex-lovers, why he isn't married yet, or what happened in the divorce. And never tease about potentially sensitive issues like weight or receding hairlines.

Treat your date with sensitivity and consideration, the way you'd like to be treated. Your goal is to keep the date upbeat, fun and playful. Remember, your date has to find you fun to want to continue seeing you.

Get her home safely

If the man has provided the transportation for the evening, he should drive the woman home. Never drop her off down the road from her house or apartment. Wait until she is safely inside before you leave.

If she has driven herself to the date, e.g., if it's a blind date or a first or second date from a personal ad, walk her to her car and wait until she safely drives off before you leave. If she has taken a cab to the date, call a taxi for her and wait with her until it comes. Leave after she is safely on her way. Don't rush her though dessert, say, "Well, goodbye," and let her walk to her car or a cab alone.

If neither of you has transportation and it's not a blind date or your first date, accompany her home in the cab, walk her to her door while the cab waits, see that she is safely inside, then take the taxi home.

End on an upbeat note

Men, it's appropriate to thank her for the date, tell her you enjoyed her company (if you did), and ask if you can call her again (if you'd like to). But don't tell her you'll call her if you have no intention of doing so. If she indicates that she'd like to see you again, don't come on too strong by trying to book her for the entire month.

If she's not enthusiastic about seeing you again, be gracious and leave the door open. Don't react in a hostile or aggressive way. Tell her you're sorry she feels that way, but you respect her wishes. Ask her to call you if she changes her mind.

When it's time to leave, gently squeeze the woman's hand between yours and give her a kiss on the cheek at the same time. If she wants more, she'll turn her head. But don't try to make out with her while you're saying goodnight.

If she invites you up to her apartment for a nightcap, be a gentleman. Don't view an invitation to have coffee or an after-dinner drink as an invitation to have sex.

Women, be sure to thank him for the date. Be considerate. Don't tell him to call when you have no intention of ever going out with him again.

If you're declining a second meeting, say so graciously, adding a positive, but honest, comment: *"Thanks for the time we've spent together, and for treating me to dinner. I really appreciate it and all the effort you put into it, but I just don't think we're compatible. I think you're a very nice person, though, and you deserve to have someone wonderful in your life. I hope you find someone compatible very soon, and I wish you all the best."* Don't refuse another date by telling him what's wrong with him. If he isn't interested in seeing you again, don't react with hostility or aggression.

And now a word about sex: Don't have it on the first date. In fact, don't have it for the first three months of a relationship, if at all possible. Sex early in a relationship makes it too intense too soon and can cause the man to bail. For more on this, see **Chapter 4—Sex!**

Follow up with class

Men, leave a message on her machine the day after the date, saying you really enjoyed her company and you'll call her again soon. Then telephone her a couple days later to arrange another date. Don't send flowers or a note after the first or second date. Don't tell a date that you'd like to go out again, then wait two months before you call or never call again. But don't decide not to call her because you have waited two months and are now too embarrassed to call. Just pick up the phone, apologize for not calling sooner and ask for a date. If you sound sincere, she may very well accept.

Women, don't make a date with a man if you're planning to cancel it later. Don't avoid answering the phone or fail to return messages, hoping he'll understand that you aren't interested in seeing him any more. Have the courtesy to return his call and decline respectfully, as outlined in the above section.

Keep the relationship casual and go out with more than one person at a time when you first begin dating someone. But don't date so many people so quickly that you confuse them and their personal data. If you need to, take a few notes right after your date so you'll be more likely to remember what you've learned (how many brothers and sisters he has, where he went to school). That way, you won't have to say, "Which one were you?" or, "Were you the one with three sisters?" when you see him next time.

Be conscientious, considerate and responsible. Remember your dates and call when you say you will.

Put your date's correctly spelled name and phone numbers in more than one place so you won't lose them. Write any plans and phone calls on a calendar so you won't forget.

Stay in touch with reality

Keep the relationship in the present, limited to what is actually happening in real life, not what you wish would happen.

Don't tell all your friends that you've finally found "the one," obsess about him between dates, or start fantasizing about your future together. Use thought-stopping (described in the Appendix), if necessary, to forget about him when you're not together.

Real-life Love@AOL letters about dating

It helps to know that other people share the same problems and concerns. When it comes to dating, hardly anyone has a completely carefree ride, and it's nice to know you're not alone. I have received many thousands of letters from AOL members on the topic of dating. Here are some of my favorites. Enjoy!

Kissing good night—how many dates?
MY AGE: 21 MY GENDER: MALE

Dear Dr. Kate,
I just started going out with this girl, and I was wondering: How many dates should I wait before giving her a kiss good night?

Dear Romeo,
What kind of kiss you are talking about?

I think it's perfectly appropriate to give someone a kiss on the cheek on the first date. When you say, *"Good night,"* you can say, *"I had a really nice time; thank you,"* reach for her hand, squeeze it gently between both of yours (don't shake it vigorously like you've just completed a business deal), then gently kiss her on the cheek. It's all one fluid motion.

If the woman wants more of a kiss, she'll turn her head toward you, or give some other signal, and you can then kiss her on the lips. If she doesn't, just stop there. Even if she does turn her head, don't keep kissing for a long time on the first date. Just give her a nice, "full of promise" kiss that she can remember later and smile.

The next time you see her, greet her the same way, gently squeezing her hand and kissing her on the cheek. This makes contact with her in a physical, but not very sexual way; it's socially safe and respectful. Keep doing this at the beginning and end of every date until she turns her head or gives some other signal that she wants more.

All the Best, and please let me know how you're doing from time to time,
Dr. Kate

Date more than one person at a time?
I feel like I'm cheating!

Dear Dr. Kate,
Maybe I'm just old-fashioned or something, but I feel like I'm cheating on someone if I see more than one person at a time. How can one person ethically have romantic emotional encounters with multiple people? Please enlighten me. Thanks.

Dear Enlightenee,
You have multiple emotional encounters with lots of people every day. You like many people in many different ways—your family, friends, acquaintances and coworkers.

To find out if you can feel romantic towards someone, you need to experience him. Dating more than one person at a time allows you to compare and contrast how you feel about them, how you feel when you're around them, and how you feel about yourself when you are with them. Everyone needs to explore other people to find out who fits them best. The only way to do that is to date them. You have to *have* a relationship to see if it's going to work.

Now, remember, I'm not talking about sleeping with them—just dating them.

The way to do it ethically is to not imply exclusivity. Don't give a man the false impression that you are *only* dating him. He should understand this if you are not always available (*"I'm sorry, I can't make it Friday; how about Saturday?"*). If any confusion arises, you can tell him you're "not being exclusive yet." However, don't give any details about your other dates because that would be rude and unkind.

Dating more than one person at a time also slows the relationship down and allows both of you to make sure you're choosing each other because you really want to be together, not because you just want to be in love. If the relationship builds slowly, you can probably trust your feelings. If it happens quickly, you just have to wait and see if the feelings last, or if it's infatuation and dies out. If you start having doubts and try to back up and be less intimate after having been intimate, it frequently kills the relationship because it's difficult for the other person not to feel insulted.

I hope this clears up the confusion.

All the Best,

Dr. Kate

Exercises to hone your dating skills

1. **Easy Does It, One Date at a Time.** Make a list of any behaviors you need to work on, using the *Discover Your Date IQ Quiz* as a guide. Rank the behaviors in order of how difficult you think each will be for you to accomplish. Start at the easiest level, and practice doing one behavior on your next date. Keep practicing until you have mastered it and can do it with ease. Then add the next behavior, practicing both behaviors until you are easily able to do both of them together.

Continue working your way up the hierarchy until you have mastered all the behaviors on your list. Then retake the *Discover Your Date IQ Quiz* to see how you score this time. If you still need more practice, keep plugging.

2. **Try Some Roleplaying.** Ask a trustworthy, opposite-sex platonic friend to read this chapter and then roleplay a date with you. If you can't find a platonic opposite-sex friend, ask one of your same-sex friends to play the opposite role. Roleplay the entire date, including flirting and making upbeat, first-date conversation. Videotape (preferably) or audiotape your roleplay, then play it back so you can see and hear yourself. Discuss the tape with your friend. Ask your friend what you did well and what behaviors you need to improve. Accept the feedback as an opinion without becoming defensive. Then practice the behaviors you need to improve. Tape each attempt.

   If you're stymied, roleplay doing everything the wrong way. Be as bad at it as you possibly can and loosen up. Laugh. Have fun with it. Be sure to keep your first video or audiotape, rather than recording over it. That way, you will be able to see your improvement. Sometimes a picture (especially a moving one) is worth a thousand words. Once you've mastered the behaviors at home, ask your opposite-sex friend to roleplay a date with you in public. Stay in character for the entire time, then discuss the experience after you return home.

3. **Get Your Feet Wet & Jump In.** Start reading the personal ads, either online in *Love@AOL* (AOL Keyword: Personals or on the web at http://www.love.com), or offline in a magazine or newspaper. Respond to one. Then write your own personal ad. Have a confidential friend (preferably an opposite-sex platonic friend) review it first and give you feedback. Does the ad describe you accurately? Will it attract compatible people? When you are happy with your ad, place it, either online in the *Love@AOL* Photo Personals or offline in a magazine or newspaper. Before you place a personal ad or reply to one, be sure to read *How to Date Through The Personal Ads* in the Appendix.

4. **Research and Choose.** Read *How To Choose A Dating Service* in the Appendix. Take this book with you and visit some dating/introduction services in your area. Ask the questions, take notes and think about which service feels most comfortable to you. When you return home, compare the responses you received from the various services, how you felt at each and which might be the best to join. Reflect on this for a day or two. Then join the one you found most comfortable that also gave the best responses to your questions.

Chapter 3

Compatibility
Taking an objective look

*I*n Chapter 1, we discussed how the soulmate myth is erroneous and how there are really many people you could love, live with and be happy with. In Chapter 2, we discussed taking the first step towards meeting a significant other by flirting and dating. In this chapter, we'll take a closer look at compatibility. Once you are dating someone, how can you tell if you're compatible for a long-term relationship?

Before you read any further, take ***The Dr. Kate Compatibility Quiz*** (located in the Appendix) for anyone you are currently dating. Score yourself and read the results. Then return here to learn more about compatibility.

Who is compatible with you anyway?

So, who *is* compatible with you anyway? Is it someone who is most similar to you? Or someone more opposite? Does the person need to believe exactly the same things that you believe? And what does that word "compatible" really mean anyway?

What compatibility is not

Let's start with a very important secret of compatibility: Just as you're not perfect, you will never find a perfect partner, nor will you ever find perfect compatibility.

> *No one is ever perfect, no one's partner is ever perfect, and no relationship is ever perfectly compatible.*

This is the real world, and in the real world, perfection just doesn't exist. Besides, just like the people who tire of the beautiful weather in Hawaii, if you never have any challenges in your relationships, you'll probably find them boring.

Added to that is the fact that everyone has different perceptions of what "perfect" is. One person might love to stay home and read at night, while another loves to be out mingling and socializing. One person enjoys working 20 hours a week; the other prefers 80. Everyone has different preferences in their life. There's a wide range of normal behavior, and just because someone is different from you doesn't make them better or worse. Unfortunately, sometimes people forget this fact in their pursuit of a "perfect" mate. I'll never forget the day I met Melissa.

Melissa's Story

Melissa, 34, was an attractive professional who came to interview at my introduction service. She was armed with a list of her requirements for a mate, and the list was quite extensive. She had obviously put a lot of thought into what she absolutely "had to have" in a mate. Unfortunately, she absolutely had to have a LOT of very specific qualities in that mate. When I interview someone, I typically ask about preferences. For example, does it matter how much education the person has, what he does for a living, what religion he believes in? Clients are asked to form their answers as either being completely open, having a preference, or wanting to completely rule out someone who has that certain characteristic.

Melissa had many rule-outs. He had to be 6'2" or taller. He had to be between 34-38 years old, never married, no children, Christian, nonsmoker, have a master's degree or more advanced education, and be employed as a professional. His goal had to be getting married and having children. She also wanted him to make $150,000 per year or more, and he had to live in the city, not the suburbs. Melissa insisted on these variables, even though she had only a bachelor's degree, not a master's, and made only $50,000 a year. She figured that when she married, she would stop working and stay home, and she would not be able to make ends meet on less than $150,000 per year.

Unfortunately, Melissa had already been to another service that told her she could have all of these things and more in everyone they introduced her to.

While much of my interview concerns personality characteristics, Melissa had given very little attention to any personality qualities she wanted the man to have. She was too busy thinking about the kind of lifestyle she wanted, and how this man would make those dreams come true. It was as though she thought she could "order up" the perfect man, and I would bring him on a platter.

Gently, I started probing Melissa to see if she could accept other people. What if the man made $100,000 instead? No, he had to make $150,000. Why did he have to have a master's degree? Because then it showed that he was capable of succeeding in life. The fact that Melissa didn't have one didn't seem to change her opinion of herself as successful, but she used a different standard to evaluate the men she wanted. What if the man was 6'0" instead? After all, Melissa was only 5'8". No, she insisted, she really wanted a tall man; in fact, she preferred them 6'4"! How about a 10-year age range? No way! Every time I probed to see if Melissa could be flexible on any criterion, she just became more rigid and more adamant that this was the perfect man for her.

When we talked about activities, Melissa was not willing to try anything for anyone, including a perfect man. Finally, when I thought she had to be finished with her list of demands, Melissa started telling me how much hair the man had to have on his chest. Well, it was all I could do to sit there without laughing. After all, how would I know how much hair the man had on his chest, unless it was sticking out his shirt?

Of course, this question had never even occurred to Melissa, in all her self-centered glory.

Now, the problem wasn't that I didn't have any 6'2" or taller, never- married professional men with master's degrees who made $150,000 in my service. I did. The problem was that I knew that any men I had would not like Melissa; they would not get along with her at all. Why? Because Melissa was not warm and friendly, positive and upbeat, nurturing and accepting. She was cold, self-centered, full of herself and judgmental of others. She just wasn't a very nice person. But she didn't even realize that. She was too busy ordering up her world. No matter how beautiful she was, her attitude would have driven men away.

When I tried to explain how important attitude is to finding someone, and how important it is to think in a more open, flexible, positive way, Melissa replied, "Well, my girlfriends tell me I shouldn't settle. I have high standards and I deserve it."

I politely turned Melissa down as a client for the dating service. She was not healthy enough. I would have offered her therapy, but Melissa would have thought she was too perfect to ever need therapy. I was as kind and polite as I could be, explaining why I didn't think we could accept her into the program. Nevertheless, Melissa grew very angry, and before she left the office, dug through her purse to locate our brochure. Then with great emphasis, she balled it up and threw it in our wastebasket before leaving. I breathed a sigh of relief. She was even more hostile than I had originally thought. Thank goodness I didn't take her!

Unfortunately, there are many Melissa's out there. So that brings us to a very important secret of compatibility:

Just because someone is different from you doesn't make them "better" or "worse."

It just makes them "different."

There is no universal hierarchy of qualities such that if you have these qualities and your date doesn't, you are "better" than he is.

When someone assumes that her preferences are universal standards, she is setting herself up for years of frustration and failed relationships.

Instead, it's best to consider that everyone has preferences for how they live their life—what they enjoy doing, what they like to talk about, how much money they spend, how much they give away, how much time they spend making that money versus how much time they spend with family and friends. Professionals are not better people than blue-collar workers, and blue-collar workers are not inherently stupid or uneducated.

They may be better at using their spatially-oriented right brain, while you are better at using your verbal, analytic left brain, but that doesn't necessarily make one or the other of you more or less intelligent.

Sometimes well-meaning therapists who don't work in the dating industry encourage their clients to make lists of qualities they seek in a mate. I understand the exercise in theory. To help the client organize her thoughts, the therapist encourages her to make a list of "things I have to have," "things I can totally live without," and "things that are negotiable."

Unfortunately, many people use that opportunity to become more extreme in their demands and end up with a *lot* of qualities in the "have to have" category. Like Melissa, they list money, house and lifestyle qualities under "have to have's," instead of important psychological variables like honesty, monogamy and trust. Their idea of compromise is agreeing to date someone one year older than the four-year age range they previously specified.

Of course, the same woman who becomes demanding in this way doesn't even stop to think that the man also comes in with his list of preferences.

On the other hand, I have also seen therapy clients who have been abused by their mates. And I have received hundreds of letters from abused women who have written to me at my *Love@AOL* Dr. Kate site. In those cases, the woman needs to be more selective in choosing a mate.

So what should someone look for in a mate? Well, look back at the scoring template for *The Dr. Kate Compatibility Quiz*. See the list of qualities to the right? Those are the variables each question addresses. Let's look at each of these and its relevance for compatibility.

Elements of compatibility
Honesty, trust, loyalty and monogamy
If you don't have these, you basically have no relationship. Becoming intimate with someone means that you share things with him that you don't share with anyone else and vice versa. If you are cheating on your mate or lying to him or vice versa, your relationship is in trouble. People can recover after affairs, but it is very difficult. Trust is an absolute must in any relationship, and even more important in a relationship with your mate.

Shared goals and plans
If you talk about your goals and they seem to be in sync, then you are more likely to be compatible long-term. If they're somewhat different, but you negotiate, you can usually find reasonable compromises. If you don't even talk about your goals, it's often because you know deep down inside that they are too disparate and bringing them up would logically lead to a breakup.

Shared goals for the relationship

Similar to your life goals, goals for the relationship should be in sync. If you want to get married, and he's comfortable just living together, you'll probably feel more and more frustrated and angry the longer you stay together. If you want to get married and your partner is already married to someone else, you are just kidding yourself if you think this is a good relationship. Similarly, if you are both married, the odds are that you won't have a future together. If you're both single and want a temporary relationship, then your relationship is compatible for such time until one of you changes your mind. However, if the two of you don't talk about your goals for the relationship, chances are you don't agree. If you're avoiding the topic because you're hoping he'll change his mind, then you may just be wasting your time in this relationship.

Financial disagreements

One of the most common things couples fight about is money—not having enough of it, and how to spend what they have. If you and your mate generally agree about money or are usually able to find satisfactory compromises regarding it, then you are more compatible than if you generally disagree. If you prefer to keep separate financial accounts, and you are both in sync with that, it can be OK. However, if one person takes the other's desire to do that as a personal affront, hurt feelings, anger and distancing can result. If you think your partner is dishonest about finances, then your relationship is in trouble for the same reasons cited above for "trust" and "honesty."

Intelligence/Intellectual interests

It's important to feel understood by your partner, and to understand him. If you and your partner are very divergent in terms of intelligence, that won't happen. On the other hand, as we noted earlier, there are different kinds of intelligence. Your partner may be better at spatial tasks, and you could be better at verbal tasks, and yet the two of you could be fairly evenly matched in intelligence. Perhaps you would need to learn to communicate better together. But just because you don't at this moment doesn't necessarily mean that he isn't intelligent enough for you.

Similarly, your mate doesn't have to share all your intellectual interests to be compatible. You can discuss poetry with your girlfriends. However, intellectual stimulation is another way to connect and have fun. If you look forward to sharing ideas with your partner and find his ideas stimulating, it should add to your enjoyment and overall compatibility.

Communication

One of the most important variables that determines whether or not two people will stay together is how well they communicate. As we mentioned earlier, no two people are ever perfectly compatible. That means that sooner or later, you will disagree about something. Research shows that it isn't the disagreement per se that will break up the couple; it's the way they disagree that counts. If you can respectfully disagree with your partner and work out compromises, then you are far more likely to stay together. Conversely, if you can't talk without yelling or screaming at each other, you will have a difficult union if you stay together. If your partner doesn't even believe that communication is important, you should rethink your decision to get together. And if your partner is physically abusive, there is no hope for this relationship.

Physical and sexual attraction

To have a healthy relationship, it's important to enjoy sex with your partner. If you find him physically attractive, that's a plus. On the other hand, most people find that when they love someone, that person ends up looking beautiful to them. This is truly a life-saving phenomenon. Since most of us are not classically beautiful, if no one had this ability, the world's population would soon die off.

Sexual attraction is a slightly different phenomenon. You can be sexually attracted to someone and at the same time, be able to say that he isn't that attractive physically. Sexual attraction has a lot to do with how playful someone is, how much he flirts with you and how much you enjoy flirting and playing back with him. In addition, how much you enjoy sex also has to do with whether you enjoy the way your partner pleasures you, as well as how much love you feel. If you love him and love giving and receiving pleasure from him, then your sex life can flourish.

In *Chapter 8,* you'll learn that sex is the glue that holds a couple together. Being sexually intimate with your partner on a regular basis helps you stay emotionally close as well. So, if you enjoy sex with your partner, you're more compatible than if you don't. If you hate sex with your partner or go out of your way to avoid it, then you're probably having relationship problems of a fairly high intensity and should seek counseling if you decide to stay together.

Culture/religion/ethnicity, support of family and friends

In general, the more similar you are on these variables, the better. One of the things that makes people feel close to one another is a shared sense of history. If your ancestors shared a similar past, and you were raised a certain way that reflects that past, then you will probably feel more at home with someone else who has shared that experience. If you were a flower child and will never forget where you were when Kennedy was shot and your boyfriend wasn't even born yet and thinks the Vietnam War was justified and the 60's marches were stupid, you may feel a distance between you. On the other hand, many happy couples have crossed the age, color, culture and religion line. Their enjoyment of each other in other areas and their mutual respect for their differences allow them to be together successfully.

However, it's important not to underestimate how much pressure family and friends can put on a budding relationship. Perhaps his mother always wanted him to have his own biological children, so she isn't wild about him dating a woman 15 years older who is already 40. Similarly, if he's 30 years older and you enjoy going ballroom dancing with him, but can't imagine him hanging out with your friends, then you also have a problem. You can't have a relationship in a vacuum. Sooner or later, your family and friends will need to mix with your partner. That doesn't mean that you should just drop someone if you think your peer group or family wouldn't approve. It just means that if you decide to stay involved with this person, you need to go into it with your eyes wide open. Be aware of the stresses and have some idea of how you will handle them. Eventually, when you are an established couple, you'll need to candidly discuss the differences and decide on a united course of action.

Similar interests

One of the major problems couples argue about is how they spend their free time. So the more you can keep this area in sync, the better you are likely to get along, and the longer you are likely to stay together. Your attitude should be that when your partner enjoys doing an activity, you'll try to enjoy it for him. Figure out a way to cheerfully go along, even if you don't enjoy the activity itself. For example, if he likes skiing and you've just had knee surgery, go with him to the resort and relax at the lodge while he's out skiing. When he returns, spend some romantic moments in front of the fire and remind him through your actions why he brought you along!

Length of time you're together

It's easy to think you're compatible when you've only been together two weeks. As we previously discussed, it takes about 3 months of seeing one another several times a week to get to know your partner better and to pass from the infatuation stage into love. If you have been together less than 3 months, your opinion of each other may still change drastically.

Conversely, if you have been together many years, there's probably not much you don't know about each other. So if you're still together, there must be something strong holding you there.

Overall fun and chemistry

This is probably the most important variable in compatibility. If you can play with your partner, if you have fun being with him, and he feels the same, then you're highly compatible and likely to stay together despite other variables not being in sync. If you each view time spent with the other as the highlight of your day, then you are more likely to compromise on other issues that are not in sync. Conversely, if you feel bored or uncomfortable around your partner, then you either lack respect and are having serious relationship problems that require professional intervention, or you are simply not compatible.

Perseverance

Last, but not least, how much you are willing to work on a relationship has a lot to do with whether or not it will last long-term. If you and your partner have been raised to believe that you should always work hard on everything and hardly ever give up, then you will treat your relationship in a similar fashion. One reason long-term married couples stay together is they know that when their relationship goes into a slump, it will eventually improve—if they just hang on.

Conversely, if you think that everything in life should be easy and you give up quickly when it's not, chances are you'll never stay very long with anyone. While it isn't good to persevere in an abusive or completely incompatible relationship, perseverance is extremely important in weathering problems that occur in any normal, healthy, compatible relationship.

When to be more picky

You'll notice as you look at the compatibility quiz scoring and results that if your partner is physically abusing you, you are not at all compatible. There is absolutely no justification for physical or sexual abuse. A woman who stays in a relationship with an abusive man is not being picky enough about compatibility. In order to have an intimate relationship with someone, you have to be treated with respect. While many partners feel they are giving a little more than their partner is, the discrepancy in an abusive relationship is monumental. The abuser holds a double standard for his behavior and that of his victim, being critical and intolerant with her. He doesn't love her; he wants to possess and control her, and that's very different. When you love someone, you want her to have freedom. If you find yourself attracted to people who physically abuse you, be sure to read **Chapter 10—Tough Times**, which includes a section on abuse.

Similarly if your partner is married and you're dreaming about being together, you are kidding yourself. Most affairs end up hurting everyone. If you're dating a married man, you should be more picky. How often a woman has told me, "He's handsome, charismatic, fun, charming, intelligent, witty, really good to me and lots of fun. There's only one problem... he's married." Only one problem? The problem is that he isn't emotionally available. So, you have almost **no** chance of being compatible long-term. That means he's not compatible AT ALL. Women who date married men should be more picky—they should limit themselves to the pool of single, emotionally available men. I know the other ones can look good, but they are just not viable candidates. So why hurt yourself by getting involved with them? If you have this problem, be sure to read Chapter 10, which includes a section on cheating.

Some common myths about compatibility

Now that we've talked about some of the most important elements of compatibility, let's consider some of the compatibility myths that cause people a lot of grief.

Instant compatibility assessment

Many clients have told me that they can "just tell" whether or not they are compatible with someone within the first 5-10 minutes. The people who say this are frequently men employed in sales or some profession where they believe that they "use psychology" to size people up. This is an unfortunate belief.

In my opinion, what the person is actually doing is making a quick chemistry evaluation based on his opinion of your physical appearance and whether or not he'd like to have sex with you. Now, it is vitally important to have sex with your partner eventually. However, since you're not going to do that in the first 5-10 minutes, this instant assessment is unfortunate. The assessor is not allowing himself enough time to find out if he could ever like you, love you or become physically attracted to you in the future.

In addition, since someone who holds this belief usually doesn't test it by getting to know you, it's a self-fulfilling prophecy. For example, if a man only continues to see people he immediately finds physically attractive, then the women he ends up having relationships with will be some subset of that group. Similarly, if he rules out everyone he doesn't find immediately attractive, he'll never have the opportunity to find out that someone who didn't initially attract him later does—once he gets to know and love her.

This myth causes people to pass up many relationship candidates. Sure, it's possible that you can find love with one of the remaining people, but why limit yourself so severely?

In fact, when I attend weddings of people who met through The Relationship Center™, the bride and groom frequently joke about how they didn't like each other until the third date.

Diane's Story

I told this story to a female reporter who had come to film one of our weddings for a news feature on The Relationship Center™. "Oh, yes!" she said. "I know exactly what you mean." She then proceeded to tell me that for years, she had been dating men who were initially charismatic and had a lot on the ball, but they always ended up being afraid of commitment or so arrogant that they were not able to have a healthy relationship. Finally, she told her girlfriends that she would love to date a regular guy. "I just want a normal, regular guy for a change—someone who's not afraid of a relationship."

So, one of her girlfriends set her up with a friend. On the first date, the newscaster was not impressed. She met the man, but found him a little boring. However, she felt somewhat guilty about this, since she had said she wanted a regular guy, and she didn't want to disappoint her friend. So when the man asked her out again, she accepted. Once again, she didn't have a great time. But she knew he was a nice guy, so she felt even more guilty that she wasn't able to return his interest in her. She found herself asking him to a concert in Grant Park. On the appointed day, she packed a picnic basket with sandwiches and a bottle of wine, and off they went to the park, with their basket and blanket, to listen to a concert under the stars.

But instead of finding a crowd of people enjoying the music and warm summer evening, the park was empty. To her surprise and dismay, she had made a mistake about the date of the concert! Well, they decided to make the best of it and picnic in the park. And then something quite amazing occurred. The man started to talk, and the more he talked, the more she liked what he had to say. She liked it so much, she got a little nervous, hoping that she wouldn't wake up and find out that it had all been a dream. After that night, their third date together, things developed smoothly, and they ended up getting engaged.

Why is the third date the charm? Who knows. We can speculate that people are just too tense when they meet each other. First dates are usually a little strange; it takes people time to relax. It's more difficult to tease or joke, because you don't want to offend. When people are nervous, they also talk too much or too little. Many people tell me they're a little shy and reserved at first, but after they open up, well…!

So the bottom line is: You either have to go out with someone a few more times to be sure that they're not compatible, or you take the risk of passing up someone who could have been very compatible. Since that's a more serious risk, I always advocate seeing someone three times before giving up.

Now, that's at my introduction service, where the people are all safe, respectful and quite compatible with one another. When you meet through other means and no one has interviewed your date, three dates may be unnecessary to know that you are grossly incompatible. However, I think it's important to remember the three-date philosophy and use it whenever it seems appropriate.

People sometimes reject out-of-hand people they are not used to being with, and those who don't fit their image of an ideal man or woman. For example, maybe you have always been attracted to tall, dark-haired men. Then you meet a shorter, redheaded guy who's really funny. Your initial reaction is, "Oh, this will never work." If you never see him again, you're right. It won't ever work. On the other hand, if you let yourself experience him for three dates, you might find yourself having so much fun, you continue dating him. Then one day you look at him and think, "How come I never noticed how attractive he was before?" Well, he hasn't changed. But you now see him a different way, and you have become more compatible with him. In a world where compatibility is difficult to find, I believe it's best to make use of these opportunities.

More When Harry met Sally than Sleepless in Seattle

When I examine the feedback sent in by people who meet people through my introduction service, I can see that the largest group of marriages occur between people who gradually got to know one another and fell in love over time. They didn't know right away that this person would end up being their mate. In fact, they may not have even liked each other much on the first meeting. They might have preferred someone else. But over time, they find that the most attractive or funniest or most successful match does not have the "other things" they need. So that person drops out of the picture, and instead, they fall in love gradually with someone else who not only is attractive, funny and successful on a more subdued level, but also has the other qualities they need in a partner.

The person you end up marrying is not the person you meet on the first date. So a first date quickie assessment is often not in your best interest.

No love at first sight

Just like you can't necessarily assess your compatibility with someone on the first date, you also can't trust any attraction you feel for someone at first sight.

If you don't know someone yet, you can't possibly **love** him. You can have lust at first site or infatuation at first sight, but not love. You see someone and get excited about him, but you still don't know him very well. You like what you see, but there are many holes in the picture. People tend to assume that those holes will fill in with data that they will also like. However, that may not be the case. As you get to know someone and learn more about him, you may not like some of that information. You may push that knowledge out of your awareness for awhile. The longer it has been since you've fallen in love and the more you want it to happen, the more likely you are to ignore the information you don't want to see. However, in time, when you receive enough incompatible information, it will cross threshold into your awareness, and you will suddenly "pop out" of your infatuation. You'll realize that you weren't in love with your partner, but rather, with whom you hoped he would be.

It takes at least 3-4 months of seeing someone several times per week before you really know a person well enough to know that you really love **him**, not just the person you hope he'll turn out to be. If the feeling remains strong and grows, it's likely to be love. If it drops off suddenly, it was infatuation, not love.

Really compatible or dysfunctional hook?

You can also be highly attracted to someone very quickly because they are a "hook" from your dysfunctional past. Remember Matt from Chapter 1? He was instantly attracted to his girlfriend because she showed him very quickly that she was going to play hard to get. That immediately cued him into his dysfunctional past and hooked her forever into his heart. So when you get a strong feeling immediately upon meeting someone or shortly thereafter, it can also mean that you have met someone who exemplifies the dysfunction from your past. In other words, instead of getting closer, that person is very **IN**compatible with you, and you should beat feet to get away from him as soon as possible.

It's quite possible that many of those people who think they are falling for their soulmate are really just hooking into pathology from their past. How can you tell the difference?

Take the compatibility quiz for that person and find out how you stand on the qualities we discussed in this chapter. Then step back from your life and ask yourself: Does this person generally contribute to my life? In what ways? Has my life gotten better since I met him? Does he respect me and my differences? Or is he trying to control me or make me into the image of what he wants me to be? Does this person remind me of anyone in my family? Who? In what ways? Does he remind me of anyone I have ever dated before? Who? In what ways?

Review the notes you took when you plotted your relationship history for the Chapter 1 exercise. The more qualities your mate has in common with people who ended up being dysfunctional for you, the more likely he is hooked to you in an unhealthy way.

Abusive men

An abused woman will often comment that the man wasn't abusive when they first met. He was charming, solicitous, funny and really seemed to care. However, when she describes the behavior he did that led her to believe he cared, it generally includes some incidents of overstepping boundaries. Not flirtatious overstepping of boundaries, like we discussed in Chapter 2, but more pathological overstepping.

For example, he might call in sick for you, without asking you in advance. The real reason he does it is because he wants you to stay home with him—for his sake—not because he's concerned about how you're feeling. Women with abusive boyfriends usually overlook those first signs of the man's disrespect, over-control and overstepping.

Opposites can attract, then repel

Another commonly held belief is that "opposites attract." The truth is it depends on which qualities are different, how intense those differences are, and how that interaction plays out in the long run.

For example, if you have a tendency to be melancholy, it might be better for you to be with a partner who is usually perky and upbeat rather than someone who is more similar to you on this variable. Someone who also has a tendency to think negatively and be melancholy might be very empathic when you are feeling down, but then end up feeling down for you. Then you'll feel sad for him because he's feeling down, and so on and so on. On the other hand, the partner who is usually upbeat and positive may be less bothered by your tendency to think negatively. He may just kind of tune it out, and instead, make positive, upbeat comments about life. Those comments might help you feel better and eventually, you might even find yourself learning to think more positively.

On the other hand, if you are really clinically depressed and sit around and mope all day instead of getting treatment, your positive, perky, upbeat partner may become totally frustrated with you and decide to move on.

If you are very social and your partner is very withdrawn, you'll want to be out and about socializing with many people, and your partner will prefer to stay home alone with you. That is not a good combination. On the other hand, someone who is a little more quiet may go better with someone a little more talkative, because the quiet one will listen when the other ones talks, and the outgoing one likes to talk a lot!

With intelligence, religious goals, values about life, and all the qualities we discussed in the compatibility quiz section, it's better if the two of you are more similar than different. It's also helpful if you share similar ideas about money and how to spend it, similar ideas about raising children, and similar short- and long-term life goals. The more you see eye-to-eye, the easier it will be to live together as a couple.

It's been my observation that when two people are very dissimilar, but are tremendously attracted to one another, the attraction is more sexual in nature. You are powerfully attracted, but other than having sex together, there's not much room for the relationship to grow. Living together, because of your great differences, is not going to be feasible.

Distance doesn't really make the heart grow fonder

We do tend to take people for granted when they are too accessible, and miss them when they aren't always immediately available. However, in order for a relationship to flourish, the couple has to spend time together on a regular basis. Part of intimacy involves sharing day-to-day experiences, joys and sorrows with one another. You can talk on the phone or use email, but it's much easier to misunderstand one another that way, because many of the cues you have in person aren't present. You can't see your lover's face to tell that he's joking or touch him on the knee to soften a remark.

It's also important to be physically close. Everyone needs to be touched, and of course, lovemaking is important for both emotional and physical reasons.

So if you have to be separated from your partner for a period of time, keep in touch by phone, email and snailmail and any way you can. However, if you want to stay close, you'll also need that valuable in-person time.

In my opinion, it's very unwise to start a relationship long-distance. A new relationship is very fragile, and with the distance, it's likely to fall apart. Long-distance relationships are very difficult and expensive to maintain, and one person has to eventually move to be with the other, or the relationship will break up. Besides, there are compatible people for you in your own backyard. So why not concentrate on finding them instead?

So how picky should you be?

Picky enough to rule out anyone who is unhealthy for you, anyone who is so vastly divergent in relationship goals that you would not be able to find a suitable compromise, and anyone who has severe psychological or other personal problems such that your relationship could never be successful until those problems are fixed.

With healthy people, whether or not you are compatible is going to depend on how close you are on all those variables we discussed earlier. On the other hand, when deciding whether or not someone is compatible enough, it's also important to understand how age and sex can affect your decision.

More younger men and older women

Basically, there are more men born than women. However, males die faster all the way up the lifecycle. They die faster in childbirth and childhood. Then when men get close to 40, they start dying from heart attacks in greater numbers than women. When they get closer to 50, they start dying from strokes in greater numbers. In short, they die faster than women all the way up, at least until the 80's, where more women are expected to die from Alzheimer's than men.

So when a woman is in her 20's, she's really outnumbered by men. I know, you don't feel like it, but it's true. However, when she gets closer to 40, she starts to notice that there seems to be less and less available men. That is also true. It becomes more and more difficult for a woman to find a compatible mate the older she gets because the pool of available men keeps shrinking.

The other problem is that women traditionally notice more details than men. As the woman ages, she gets even better at noticing details. The culmination of this is that if she allows herself to, she can start ruling out more men than she formerly would have. If she's ruling them out for frivolous reasons, it's very unfortunate; the pool is smaller, and it would be much better if she didn't waste her opportunities!

So, if you're a younger man looking for a woman, don't despair. Your odds of finding a compatible mate should increase the older you get. If you're a woman between 28-35, it's very important to use your time wisely. If you want to get married and start a family, don't waste your time dating anyone who isn't marriage material. And definitely use an efficient method to meet single, emotionally available men—an introduction service, the personals or both.

A report in *Time* magazine discussing longevity stated that since more women are expected to die from Alzheimer's in their 80's, a woman who lives past 100 should once again be outnumbered by men! In the meantime, however, if you're a woman over 40 looking to meet a compatible male for a long-term relationship or marriage, it's very important to focus on the important aspects of compatibility and not rule out potential mates for frivolous reasons. For more about older women and compatibility, see *Chapter 12—Starting Over.*

Real-life Love@AOL letters about compatibility

As you may imagine, I have received many AOL letters asking about compatibility issues. Below are some of my favorites. Enjoy!

Sexually abused his daughter...men to avoid! MY AGE: 41 MY GENDER: FEMALE

Dear Dr. Kate,
My 43-year-old boyfriend recently told me that he was convicted of sexually abusing his daughter over 6 years ago, when she was about 14. He says he is "cured" of his obsession with her. But she acts jealous of me and wears skimpy clothes and dances suggestively around him. He also has porn movies featuring girls who look very much like his daughter. What do you think?

Dear Girlfriend Of Ex-Child Molester,
I think you should get yourself a new boyfriend. Here's the bottom line: No one is perfect. No relationship is perfect. However, some problems you can work with, and others, you should just avoid.

In general, totally avoid men who are currently involved in or have any history of sexual abuse, physical abuse, child molestation, sexual addictions, paranoia, violent tempers and psychopathic (con artist) behavior. Also totally avoid current alcoholics, drug abusers, gambling addicts and psychotics (people who are out of touch with reality). Be very cautious of anyone with a history of alcohol or drug abuse, gambling addiction, bad judgment, lying, infidelity, intense family pathology or an inability to commit.

Your boyfriend has a history that includes bad judgment, sexual abuse, child abuse and incest. He was 37 when the incident with his own daughter happened. How many others did he molest or think about molesting before that? It takes a lot for an adult to completely throw away his judgment and molest a child. Don't underestimate the pathology involved.

In contrast, men who are "workable" are: Men who are shy and need help opening up, men who basically want commitment but need a little help learning to express their feelings, overweight people or people who smoke, men who dress badly, men who basically have good intentions and treat others well, but who may have a few issues of their own (e.g., lower self-esteem, anxiety, non-psychotic depression, or problems that don't threaten or malign other people).

You are 41 and you can still find a man who is much healthier than your boyfriend. With someone like him, you'll never have a stable future anyway. So why do that to yourself?

All the Best. Please let me know what you decide to do and how it works out,

Dr. Kate

Con artist ruins fairy tale...how to trust again?

Dear Dr. Kate,

I am a very confused young lady who wants to believe in the fairy tale, but at the same time, believes that there are no good men out there. About four months ago, I got out of a three-year relationship. The man I was dating turned out to be a real con artist. He slept with everything he could get his hands on, stole my money and was still able to look me in the eyes and tell me he loved me. How am I ever supposed to trust a man again?

Dear Confused Young Lady,

I'm very sorry you had this experience. One of the ways to learn to trust again is to learn how to differentiate men you can trust from those you can't.

The first lesson is how to recognize a con artist. Also called psychopaths, sociopaths or antisocial personality, a person with this disorder commonly seem charming and very socially-skilled at first. He's intelligent, verbal and articulate, and seems to know exactly what to say. He can be charming because he doesn't care whether or not he is telling the truth. He says whatever it takes to manipulate you. He plays into your desire for romance and seems to be your every wish. He pretends to be loving, devoted, romantic and smitten. You only find out later that he says the same thing to every woman he meets. When he says, "I love you," or, "I'm sorry," it's because he knows it's socially appropriate to do so. He doesn't really mean it; it's a means to an end.

In reality, a man like this doesn't want to be married, monogamous or have any responsibilities. Instead, he loves the excitement and risk of being with several different women. He likes to live on the edge. He doesn't care what society says; he makes his own rules. He puts himself and his needs ahead of everyone else's and views others as objects to be manipulated for his own ends.

Many women have difficulty resisting such men, because they are so charming. Some women even have trouble getting over such a man after the affair ends, even though they know the man is not healthy for them.

The problem is that in comparison to "normal men," the psychopath often seems much more fascinating, enchanting and irresistible. Other men seem boring in comparison. However, once you have been burned by a psychopath, it becomes much easier to value someone who tells the truth, even though he may not be as charming because he is more honest.

So, in the future, if something seems too good to be true, ask yourself if it really is. Talk to the man's friends. If he doesn't have any long-term, close friends, if he refuses to introduce you to his family or friends, if they make references to him making up stories or manipulating people, or if they don't treat you as very important (because he's introduced them to so many women before), then there's usually a problem. If he also tells any small, seemingly meaningless lies, that's also a warning sign.

To get over such a man, simply imagine that he is saying the same romantic things he says to you to all the other women he beds. That should break the romantic bubble and help you see him for the con artist he is.

It's important not to totally distrust all men because of this one person. While there are many psychopaths out there, there also many nice men who say what they mean and mean what they say most of the time, and who do not manipulate, steal or lie. If you allow this one experience to color your whole approach to men, you will, in effect, be allowing this man to hurt you more than he has already.

So learn the appropriate lesson from this: When you're dating, calmly and objectively differentiate the honest men from the dishonest, then act accordingly.

I'm sorry you had this problem. Learn what you can so it doesn't happen again in the future, and the experience will not be a total waste.

All the Best, and please let me know how you're doing from time to time,

Dr. Kate

Exercises to learn more about compatibility and your relationship stages and patterns

These exercises will build on the relationship history you started in your Relationship Notebook for the Chapter 1 exercise.

1. To learn more about your relationship stages and patterns, take **The Dr. Kate Compatibility Quiz** for each of the partners you listed in your relationship history. Compare the results and look for patterns. What do you notice about your pattern? Have you been looking for the most important qualities in your partner? Do you find yourself drawn to people who are compatible in some ways and not in others? Which qualities? How does that work out in the long run? Have you been too picky? Or not picky enough? In what ways?

    Skim back over the myths of compatibility. Have you passed up any people because you believed in love at first sight? Instant compatibility assessment? Have you bet too often on long-distance relationships? How did they work out?

2. Take **The Dr. Kate Compatibility Quiz** for each of the people you are dating now. Compare those results to your results from #1 above. What do you see? Do you notice any patterns?

3. Without looking, make a list of the most important qualities to find in a compatible mate. Don't look at the book. Just think it through for yourself. Then review that section of the book and see how well you did. Writing the important

qualities down and reasoning them through will help you remember what's important when you're actually out and about meeting people.

4. If you need to decide which of two people is more compatible, try this exercise:

    A. Take **The Dr. Kate Compatibility Quiz** for each of the people you're seeing. Compare the results. Who seems more compatible?

    B. Take two pieces of paper, divide each in half lengthwise and label one half of each page "*Pros*," and the other "*Cons*." Label each page with the name of one of the people. Then proceed to list the pros and cons of being with that person. When you're done, go back and assign a "weight" (a rating of importance) to each item on a 1-5 scale, with 5 being the best. For example, if one person wants kids and the other doesn't, and you want kids, one person gets a 5, the other a 1, and the weight is a 5, because it's very important to you to have kids.

    Do the same with the items in the "con" columns. Then multiply each score by the weight you gave it, total the positives (*pros*) for each person and subtract their negatives (*cons*) to see how they compare.

    You'll probably find that this scale doesn't work in a precise way. For example, you might suddenly realize the one who gets the best score isn't really the one you want. It's perfectly OK to make a decision that is different from what is suggested by the numbers. The goal of this exercise is just to help you decide. Most of my clients who have used this technique have found that by breaking the comparison down in an organized way and exploring their feelings in each category, they are able to tell which choice is best for them.

    Once you have decided, though, try to stick to your decision. If the two choices are very close, as soon as you decide for one person, the other person will look better. However, if you make a decision for that person, the other person will look better, too. So just stick with your first choice.

Chapter 4

Sex! Getting closer?
Getting physical

S ex! "Say it loud and it's music playing, say it soft and it's almost like praying…" Well, not quite. But say the word **SEX!** And people immediately perk up and become interested (kind of like that old E. F. Hutton commercial—"*When E.F. Hutton speaks, everyone listens…*"). The room goes quiet, all eyes are on the person discussing sex and you can hear a pin drop—or you pretend to continue your conversation with the person you're talking to, but in reality, you've got one ear on the sex conversation as well. Why?

Because most people are very interested in sex.

But before we discuss sex any further, you may be wondering what my background is. I would be, if I were you. It's good to ask those kinds of questions, especially since there has always been a lot of misinformation distributed about sex. After all, not knowing anything about sex surely didn't stop Freud from making all kinds of assumptions about it! From Freud's *Three Essays On Sexuality* to the primitive sex manuals of the 30-50s, much of what was published on sex was incorrect information. Yet a great deal of this data has been absorbed into cultural lore, and has caused grief for people of both sexes.

My sexual research

Like most people, I've been interested in sex since I was born (or shortly thereafter). I was also fortunate to be aware of what was going on during the sexual revolution of the late 60's. And certainly, by the time I had decided to become a psychologist, I was curious to learn more. One of the fun parts of psychology is the ability to do research and practice in the area of sex. So in 1974, I conducted the first ever sexual research at Rosary College to study sexual humor. I later completed a major review of the sexual literature, including the best treatment procedures for sexual problems. I studied Masters and Johnson's methods, as well as the work of other sex researchers and therapists. From there, I went on to evaluate the first ever Sexual Attitude Reassessment Module at the University of South Dakota. I did two research projects in the area of sex, and studied sex therapy as well.

Since then, I have treated many couples for sexual problems, from premature ejaculation to ejaculatory incompetence to impotence, to female orgasmic problems to painful sex—you name it. I have seen people who wanted to ask questions and get straight answers—everything from "Does oral sex cause cancer? How do you do it anyway?" to a 30-year-old man with mild retardation wanting to know "why women take longer to go to the bathroom." The same man thought all naked women looked like *Playboy* models (since that was his reference point), and that they all wear garters and nylons.

I have treated couples who have not had sex for decades, as well as male and female virgins ranging in age from 28 to 50. And of course, there were many couples who just varied from each other on the frequency of sex, the timing of sex (morning versus nighttime), and how they liked their sex. I have seen couples who came in for sexual problems, but turned out to have communication problems instead. (If you're so angry at your partner you could spit, of course, you are going to have trouble making love! Makes sense, doesn't it?)

I have also seen people who have had more serious sexual deviations, like the man who sexually abused his children, belonged to swinging clubs, and couldn't walk to my office without stopping off at the porno place to watch movies, eat several hotdogs, have a smoke and a couple of drinks. His wife couldn't stand him, his kids refused to talk to him, and he finally came in for treatment when he was on the verge of losing his job due to his unusual habits.

I have evaluated transgendered people for surgery, interviewing and testing a biological man who wanted to become a female by getting breast implants and later having his penis converted into a vagina.

At my AOL site, I have received thousands of letters about sex—everything from people asking simple sexual questions, e.g., about birth control, the menstrual cycle, common misperceptions about sex—to letters from crossdressers, swingers, sadomasochists, pedophiles, you name it.

I've discussed sex on the radio and on TV—everything from keeping the passion alive to oral sex to videotaping sex. I've given hundreds of magazine and newspaper interviews on related topics.

The bottom line is that there is so much to say about sex, it's impossible to cover it all in this book. Besides reading this chapter, be sure you read Chapter 8 about sex in a long-term relationship. Then I invite you to read my next book, *Sex Secrets!: Dr. Kate's Guide To Sumptuous Sex*, which will be entirely devoted to this incredibly important and interesting topic of **SEX!**

In this chapter, I'm going to touch on some of the most important secrets that people need to know about sex early in the relationship, and how you can make it a positive experience.

So now that you know that I have studied sex extensively, have researched it as well as practiced sex therapy, you can rest easy and open your mind to the rest of this chapter.

Sex is a normal drive

Sex is a normal human and animal drive, just like eating and sleeping. Sex is good. In this chapter, we're going to explore the differences in the way men and women approach sex, and how this sometimes causes problems. But that doesn't make sex bad. It's important to remember that just like our other drives of eating and sleeping, sex is a very important and pleasurable part of life.

When, where, how and with whom?

Sex is a very important onstage in the relationship. Some of the key issues include questions of when, where, how, how much and with whom.

When—At what point in the relationship should you have it? What happens if you have it before or after that?

Where should you have it?

How should you do it? What's the best method? What's normal versus too off-the-wall or deviant? What do you do if your partner likes it one way and you don't?

With whom should you have it?

Let's take the last one first.

With Whom

I believe it's best to limit sexual encounters to people you really love. Keep in mind that strong feelings early in the relationship may be infatuation or "lust at first sight." If the feelings last and grow stronger after seeing one another several times a week for at least 3 months, they're more likely to be love. If you delay sex this long, and the man is still around, it's highly likely that he really does love you. Partners who aren't serious about a relationship will usually fall by the wayside way before that time.

Also, if you limit your sexual contacts to people you really love who also love you back, you will greatly reduce your number of sexual episodes, which will then lower your risk of contracting a sexually transmitted disease.

OK, so you're saying you could never wait three or more months. I certainly live in the real world and understand that many people don't wait this long. However, as you'll see in the next section, sex too soon can be very problematic. So if you decide not to wait this long, it's very important to understand the risk you're taking and go into it with your eyes open.

When

When should you have sex for the first time ever? And when should you have it in any particular relationship? Those are important questions that must be considered carefully.

SEX FOR THE FIRST TIME EVER

If you've never had sex before, then making a decision to have sex with someone is a big step. *You will always remember your first sex partner*, so try to make the experience meaningful. You should never make a big decision like that on the spur of the moment or while under the influence of drugs or alcohol. Rather, deciding to have sex for the first time should be something you do after reflecting on your relationship and whether or not you and your partner can emotionally handle sex, and whether your relationship is ready for it.

SEX FOR THE FIRST TIME IN A PARTICULAR RELATIONSHIP

So at what point in a relationship are you ready for sex? In my opinion, the best time to have sex is when your relationship has progressed to the point that you and your partner are emotionally involved enough to warrant the seriousness of sexual intimacy. In other words, sex is very intimate. It's the most intimate thing you can do with someone physically. The man gets inside the woman. You can't get any closer than that from a physical point of view. So in order to warrant that kind of physical closeness, your emotions should be just as seriously involved. If they're not, or if one person's are and the other's are not, then you may be in for a big let down when the relationship doesn't flow as you'd like.

If you allow yourself to get caught up in the passion of the moment with someone you just met, realize that he may not be there for you later. If you decide to have sex on the spur of the moment when you're under the influence of alcohol or drugs, it's even more likely that you will regret it the next day when you are sober. If you don't, your partner might. So if you choose to do have sex so soon under those conditions, realize that you're taking a risk, and go into it with your eyes open. That way, if your partner does disappear the next day, you won't be shocked or hurt.

Why is sex on the spur of the moment an emotional risk? Because men and women often have sex for different reasons. And since they generally don't discuss those different reasons in advance, this discrepancy can make for a lot of misunderstandings, confusion and hurt feelings.

Men and women often have sex for different reasons.

A man may have sex mainly to satisfy his sexual needs, while a woman rarely has sex just for the sake of having sex. She's far more likely to do it when she's really interested in developing a relationship with the man. A major problem then occurs when she assumes that what she's feeling is the same as what the man is feeling. As Masters and Johnson noted, men tend to be biophysical in their approach to sex, focusing on the biological and physical factors of the act, while women tend to be psychosocial, valuing sex for the psychological and social value.

The following chart shows these differences and other important ways that men and women vary in their approach to sex.

Men, as a group, tend to or are more likely to:

Be biophysical, focusing on the biological and physical aspects of sex.

Be able to separate physical, sexual feelings from emotional, romantic feelings.

Be able to have sex mainly to satisfy sexual needs.

Have a much easier time having sex with someone they don't really care for, including bad dates and 1-night stands.

Be practical about sex. May have sex with a date just so the evening isn't a total waste of time and money.

Don't fall in love just because they have sex with a woman or are impressed with her ability in the bedroom.

May say, "I love you," when they mean, "At this moment, I am so excited (or sexually frustrated) that I really, really, really want to have sex with you."

Peak sexually in the late teens–early 20's.

Push like crazy for sex when peaking, but don't really want the woman to give in.

Not understand that a woman might have sex with a man because she thinks he's special, not because she's just "easy."

Imagine that the woman is having sex with every guy she dates, and hence, don't want to see her again.

Be less able to adapt to the incongruity between what they expected to occur and what actually did occur. More difficulty assimilating unexpected behavior into their self-concept. If man unexpectedly has sex, he may blame the woman and lose interest.

When embarrassed and confused, more likely to run away.

Find it easier to dump woman to avoid thinking about their actions that night.

Women, as a group:

Tend to be psychosocial, focusing on the psychological and social aspects of sex.

Usually connect sex with love, caring and romance.

Rarely have sex just for the sake of satisfying sexual needs.

Generally prefer to be in love with a man before having sex with him.

Think about sex as **making love.** Have sex if date is special and don't think about the time and money involved.

Far more likely to: Have sex to be accepted or make man love her, and to fall in love with man after having sex with him.

Take the words literally, believe man loves them and become even more infatuated with him.

Peak in the late 30's-early 40's.

Believe the man really wants them to have sex, and they feel guilty for refusing.

Have unexpected sex with man because they think he's special and they're interested in developing special relationship with him.

A woman tends to assume man is having sex because he feels she's special. Never imagines he thinks she's easy.

Women find it easier to accept their decision to alter behavior. Assimilate unexpected behavior into self-concept by saying they didn't expect to sleep with him, but did so because thought he was special. Accepts responsibility for decision.

When embarrassed and confused, more likely to talk about it than run.

Look forward to making emotional relationship catch up to the physical intimacy. Don't understand when the man disappears.

So given these differences, it's important for men and women to realize that they may not be thinking about having sex with one another in the same way. To avoid misunderstandings and hurt feelings, it would be much better if they would talk about it first. In my opinion, if you don't feel you can do that with your partner, then you are NOT emotionally close or intimate enough that you should be participating in the act together. However, if you decide to do it anyway, just remember that you took the risk with your eyes open. If it works out as you'd like, fine. If not, try to learn from the experience and apply it to your next one.

It's OK to say, "No"

Young women also need to know that if they say, "No," to a man, he will, in fact, live. Don't be swayed by guilt or any accusation that you have "led" the man on. If you feel you have led him on, apologize. But don't have sex with him just for that reason. I can guarantee you that the same man who is willing to accuse you in that way will not be there for you if you get pregnant or come down with his STD.

Where

Have sex someplace private where you're comfortable and relaxed and have time to focus on your partner, and where your partner is comfortable and can concentrate entirely on you.

Your first sexual experiences with your new partner should be special and wonderful. Hurried sex also does not allow time for the foreplay the woman needs to get ready for orgasm. In addition, frequent hurried sex can cause a man to develop premature ejaculation, or if the man is very nervous, failure to maintain an erection.

How

HAVE FUN

Focus on giving and receiving pleasure, the sensations involved and having fun. Experience the whole act of lovemaking and enjoy every moment of it, rather than focusing on orgasm as the primary goal. Having fun is the bottom line. If you and your partner are both enjoying what you are doing, it isn't necessary to orgasm. Sometimes a man becomes obsessed with whether or not the woman had an orgasm. That puts way too much emphasis on performance and inhibits her ability to relax and enjoy. In addition, anxiety decreases or eliminates a man's erection, too.

So take sex seriously as far as deciding when to have it and using adequate protection. But once you are having sex with someone, don't approach it like a serious project or worry about your performance. Instead, make love with enthusiasm, energy and a spirit of fun. In fact, sometimes funny things happen during sex, and when they do, it's OK to laugh about them together and take them in stride.

BE POSITIVE

At the same time, never say anything during sex that can be construed as critical. Everyone wants to be a good lover, and critical comments can really take the wind out of someone's sails. They can also cause someone to develop erection or orgasmic problems. So be sure that whatever you say during sex, it is positive and encouraging. And for heavens' sake, NEVER talk about your ex-lovers or sexual experiences with other people during sex.

GET INTO IT

Now, that doesn't mean a woman should be silent and lay there. Men hate a woman who does a log imitation during sex. Nothing is more frustrating than doing your best to pleasure someone, only to have her act like nothing is affecting her. So get into the sensations, and let your partner know when you like something he's doing. Let yourself make noise, moan or sigh. Say something like, *"Oh, that feels wonderful!"* You can also touch and direct your partner's hand or head, or alter the pace with comments like, *"Slower," "faster," "harder" "softer" "higher," "lower," "right there,"* etc.

If you don't like what he's doing, don't say, "I hate that." Just redirect his hand or head until he is doing something that feels good and say, *"That's better. I like that."* Keep all your comments as positive as possible, and he will feel like giving you pleasure.

LEARN YOUR PARTNER'S RESPONSES

Similarly, be aware of his physical and verbal cues to learn what he likes best. Note any altered breathing patterns, involuntary gasps, shivers and twitches. If he isn't saying anything while you are pleasuring him, say, *"Tell me what you like,"* or, *"Let me know when I do something you like."* In time, you will learn what he likes best and how to pleasure him to give him an optimum experience.

Never assume that your partner will enjoy what your last partner enjoyed. Everyone is wired somewhat differently. What one person finds extremely pleasurable, another can find irritating or painful. So think of each new person as starting over from scratch. Explore sex together and learn what you each like. Then in time, you can become wonderful lovers for each other.

HAVE SEX RESPONSIBLY

It's vitally important to **always** use two forms of birth control to protect against pregnancy, since no one method is foolproof. One should always be a latex condom, since the latex condom also helps prevent sexually-transmitted diseases. The other should be another highly effective form of birth control (e.g., the contraceptive pill, shot or implant, IUD or diaphragm) to further help prevent pregnancy. Be aware that there is no such thing as perfect protection against pregnancy or sexual disease. The condom does not prevent all STDs (it will not keep you from getting genital warts, crabs and scabies, for example) and most sexual diseases (including herpes, genital warts, syphilis, gonorrhea, chlamydia) can be passed through oral sex. So while you should use a condom for any episode of any kind of sex, the bottom line is that there is always some risk. Choose your partners carefully discuss your sexual histories in advance, and don't have sex with someone unless you really believe he's worth taking that risk and would feel the same toward you.

If something goes wrong even though you're using two forms of birth control (e.g., the woman forgets to take her contraceptive pill and the condom breaks), call the gynecologist immediately and ask for "morning after pills." These can prevent you from getting pregnant. However, they are only a backup method and should not be used as a primary method of birth control, since they may or may not work.

Also, be honest with yourself about your libido. Don't deny that you might have sex when, in fact, you're very close to having it. Nothing is worse than getting drunk or being overcome with desire, and having unprotected sex in "a moment of weakness." Better you should be honest with yourself that you may be having sex soon, get on birth control and carry latex condoms with you.

Now that we've discussed some of the key issues in sex, let's talk about some of the myths that have complicated sex for centuries.

Secrets to sumptuous sex

A good time does not always mean an orgasm

The first secret is that you need not have an orgasm for sex to be enjoyable and worthwhile.

Focusing on orgasm as a goal adds anxiety and makes sex far less enjoyable and fun. If the anxiety gets too high, it can prevent you from having an orgasm. Focus instead on giving pleasure to your partner, on the wonderful feelings of intimacy. Then, whether the "Big O" comes or not (and it's more likely to when you do this), both of you will be far happier.

Go ahead—fake it!

Some people believe that you should never fake an orgasm. However, I strongly disagree. Acting *as if* you are having an orgasm can allow you to relax, feel the sensations more intensely, and get into the sexual experience with your partner. Your acted-out excitement can be a turn-on for your partner, too. He's been trying hard to please you and it rewards him for his effort. It also makes it far more likely that he will look forward to pleasuring you in the future. In contrast, acting like you're not affected can cause your lover to question his abilities and gradually lose interest in being intimate with you. At the same time, don't lie and specifically say that you had an orgasm. Just act it out. If your partner asks, say, *"That felt grrrreeeaaaaat!"* Besides, that's the bottom line anyway—having fun and feeling great. Whether or not you actually experienced the full physiological phenomenon labeled "orgasm" is not important.

Lack of experience is OK

Some people fear that their lack of experience in sex will be a turn off to their partner. The truth is that sex is a great equalizer. Everyone is wired somewhat differently, so they find different sensations pleasurable. What one person finds pleasurable, another might find annoying or even painful. A good lover knows to start fresh with each partner, learning what that person likes and doesn't like during sex.

The worst thing in the world is a lover who thinks that you should like having a certain body part rubbed a certain way because his last partner liked it that way. Less-experienced lovers don't usually make such assumptions. They also tend to spend more time in foreplay and afterglow and be very enthusiastic about sex and learning their partner's preferences. And everyone loves that! So if your experience level is low, don't fret. Just remember to pay attention to your partner's verbal and physical signals to find out what he likes. And be sure to give him signals to let him know what you like, too!

Size does not matter

Another common myth is that the size of the man's penis is important. The truth is that the way the man uses what he has is far more important than his exact size. A woman can contract her vagina around a smaller penis, and it will naturally stretch to accommodate a larger one. While a large penis might initially seem preferable, it can make oral sex more difficult and necessitate the use of lubricants or a lot of foreplay prior to intercourse. All things considered, the man's sensitivity to the woman's needs, both inside and outside the bedroom, and how he makes love to her, including how much quality foreplay he gives her, can more than make up for a smaller penile dimension.

Intercourse does not equal orgasm

Another secret is that many women cannot orgasm through intercourse alone. If you fall into this category, there is no reason to feel inadequate. You are far from alone. During intercourse, stimulation of the clitoris is much less direct; it slides under the clitoral hood during thrusting. Many women find that they orgasm much easier through oral sex or manual manipulation, because both provide more direct, concentrated and controlled stimulation of the clitoris and surrounding area. However, sexual intercourse usually has more emotional and romantic meaning to the woman than oral sex; it represents a coming together of her and her lover in a very intimate way. So even though a woman may not have an orgasm through sexual intercourse alone, very few would actually opt to skip it.

Real-life Love@AOL letters about sex

I have received many thousands of letters from AOL members on the topic of sex. Here are some of my favorites. Enjoy!

Partied and had sex...what do I say to save face?   MY AGE: 18 MY GENDER: FEMALE

Dear Dr. Kate,
I have been in love with this guy at school for months. At a recent party, we both had a lot to drink, and ended up fooling around. He never called me, and he told my friend he made a big mistake. The thing is—I think I knew he was using me, but I wanted to be with him anyway. What do I say when I have to face him at school?

Dear Saving Face?,
Just say, "*Hello*," and act as you would toward anyone else. Be friendly and polite, but no more or less friendly than you are to any female or male platonic friend. Act classy, like you like yourself. Don't bring it up or try to talk with him about it. Don't apologize for your behavior. Don't act like he did you a favor, or like you feel badly about it. Just act like it never happened.

In general, men have a difficult time talking about awkward situations like this. And young men generally have almost no skills in this area. So if he brings it up, tell him you enjoyed it. But don't say anything more unless he talks about it in a mature way. He may be putting a negative spin on it in his head because he's embarrassed. Or perhaps he had a commitment with someone else, and feels a bit guilty for getting involved with you. But no matter what he feels, there is no reason for you to feel badly or apologize to him for your actions.

On the other hand, please learn from this. In the future, don't let yourself sleep with anyone after a party. It's usually *not* a good idea, since it is most likely an impulsive act, well-fueled with alcohol, and one which you or your partner may very well regret later. With STDs running rampant, you just can't afford to have that many sexual partners these days. So one-night stands are not only emotionally questionable, they are also physically risky.

Best Wishes, and please let me know how you're doing from time to time,

Dr. Kate

Got drunk, had sex, now no phone call!: Sex early in dating, part II

MY AGE: 55 MY GENDER: FEMALE

Dear Dr. Kate,
I knew him 6 weeks, and we had dated sporadically. The chemistry was there for both of us, but we had only kissed, nothing more. I'd gotten a bottle of vodka for a Christmas gift, and he came over for a holiday drink. Neither of us are drinkers, but we both had too much that night. Before I knew it, clothes were flying, and I was sort of "in and out"—blacked out, but also aware some of the time. He had sex with me, but there was no pleasure involved. Up to now, we'd only kissed. He went home that night—10 days ago—and I haven't heard from him since. What should I do now?

Dear Conscious, But Embarrassed Now,
If you have not heard from him by the time you get this email, call him. Try to speak to him directly (not via the answering machine). Ask him how's he's doing, and then ask him out. Invite him to a casual event (not your house or any intimate location) where you can relax together without thinking about "it." A sports game or comedy club, with a casual dinner afterwards, might be good. That way, he'll have time to sit with you, warm up and get over his embarrassment; he'll also have time afterwards to chat with you and be friendly.

Men are frequently put off when something happens that they didn't expect. He didn't think he was going to end up sleeping with you, so he's probably embarrassed and confused by the incident. People who are confused often avoid dealing with issues. So you want to gently help him get used to you again, while letting him save face.

Men often have a difficult time talking about awkward situations like this. If he were a young man, it might be better not to talk about it. However, he's a mature male and has hopefully progressed. You just need to give him some encouragement.

So wait until he brings up the last evening you spent together, then tell him you enjoyed it. If he sounds embarrassed, you can reassure him that there is nothing to worry about. Although you would like to go slower in the future, you did enjoy the evening and his company. He's going to be very influenced by how you act, so don't act embarrassed.

Embarrassment is a useless emotion; it implies that you have done something wrong and someone noticed. But you didn't do anything wrong. The two of you are adults and if you want to have sex together, it's OK. Besides, the only people who noticed were the two of you, and you were both involved! True, it's best not to drink so much beforehand, but so what? In the future, act the way you want and then don't feel badly about it afterward. Or—if you're going to regret it later, don't do it. But don't do something and then feel embarrassed. Make sense?

It's important to demonstrate the behavior you want to see in him. In other words, act confident, secure and calm about what happened so that he can, too. If he doesn't bring up the evening, but seems to relax around you, you can let it be for now. If he seems to want to talk about it, you can gently broach the subject. However, it's important to be sensitive to how comfortable he feels, as if he feels trapped into discussing the evening, it will only make things worse.

All the Best, and please let me know how it works out,

Dr. Kate

I'm very hot...Afraid I'll go too far!: Sex for the first time?

MY AGE: 18 MY GENDER: FEMALE

Dear Dr. Kate,
I'm a virgin, but lately I've been very, very hot. I'm not in a steady relationship, though, and I'm afraid I'll just get carried away on a date and end up doing it. How can I control myself? Thanks.

Dear Hot and Bothered,
1. Get some latex condoms, as well as another form of birth control (e.g., spermicidal cream or jelly, or see your doctor or Planned Parenthood for the pill or an IUD). I know you're telling me you don't want to have sex, and I hear you. However, since you are thinking about it so much, it's best to be safe by making sure you always have protection with you. Keep the birth control in your purse, *always* with you.

2. Avoid being alone with your date in any private place (his bedroom, his house when nobody else is home, the park) where sexual activity could progress.

3. Don't drink too much or do drugs on your dates. That way, your judgment won't be impaired, and you'll be better able to resist temptation.

4. Always bring money with you. If the guy gets angry because you won't perform sexually, you'll have cab fare home.

5. If your date tries to go past kissing, say, *"No, please, not now. I like you and if we get closer, that may be a possibility, but I don't get sexual with someone unless I'm in a relationship. So let's get to know one another better and see what develops, OK?"*

6. When you say, "no," act like you mean, **"NO."** Don't laugh, smile, or feel him up at the same time, or he won't realize you're serious. Make sure your words and behaviors are in sync; give clear signals.

7. If things get too hot, ask to do some activity that is impossible to do at the same time you are getting sexual, e.g., take a walk, watch TV with his parents, go to a club, socialize with others.

8. Once you and your date become sexually excited, it can be difficult to stop. So say, "No," sooner than later.

9. If you forget to do #5 and #8 and your date becomes excited, don't fall for the line that since you got him that way, you have to "finish him off." It's the oldest line in the book, and millions of teenage boys have used it on teenage girls since the beginning of time. Don't feel guilty; stop anyway. He will survive, trust me.

All the Best,

Dr. Kate

And just because sometimes you just gotta laugh…(never forget to find the humor in life—and sex!)

His condom fell off!
MY AGE: 31 MY GENDER: FEMALE

Dear Dr. Kate,
My fiancee and I were having sex when the condom came off. And now we can't get it out!!! HELP!!! Should I call my doctor or keep trying?????

Dear Condom-full,
Call your doctor immediately. What goes up must come down, or there will be a whopping infection before long.

All the Best,

Dr. Kate

Will menthol cigarettes kill my sperm?
MY AGE: 21 MY GENDER: MALE

Dear Dr. Kate,
I've heard that menthol cigarettes stop you from having sperm, and that they also kill your sperm. Is that true?

Dear Worried Smoker,
No, menthol cigarettes will not prevent or kill your sperm. However, menthol cigarettes can kill you, and that in turn, can kill your sperm. A woman can also harm the fetus by smoking during pregnancy.

Instead of worrying about this, why not give up smoking? You're still young, and it will be easier to quit now than it will be years in the future when you are even more addicted. As a matter of fact, if it helps, maybe you should continue to think that you are quitting to save your sperm—what a motivator!

All the Best,

Dr. Kate

Masturbation and little green men...?

MY AGE: 18 MY GENDER: MALE

Dear Dr. Kate,
If you masturbate too much, can you reduce you sperm count?

Dear Concerned,
No, masturbation does not permanently reduce your sperm count. When people are trying to get pregnant, it is often recommended that they have sex once every two days around the time of ovulation. During that 2-day time period, the concentration of sperm continues to build, so chances of impregnation are better when the man ejaculates. However, you're not trying to get anyone pregnant at this time.

Masturbation does not permanently reduce sperm count, nor does it cause incompetence, impotence, blindness or little green men to cross your visual tracks. I think I'm going to write a book sometime about what masturbation does **not** do. It is clear to me that our society instills a great deal of guilt about this activity, as evidenced by the amount of mail I get on the subject, and the number and variety of possible disorders and anomalies people worry about in association with it.

So, don't worry. If you masturbate in private, alone, and fill your head with positive sexual images and not sadomasochistic or other problematic fantasies, and as long as you are not doing it so much that you are wearing off your skin, avoiding sex with your wife (when you have a wife), or failing to live life in a productive and meaningful fashion, there's no reason to be concerned. So, now, relax and enjoy!

All the Best,

Dr. Kate

Big foot strikes again? Here hair, there hair...

MY AGE: 41 MY GENDER: FEMALE

Dear Dr. Kate,
What is the best way to remove all public hair? I see many hairless people and I would like to try this, but I don't know if waxing or shaving is the best way. I certainly don't want to have stubble. This is very important to me, so please get back to me ASAP. Thanks.

Dear Hairy,
I don't think it's a very good idea to try to remove all public hair. You might get arrested. ;)

On the other hand, you can remove your own pubic hair through the careful use of scissors and a razor. Waxing, creme hair removers and other chemicals would probably be way too harsh for that sensitive skin and you wouldn't want to chance getting them into places they shouldn't be.

Regardless of the methods you use, however, you are going to have stubble. It will grow back. And when it does, it will also itch like crazy until it reaches a certain length. So, consider that before you decide to opt for the bald crotch look.

All the Best,

Dr. Kate

Exercises to make your sex life spark

It's time to examine your sex life in the daylight! Put aside your defenses, inhibitions and insecurities for a few minutes and take some time to review this important area of your life and how much fun you're having—or wish you were having. Turn to the **Appendix** and do the sex exercises.

Stage 2 of The Love Cycle—

Making the relationship work

Chapter 5

Making a commitment
Living together & moving toward marriage

In the previous section, we talked about the early stages of finding love—flirting and dating and then deepening that attachment through sex. With this chapter, we'll begin discussion of **Stage 2 of The Love Cycle—Making the Relationship Work.** We'll consider what happens when the couple continues their relationship and deepens their attachment even more, making a commitment to each other. In this stage, some couples choose to live together or move toward marriage. By this time, they've usually passed into the nesting phase of their relationship as well.

You'll recall from Chapter 1 that individual relationships themselves have stages. When you first meet, you're in the infatuation stage where your endorphins are firing and you are very excited. Then you eventually enter the nesting stage, where you feel more cuddly and relaxed, and less excited or anxious about your relationship and your lover. You begin to trust that your partner will be around tomorrow, day after day, week after week, and that's good. It allows you to make longer-range plans, and to relax and be yourself more.

As the feelings between you and your partner deepen, you begin spending more and more time together. For most people, this means spending more and more nights together, then rushing home to change clothes and go to work. Eventually, you start thinking that it would be easier just to move some of your things in. So little by little, you start moving a few things around. Eventually, even that seems kind of wasteful. Wouldn't it just be easier to live together? Then you could save a whole rent, and avoid all the hassle of remembering where everything is, or having to have two sets of toiletries and clothes in each place. You're usually together anyway, so why not?

Sometimes living together can be a good idea. Sometimes it's not as helpful. Let's look at both of these and talk about when it's helpful and when it's not.

Living together—when it's helpful
So, when is living together a good idea?

When you've dated enough, but are not yet ready to get married

If you've dated a lot, have a good idea what you're looking for in a marriage partner, but are not yet ready to get married to anyone, living with a romantic partner can be a good learning experience.

It's better if you marry after you and your partner are both emotionally mature. If you marry before that time, you will both change a LOT by the time you do fully mature. If that growth is not in the same direction, you may find that you are married to a totally incompatible person in 10 years.

In my observation, women tend to mature around age 28 and men around 30 plus. So, if you have had enough dating experience, and are 23-27, it can be a great learning experience to try to live with someone. It sensitizes you to how difficult it can be and usually teaches patience, tolerance and other virtues you'll need to cohabit in marriage. You can also use your experience in the future to help you decide who would be a good marriage candidate.

Enduring a temporary, long-term, stressful situation together

When you're going through a temporary, but long-term, stressful situation and don't have time to date, living with someone for emotional support can be a good move. It keeps you stable and grounded while you handle the stress.

For instance, graduate school can be a great time to live with someone. In graduate school, you are working so hard you don't have time to date around. At the University of South Dakota, for example, the students worked 16-hour days, then had a party once every three weeks where the music was turned up and everyone let loose to de-stress. Our school was not as stressful as most, but all graduate schools are stressful. You're poor, studying more than you ever thought possible, holding down a job on the side to make money to live on, seeing clients and doing research all at the same time. There's a lot at stake; you've put a lot into this, you've got to please a lot of people, and there's a time limit on getting through the program.

People often paired up at the USD graduate school, partly because it was so COLD out there. Blizzards started in October and the last occurred somewhere around March. When a blizzard hit, there was some warning. You got food, found a person you liked, and spent three days partying and relaxing while the blizzard and its 80-mph winds snowed you in. There was one plow in town, but they didn't start plowing until the winds stopped. So it was basically a free three-day holiday, which was quite enjoyable— provided you had the right companion and basic supplies and didn't try to work.

Out of a total of 25 clinical psychology graduate students, I was astounded at how many of them ended up marrying or living with someone during their three to four years on campus. (Just because you have 25 psychology grad students together in one place, why would they be that compatible?) They kept each other warm during the cold nights, made digging out a lot more fun and helped each other through the incredible stress. Following graduation, almost all of the people who paired up or married during graduate school broke up or divorced. Graduate school also broke up many of the marriages of those who married before grad school, while those who married *after* getting their Ph.D.'s fared better.

My conclusion? If you're going to go through hell and back again with someone, it's usually better to live together and wait until hell is over to see if you really have enough in common to stay married long-term. If you don't mind getting divorced after it's over, that's fine. But avoid having children, because that complicates the situation and adds stress rather than relieving it.

Similar stressful situations where living together might be the best choice include: Being in the army together, going through a war together, being abroad in the Peace Corps together. In short, any situation that puts you in a stressful foreign environment where you will have to live and interact with people for a time, but from which you will eventually return to a more normal, relaxed environment is usually a good place to cohabit with your significant other.

You don't have time to date anyway, and having a steady partner at home to share your joys and sorrows and allow you to vent as needed is extremely valuable. Your partner validates you through emotional support, and reminds you that you're a wonderful human being. He also reassures you that before long, this stress will end and things will be more pleasant.

When you're moving from place to place to further your career

Another good time to live with a significant other is when you have to move around for awhile to further your career. A couple of years here, another couple of years there. Often the relationships end because the careers of the partners take them to different cities. Perhaps you work for an international company, and the next step up the corporate ladder for you is in some town where your partner can't advance or even stay level in his career. Or perhaps you work in the arts or professional sports, and there's so much competition, you just have to go to where the work is.

TV producers, sportscasters, newscasters, radio professionals, writers, editors, newspaper journalists, and anyone who works in the media typically find themselves in this position. It's a highly competitive market, and you need to go where the jobs are, transferring from city to city as you climb up the market shares. People who work for large national and international companies often find that their next promotion carries more money and prestige, but also a move to a different city. Even academics who want to climb the university hierarchy find moving necessary.

Now that women enjoy careers that are just as demanding and powerful as men, the situation has become more complicated. Achievement-oriented dual-career couples often find themselves pulled in different directions.

Marrying someone during this time would either mean that your spouse would move with you, giving up his career and family to follow you around—or stay in your hometown without you. Living with someone in different cities in between might make more sense, until you've finally acquired a position substantial and stable enough that you could be happy with it as a permanent job, at least for the foreseeable future.

Many of the clients at The Relationship Center™ have remained single into their 30's because they pursued advanced degrees, then moved a few times to establish their careers. Each time they moved, their long-term relationships broke up to allow them to pursue separate career paths.

To stay financially independent

Stars in Hollywood and other people with large incomes often stay single so as not to complicate their finances more than they have to. In a city where marriages die quickly, it may also help some work harder to keep their relationship thriving. Prenuptial agreements are often used to delineate separation of funds in case the marriage should fail, but prenups can be challenged. While most of us don't have that kind of money, people with very little money or those receiving funds from the government often consider the negative effects marriage might have on their finances. For example, sometimes senior Americans find that they can receive more Social Security money if they remain single. While it's unfortunate that such concerns would prevent a couple from marrying, it is certainly understandable.

Recently divorced, no kids, not ready to remarry

It usually takes two or more years to recover from divorce. If you meet someone before you're really done recovering, it's a mistake to marry. It could be a rebound marriage, based on your neediness rather than compatibility, and end in another divorce a few years later. Living with that person instead could allow you to get close without risking another divorce. If you have children, it's usually not a good idea to live with someone, because it can confuse them and cause them to become attached to someone who doesn't end up remaining permanently. On the other hand, if you are divorced, without children and not yet ready to remarry, living with your love interest may be a way to ease back into a safe nesting environment.

Sam & Teri's Story

Sam and Teri met when she was going through a divorce from her second husband. She had been married most of her life, and had never really lived on her own. Sam had married in his teens when his girlfriend got pregnant, and divorced a few years later. He stayed single a long time, then lived with someone for many years in a troubled relationship.

Sam and Teri hit it off because they had a lot in common. They also shared a skittishness regarding the institution of marriage. Neither had had a positive experience with it, and Teri had gotten the short end of the stick many times. She even helped her second husband pack so he could "go find himself," only to find out later that he was really leaving her to live with another woman, someone who had just had his baby. Teri hadn't even known her husband was cheating. She had really tried to be a good wife. When she discovered the truth, she felt betrayed, embarrassed, put down. She lost much of her belief in people; she doubted their honesty. She had a bad track record with husbands who lied, cheated and took advantage of her.

But Sam was a good guy, and gradually, Teri learned to trust him. Seven years later, she finally moved in with Sam. Teri had three kids and Sam one, but they were all grown. There was no family pressure to get married. But Sam thought marriage was a natural progression of their relationship.

However, his presentation of an engagement ring a few years later made Teri so nervous that it caused problems in their relationship. So after one of their fights when Teri threw the ring at him—again, Sam took the ring, put it in the bank safety deposit box, and decided to appreciate his relationship as it was. Teri was not going to feel comfortable being married again, and he would stop banging his head against the wall trying to make it happen. As far as he was concerned, they were a couple—and happier than most. Their relationship worked as a live-in, both were happy with one another, and they were viewed as a permanent couple by others, so why rock the boat?

Ed & Mona

Ed and Mona also found that they preferred living together. They met in graduate school, moved in together and gave each other emotional support through the tough times. Following graduation, they married and moved to a new town where Ed set up a lucrative practice. But Ed and Mona really didn't enjoy being married. They found that they didn't get along as well when they were married. Both felt a little trapped when the legal papers existed. They had a fierce sense of independence, were somewhat unconventional in general, and were rather unique in not feeling pressured by society to be married. Neither had any children, nor did they want any. Ed and Mona finally divorced and went back to living together—happily.

So, if having the paper isn't important to you or your partner, then living together may be the best option. This usually only occurs when both parties have been divorced or wary of commitment, or where both partners are fiercely independent and unconventional. But it doesn't always or even usually occur in these situations. For every Sam and Teri and Ed and Mona, there are thousands of couples where one person wants to get married and the other doesn't. In fact, one of the most common causes of stress in a relationship is when the two people don't share relationship goals.

Living together = all the negatives of marriage

When you live with someone, they get to see you at your worst—in the morning, no makeup, stinky breath, when you're sick, when you're stressed out. They get to interact with your family, in-laws and kids, and generally share finances and financial pressures. They get the "all-the-time" you, not the "date-and-romance" you. Yet they don't get some of the advantages of marriage.

People treat married couples differently. When you're married, people recognize you as a legitimate couple. They invite you to family and work celebrations as a couple, and include you and your spouse on holiday cards, wedding invitations and birth announcements. When you're living together, but not married, other people don't know if you're really committed to one another yet; perhaps that's why you're not yet married. Other women may even hit on your partner, thinking that he's fair game. After all, if the man wanted to marry you, he would have. So something must be off. He must be available, at least somewhat.

The status of marriage and the pleasantries people extend to you when you are married help bond you together as a couple. People see you as a couple, act that way toward you, send mail to you as a couple, address you by titles that reinforce that you are a couple ("Mr. And Mrs. ____"), so you consequently *feel* more like a couple.

These pleasantries help add to the magic of the early years, something which living together doesn't provide. The legitimacy, romance and status of being a couple offset some of the unpleasantness of living with someone day-to-day.

So what about the idea of living with someone as a step toward marriage—to see if you're really compatible on a day-to-day basis?

When not to live together
To determine marriage compatibility with your roommate
Studies have shown that most people who live together do end up married, but to other people. In addition, couples who do live together before marriage get divorced at about the same rate as couples who don't.

So the reason many people decide to live together before marriage—to determine whether or not they can be compatible in marriage—is not all that valid. In truth, what often happens is that the people go on to marry other people who don't make them "audition" by living together.

When one of you is afraid of marrying and the other really wants marriage
Another reason for *not* living together is when you and your partner have conflicting relationship goals. Take Neal and Carly, for example.

Neal & Carly's Story
Neal was an extremely successful businessman in his late 40's. He was a very large, tall man, 6'6", handsome, intelligent and highly competent. He regularly moved millions of dollars around without becoming anxious. He made about a quarter million per year himself. The problem was that Neal was phobic of mmmmmmarrriage. As soon as the word was spoken, his stomach would start rumbling, and could even be heard 10 feet away, where I was sitting. Neal would tense his forehead, furrow his brow and start rubbing his eyes with his hand. He was terrified of marriage. He came to me for therapy because his girlfriend, Carly, insisted.

Neal had been living with Carly for five years. However, he was making no effort to propose, and Carly was very angry. She interpreted his reluctance to get married as a personal rejection, and it threatened her self-esteem. She was insulted and hurt that he didn't want to "keep her," which is how she viewed his reluctance to get married.

Neal's previous relationships with women had all lasted about 5 years. He stayed faithfully with each woman until she eventually tired of his reluctance to get married and moved on. The woman always broke off the relationship because Neal could not bring himself to marry her.

During our conversations, he explained that his father had deserted him and his mother when Neal was very young. He grew up thinking he had to make his mother happy. But, of course, since no one can make anyone else happy, Neal was unsuccessful in this endeavor. He later married and had children, but the marriage ended in divorce. In his eyes, he had failed again. At that point, his phobia for marriage—his irrational fear of marriage—was sealed. Neal learned that even though he tried hard, he was a failure at marriage because he could not make his wife happy. So he vowed never to marry again. It was too painful and too frustrating.

Therapy included talking about what marriage meant to Neal. We explored what would happen if he got married to Carly. What was his worst fear? For Neal, it was feeling as though he had to make her happy and thinking that he couldn't possibly succeed. So we then talked about the irrationality of thinking that he could *make* anyone happy. Marriage is a union of two complete people who are responsible for themselves and their feelings, but who choose to share their lives with each other.

We also discussed what marriage would mean for Neal. Would it change his life? How? We talked about how he was already being faithful by choice with Carly. Did he want to date others? No. Did he want to sleep with others? No. So what would be different in that respect if he did get married? Nothing. Was this a new behavior? Let's look at your past relationships. Did you cheat on those women? No. Did you want to? No.

The fact is that Neal had basically been living like a married man in each of his five-year relationships. He just did not go through with the ceremony. I pointed out that in all probability, making his relationship legal would not change his home life in any negative respect. Instead, if he married, Carly would be happier, and there would probably be fewer problems between them and a more relaxed, cheerful environment at home.

Over the course of several months, we continued to talk about what marriage would mean for Neal. One day, I noticed a big change. He was talking about marriage, but his stomach wasn't rumbling any more! I brought this to his attention and we saw it as a sign that he was beginning to get better.

Neal's phobia actually ended before I thought it would. I had prepared Carly by telling her that he might become ill or vomit when it came time for the ceremony. Instead, Neal surprised me. He told me the phobia ended when he told his adult children he was getting married. At that point, it became official. He was going to do it. Once he made the decision to marry and followed it up with action (telling his children), he had overcome his fear. Neal 1, phobia 0. A few months later, Neal and Carly were married; they sent me a picture to prove it.

There are many Neal's out there. The story is slightly different with each, but the pattern—avoiding marriage due to irrational ideas—is the same. Let's look a little closer at how marriage and commitment phobias develop.

Commitment phobia = an irrational fear of commitment

So how do commitment and marriage phobias get started?

Several factors seem to play a role. First, let's look at one key difference between men and women:

Women tend to define themselves by their relationships, whereas men often define themselves in terms of their career, power and wealth.

Women are raised to judge themselves by their relationships. They can now choose to have a career if they like, but it's optional. People tend not to talk about how successful a woman is in her career. Instead, they're more likely to judge her by whether or not she's married, has a nice home and family life, and happy, talented children.

Men are raised to judge themselves by their careers, how powerful they are in the business world, and how much money they make. They can choose to get married and have good relationships, but other people don't usually judge them that way. And consequently, they don't usually view themselves that way. In contrast, they must be successful at their jobs. They are judged by their career status, money and power.

So given this history, it makes sense that a woman would be more eager to get married and obtain success in that area of her life than a man. But there's a lot more to the story.

A man learns that intimacy & closeness are not always safe

Both male and female babies attach to the mother when she feeds them. For the woman, this relationship remains primary. She learns that intimacy and closeness are comfortable, safe and desirable.

However, while the male child initially bonds with the mother, who is feeding and taking care of him most of the time, he must eventually learn to detach from his mother and identify with his father. He's allowed to hold onto his mother for awhile, but eventually is told to, "Be a big boy! Stop hanging on me!" No parent wants a sissy for a son, so they encourage him to leave the protection of his mother and start acting like his dad. When a child is so young, this represents a major upset. At a young age, he has learned that intimacy and closeness are not always safe; sometimes there is a shift. As a result, he grows up to desire closeness, but also to fear it somewhat. He has mixed feelings and some confusion about it. It's not as straightforward or clear for him as it is for a woman.

A boy grows up to desire closeness, but also to fear it.

To complicate this, a man is also taught that he can express anger, power, achievement, ambition and competition, but he is not allowed to show vulnerability the way a woman can. He should not cry or show fear. So a man hides his feelings in an effort to be a man, making it much more difficult to become intimate and close to someone. In addition, covering up his fear of intimacy and closeness just makes it more difficult to resolve it. Before you can fix something, you have to know it's broken and worth fixing. The mixed messages a man receives about intimacy often cause him to bury the issue rather than face his fear of it.

A man often buries his fear of intimacy, rather than trying to face it.

A phobia is an irrational fear of something. If you're afraid of a poisonous snake, that's not a phobia. A poisonous snake can kill you if it bites you. On the other hand, if you are deathly afraid of a non-poisonous snake, even though you know it's harmless, that's a phobia. Your fear is irrational. Men who fear marriage are irrationally afraid of marriage for some reason that isn't real. Usually, they're not even consciously aware of why they are afraid. The fear exists on an unconscious, gut-wrenching level. All he knows is that the thought of getting married makes him extremely uncomfortable. And when people are afraid or uncomfortable, they go out of their way to avoid whatever they fear. Each time a man goes out of his way to avoid marriage, he indirectly tells himself that there really is something there to be feared. By avoiding what he's afraid of, he never gives himself the opportunity to learn that there's nothing there to fear.

If his childhood was marked by his parents' marital strife or divorce, he may fear that the same thing will happen to him if he marries. If he then marries someone despite his fear and his marriage ends in divorce, the fear he already has is then reinforced. He was afraid to get close, but he did, and then he found out that it hurt like hell, so now he is even more reluctant to get close.

To complicate matters even further, divorce does cause many negative changes in anyone's life. It is stressful, and the man usually ends up taking a financial hit when he gets divorced. To someone who has learned that he is being judged by how successful, powerful and wealthy he is, that can be even more upsetting than the emotional pain of losing a loved one. Together, the desire to avoid the real financial and personal losses, combined with his irrational fear of marriage make the whole issue huge and scary for him.

So, the man starts out with a weaker, more conflicted drive to become intimate with someone, and he learns to desire closeness, but also to fear it. Society reinforces him less for facing his fear, so he is less likely to try. If he has witnessed bad marriages, the fear is even stronger. And if he faces his fear and then ends up divorced, his desire to avoid marriage often becomes very strong. Since there is no incentive for him to face commitment, the object of his fear, he often avoids it. It's just easier.

Meanwhile, the woman, who has learned that she is most comfortable and safe the more intimate and close she is to someone, and who has been reinforced all her life for finding and maintaining close romantic ties, feels a very strong drive to get married. Her approach is very straightforward and strong, while the man's is convoluted and conflicted.

So what happens in a relationship between the two?

The man often acts in such a way as to get closer and more intimate with his girlfriend. Then when he gets too close, he becomes afraid. He then pulls back until he is more comfortable, then starts to approach her again until he becomes too afraid, then pulls back until he is more comfortable...etc., etc., over and over and over again. This seesaw or yo-yo behavior is called an "approach-avoidance conflict" and is quite common in men.

The partner of such a man is often at her wit's end trying to make sense of his behavior. Why does he suddenly pull away, just when everything is going so well? Why does he come on so strong, and then just when she's ready to relax and go with the flow, run the opposite way? When he's chasing her, he's OK, but when she reciprocates, he runs— why? Madeline experienced this problem and more first hand.

Madeline's Story

Madeline, in her early 40's, came to therapy feeling very frustrated. She had been dating her boyfriend Brent for several years. Brent seemed happy enough and said he was happy, but he just didn't want to get married. Although he had hinted at marriage and acted in ways that suggested he was moving forward toward it, it became obvious at about 3 years that he was not acting to finalize their relationship in marriage. Brent was afraid of marriage because he feared that he would be consumed by it and lose his identity.

Madeline gave him an ultimatum, and Brent chose not to marry her. So Madeline started dating Mac. Mac was an even better match for Madeline; besides having a lot in common with her, he also wanted to get married some day. Madeline still had feelings for Brent, but now she developed feelings for Mac as well. However, as soon as Brent figured out that Madeline was dating Mac, he started coming around again. He promised to marry Madeline if she would just leave Mac for him.

After much thought, Madeline decided to leave Mac for Brent. Mac was devastated and took another job in another state to get away from his pain. However, as soon as Mac was out of the picture, Brent started to back off again. Instead of setting a wedding date, he hemmed and hawed. Madeline finally came to me in desperation.

The problem was that Brent had started to overcome his phobia when presented with competition in the form of Mac. His drive to compete with another man and not lose the prize (Madeline) was very strong. That competing drive gave him motivation to face his fear of marriage and do something about it. However, Madeline gave in too quickly. In agreeing to break up with Mac, she basically took away that motivation, and helped Brent feel comfortable with not getting married again. Once his competition was safely out of the picture, Brent started to relax, and when Mac left the state, Brent really relaxed. Unfortunately, Madeline had kept Brent apprised of Mac's actions and that was also a mistake.

In this case, it would have been better if Madeline had told Brent that she was dating someone who wanted to marry her, but had not told him anything else. That would have raised his desire to compete with Mac. She should have refused to break up with Mac unless she and Brent got married immediately. She could have married Brent and planned a celebration for family and friends at a later time, after they were married. That would have kept Brent moving forward to marriage. Once he got married, he would have had the opportunity to find out that marriage was good, that he wouldn't be consumed by it. The phobia would have been broken, and Madeline and Brent would have been happy.

Or Madeline could have stayed with Mac and refused to break up with him for Brent. Instead, the way the scenario played out, all three parties came up short.

Overcoming commitment phobia

To cure a phobia of any kind, it's necessary for the person to do whatever he's afraid of. So to get over a fear of marriage, a man would have to get married. But how can he do that if he is so afraid?

If the man will come to therapy, we can treat his phobia, as we did for Neal. However, people often refuse therapy for phobias—because therapy means sitting and talking about what scares them, and that's uncomfortable. It's just easier to avoid thinking about it. So if the man won't come in for therapy, I usually advise the woman to continue dating other men until her mate has proposed and set a firm date in the near future.

Men are trained to fear intimacy, but they have also been trained since childhood to compete. A man's drive to compete with another man can be so strong that he gets caught up in competing with the guy threatening to take away his woman, and forgets to be afraid of marriage. Once he wins the competition and marries the woman, he finds out that marriage is good and there's nothing there to be afraid of. He has done what he is most afraid of (gotten married), and the phobia has been broken. Now the man is free to be happy in that marriage.

Fear of marriage or healthy apprehension?

There is a difference between being irrationally fearful of marriage (being afraid to marry *anyone*) and feeling doubt about marrying a particular person because you're not sure if you're compatible enough. People who are phobic of marriage hold irrational ideas about what **marriage** really means. Someone who doubts his compatibility with his girlfriend does not have these irrational ideas; it's marrying this particular woman and the problems that surround it that concern him.

There is also a difference between being phobic of marriage and not being emotionally ready for marriage because you are too young and don't have enough relationship experience yet, or because you don't know each other enough yet, or because you're just freshly divorced and not ready to meet and marry anyone. Men and women of average intelligence who have dated since their teens-20's should be emotionally mature enough to get married in their 30's.

So if the person you're dating is:

- 💜 over 30
- 💜 has dated normally throughout his youth
- 💜 has not been divorced in the past 3 years
- 💜 seems loving and free of severe personal problems
- 💜 has been with you for more than 2 years
- 💜 seems to enjoy the relationship
- 💜 is committed to you and does not voice any major objections to your behavior (or the objections seem like convenient smokescreens),
- 💜 but still does not want to move forward to marriage,

It's quite possible that he's phobic (irrationally fearful) of marriage.

If you do your best to work out any other relationship problems, but he is still reluctant to get married, then it's even more likely that he is phobic of marriage.

And there's certainly a difference between marriage phobia and the slight anxiety you feel right before you get married. If you've been looking forward to getting married and are just now becoming a little nervous, that's normal. On the day of your wedding, you'll probably not be aware of much besides friendly, smiling faces. That's why it's a good idea to have a photographer and a videographer. You can watch your own wedding later, after your feet touch ground again, and enjoy all that took place.

Other reasons people don't marry

Most people consider marriage because they enjoy companionship, and want to go through life with a partner. Some want children, some don't, but as humans, we are social creatures and as we talked about earlier, we de-stress and live longer with a good partner. But some people like being alone, doing things by themselves, having total freedom and not being responsible to anyone. Some people don't want to assume the financial burden, or they don't want to compromise. When they want something, they just want to have it, without having to consider anyone else's feelings or needs.

Others enjoy living on the edge, and don't ever want to be sexually faithful. They enjoy having many partners and superficial relationships. Many of these men can be found in bars trying to pick up women for one-night stands. One man told me, "I like my life as it is. In order for me to get married, she would have to bring something to my life that I don't already have. That's a tall order."

Some people just hate making final decisions. They're worried that a better catch might come along after the wedding bells have rung. Others simply see the disadvantages of marriage as outweighing the advantages.

Others feel no push toward marriage because they get their love and companionship from sources other than marriage partners.

A man like this came to The Relationship Center™ and joined the introduction service, but never really used the service. He came from a large Catholic Irish family of eight children, including a set of triplets. He was one of the triplets. This man was a teacher and loved to help the older people in the neighborhood. He never felt alone or lonely because he was always surrounded by so many people, including two duplicates/clones of himself. His sex drive was not very high, so he was not motivated to date and marry so that he could have a regular sex partner. If his sex drive had been higher, his drive to date might have been higher and his religious family would have most likely urged him to marry. He would have received significant family pressure if he dated someone for a lengthy period of time and didn't move toward marriage.

In contrast, another client, an only child born to older, sickly parents was keenly aware that he needed to date and marry so he could begin his own family and build his base of supportive people. If you find yourself living alone, it's natural to seek other people out. If, on the other hand, you are surrounded by other adults, the pressure is much less.

So, now that you know the rational and irrational reasons why people don't get married, let's talk about the people who do.

When not to get married

Although the biggest reason people marry is to find a life partner and start a family, many other factors contribute to when and why people marry. Some of those factors can lead to trouble down the road.

Have you ever noticed that people tend to marry at certain times in life? It's been my observation that a great many people marry because "it's the right time"—like after high school or college graduation. They've been dating someone for a few years, and have now finished school. They feel ready to start an adult life, all their friends are getting married, and people just naturally expect them to follow suit. Many good-natured, well-meaning people question them on when they're finally going to "tie the knot." Marriage is a rite of passage, and people marry when they feel they are ready to step into that new role and be recognized as adults. They see marriage as a step toward growing up. They may have dated a little or maybe only one person their whole life. Yet it's time to get married and that's whom they're going with at the time, so that's whom they marry.

Others turn to marriage to escape poverty or a chaotic and unhappy home. Some marry to escape controlling, critical, restrictive or abusive parents, or parents who are alcoholics or psychologically or physically ill.

Some look to marriage to supply a critical emotional need: a feeling of self-worth, of being loved. They may be in love with the idea of being in love or being married, and they don't want to wait any longer to achieve the American Dream—spouse, kids, house and dog. Women often dream of marrying their Prince. They're especially vulnerable to the myths and fairy tales. They want to play house. They fall in love because they want to be in love. They can't wait to find that person who will be emotionally supportive and give their life meaning.

Some people marry to make someone else jealous, to save face when they're jilted, or because they're afraid of being alone. Others fall into marriage impulsively because they think it will be fun. Others feel pressured by pregnancy, age, well-meaning relatives or by the expectations of their significant other.

But how likely is it that any of these reasons for marriage will lead to a happy, lifelong commitment? Very unlikely.

In fact, a significant number of the people who have come to me for marital therapy married when they thought it was the right time. The problem is that when you're 18, you don't even know much about how people vary from one another, much less why and how much you and your partner are compatible. People date one another because they're "cute" or "have a cool car"—certainly not the best reasons for getting married! Twenty years later, you see more because you've had more experience in living and interacting with people. You've learned that he's got a cool car because he spends too much money and always wants to live on the edge. Or that she's cute, but also very ego-centric and selfish. As you mature emotionally, your ability to perceive people as they are should grow, along with your knowledge of what you need in a relationship.

So now here you are, two decades later, all grown up and married to someone with whom you have little in common. The thrill of the wedding, the presents and playing house has long worn out, and the fairy tale has been exposed as a fraud and been replaced with the problems of everyday life. That reality is even more difficult to cope with when you're living with someone incompatible because you already have a family together.

So when is marriage a good idea?

The best reason for marrying is to share your life with a loving, emotionally support-ive companion. The best time for marriage is when you have dated enough and are emotionally mature and ready for this rite of passage. Your spouse should be someone compatible whom you love dearly, and it's absolutely imperative that you have known each other long enough to be able to make that decision.

It's always a mistake to marry just because you want to be married, forcing a round peg of a mate into a square hole. You may succeed at the union for years, but in the end, once you have obtained the house, children, status, freedom and adulthood you craved, you will be left knowing that you are living with someone with whom you never really felt that much connection.

Of course, many of the people who marry too early feel that they are mature, experi-enced enough and ready for the rite of passage when they're not. So the key is to **really** be ready, not just think you're ready because all your friends are doing it. For more on marriage and how to make it happy long-term, see **Chapter 9—Marriage: Taking The Big Step.**

Exercise: Discover your feelings about marriage

1. Sit down with a piece of paper. Say the word *commitment* over and over to yourself. Write down whatever pops into your mind, no matter how nonsensical it might seem. Then do the same thing with the word *marriage*.

2. When you're finished writing, look at what you've written. If you see phrases like giving up freedom, being consumed, no going back or any other words that are negative, critical or imply irrational fear, then you may very well have a marriage and commitment phobia or other personal issues that need work. If you have written anything about your parents, in-laws or friends that is negative, it may hint at elements that have contributed to the phobia.

   If you are 27 or older, see a psychologist for help in treating your fear. If you are younger: Does this fear seem to inhibit whom you choose to date and how the relationships work out? If so, then it's time to see the psychologist. It's best if you marry after age 27, and you don't want to wait until then to start dating appropriate people, or you could be 50 before you've had enough experience with people to choose a good mate. On the other hand, if you don't think your fear has affected whom you choose or how the relationships progress, then you can wait until you are 27 before seeing the psychologist. Since it's best to marry between 28-35, if you still have the fear by age 27, it's important to seek treatment immediately.

   Review your relationship history with this new information about commitment. Have any of your relationships ended because you or your partner weren't able to commit due to an irrational fear?

3. Look at what you've written again. If you see phrases and sentences that are pro-marriage, take a good look at the reasons you have written for wanting to get married. If you want to get married, but haven't written anything about why in your Relationship Notebook, take a moment now and jot your reasons down.

   Now review those reasons. Are they similar to the healthy reasons we've discussed for wanting to get married? Or do they remind you of the ones we've mentioned as irrational reasons to get married?

   Read Chapter 9 on marriage, Chapter 10 on the problems in marriage, and Chapter 11 about divorce. Learn to view marriage realistically, not as a fantasy to be fulfilled.

Chapter 6

Happiness & relationships
Do you know the secret?

I once had a beautiful blond secretary named Lisa. Lisa would walk down the hall at the medical center, and everyone, male and female, would stop to look at her. Now, it didn't hurt that she was 5'8", blond, long-legged and beautiful. But what made people notice her was the way she walked down that hall. She usually had a sunny smile on her face, while she looked around and said, "Hi" to everyone. She walked with a bounce, with energy. She was a breath of fresh air, a break from the negativity of the hospital. She was almost always positive and upbeat, and everyone wanted to be close to the sunshine that radiated from her.

Well, how do you think she got to be that way? Did she have lots of money? Nope. She was working as a secretary and her husband was a fireman. Did she have some kind of happy gene? Nope, to date no such thing has been identified. Was her life so idyllic in comparison to other people? Not exactly.

Things will be better because...
Lisa had stresses and strains just like any other person—money problems and family problems, work problems, etc. However, she just kept everything in perspective and focused on what really counted. She didn't worry or obsess about the little stuff. In addition, she never talked negatively about what wasn't going right in her life. Instead, she always talked about why this particular change she was making was going to make things even better.

I remember her telling me how she and her new husband were going to live with Grandma in Grandma's cottage on the beach. She talked about how nice that was going to be and how much better than where they were living now, because...(of some reason). I remember thinking, *"This will never work. Grandma is about 70, and they're newlyweds."*

But when that day came and Lisa told me that she and her husband were moving out of Grandma's cottage, she didn't complain about Grandma and how the woman was driving her nuts. In fact, I don't recall her ever saying anything negative about Grandma or anyone else. Instead, what I clearly remember her saying was, *"And _____ (this particular change, e.g., moving out to a new apartment) is going to be even better because...."*

The only time I ever saw Lisa looking sad was when she returned from an appointment with her obstetrician, who told her she had to quit work and stay off her feet for the rest of her pregnancy. She couldn't afford to quit work, so on her lunch and coffee breaks, she laid down on one of the unoccupied beds and put her legs up. She didn't obsess, worry and drive herself nuts during the rest of her pregnancy. Instead, she continued being her cheerful self, and her son Kent was born without any problems.

So Lisa had her share of trials and tribulations. She just continued to look at the bright side of every situation, and then found, to her delight, that things generally did work out for the best. And because she thought this way, Lisa's ability to pull others to her never diminished.

Lisa knew the secrets of happiness. What are they? The first is:

Happiness is made, not found.

Anyone who believes that they must *find* happiness will discover that like the elusive butterfly, it seems always beyond their reach.

Happiness is a state of mind. That brings us to the second secret of happiness:

In order to feel happy, you must think happy.

If you fill your head with ideas of what's wrong with every part of your life, you can't expect yourself to feel happy. Sure, you might think that you've found happiness when you meet someone new and you're excited and happy. However, in time, that relationship will suffer stresses and strains, just like every other relationship. And even the most compatible relationship will sometimes be stressful.

If you believe at that time that you have fallen out of love, and that you must look for someone else to make yourself happy again, you will probably just drift from partner to partner, always feeling as though a happy relationship is just beyond your reach.

We're conditioned to think in unhappy ways

Ever listen to a conversation in an elevator? What do people talk about? The weather, sports and other small talk. However, if you listen closely, you'll notice that the tone of the small talk is generally negative: what's *wrong* with the weather, how *badly* a team has been playing, how *lousy* the traffic is today. Since we learn to think by listening to others talk, most of us have become pessimists by osmosis.

Unfortunately, many cultures tend to exaggerate the negative, but do not exaggerate the positive in a similar fashion. More emotional, expressive cultures will often use expressions like, "He **ruined** my life." "I'll **never** be able to trust again!" "You **always** have to have it your way!" "My husband **never** pays any attention to me." "My wife **always** does what she wants, **never** what I want to do!" "Oh, you think you're **sooo** smart, you think you're **always** *right!*"

When we use irrational expressions that magnify what is actually happening, it makes for very colorful speech. On the other hand, it also leads to volatile emotions. We also hear negative hyper-dramatic expressions repeated on TV and in movies, love songs and popular music. Try watching a soap opera and listen closely. You'll hear line after line of overdramatized speech. Dr. Albert Ellis, a brilliant psychologist who wrote about changing your irrational thoughts to more positive ones, calls this kind of speech "catastrophizing." You make a catastrophe out of everything.

And usually the person saying these catastrophic things is **not** also saying, "What a **GREAT** day! This is the **BEST** day of the rest of my life!" " You are the most **incredible** husband! I love you so much, you really **make** my life!"

And because our negatives are higher in intensity than our positives. we feel more negative than positive. And like a continuous circle, we then continue to experience life in that fashion.

So we've learned to think negatively by listening to people around us talk negatively. As children, we learn negative patterns of speech from our parents, and those negative habits become firmly entrenched when we interact with others who also think negatively. And so the pattern continues…But there is a light at the end of the tunnel.

The good news

The good news is that anyone can turn their life around. No matter what relationship stage you're in or how much money you have, you can learn to be happy.

How? Well, first let's look at what happiness really is.

The definition of happiness: what is it really?

The first thing to realize is that *happiness* means *content* or *satisfied*. It does **not** mean a *peak experience*. You can live a life where you feel largely happy, content and satisfied, with peak experiences scattered here and there and a few mildly down moments. You can't live a life that is all peak experiences. Even Hawaii's beauty can become boring to those who live there too long.

I recall a recent psychologist's conference in Chicago. I was ecstatic that the American Psychological Association convention was finally in my hometown again. Ten thousand psychologists descended on Chicago, which normally keeps the cabs hustling. However, this particular year, it rained like crazy—thunder, lightning, an intense downpour. No one could walk very well in the deluge, so people were stranded everywhere waiting for cabs. Plans got cancelled, people couldn't meet each other as they said they would, and the hotel lobby restaurants were jam-packed because people opted to eat there rather than trying to locate some other restaurant that was further away. It took hours just to get a table to sit down. I was afraid that the psychologists wouldn't want to return.

When I mentioned this concern to my California buddies, one said, *"Are you kidding! I **love** it here! **You** have **WEATHER!!!**"* Apparently his group spent the night in the restaurant on top the John Hancock Building, 98 floors up, fully appreciating and enjoying the spectacular display of thunder, lightning and rain.

So—a peak experience is by definition extra special and unique. It can't be extra special and unique if it happens all the time. If you have "weather" most of the time, you appreciate those California and Hawaii rays of pleasant sunshine. But if you have that sunny weather most of the time, no matter what the season, your peak experience might be catching real "weather" in Chi-town instead.

Common myths about being happy

Now maybe you're thinking, "Oh, sure, Dr. Kate. I was born a pessimist; I can't change." The truth is you can change yourself, but you must first accept responsibility for being the way you are, and second, take constructive steps to change your thinking. If you monitor your thoughts and change each negative statement into a realistic, but more positive statement, you can change yourself—thought by thought—to be more of an optimist. But you—and only you—can do that work for you.

Or perhaps you're thinking, "Optimism is not reality; it's a con job. I'm just more honest, that's why I'm cynical and pessimistic." But ask yourself: If you have just been given half a glass of your favorite beverage, is the glass half empty or half full? The real answer is both. However, whether you choose to look at it as half empty or half full determines to a great extent how much you enjoy the drink—and how much others choose to be with you while you enjoy that drink.

When you're at a party or on the job or just walking down the street, do you often find yourself looking at other people and thinking they're happier than you? "They're so much happier than me. Everyone is happier than me." Nothing makes people more unhappy than thinking everyone else is happier than they are. But the reality is that everyone has stress, no matter how much money they have or what kind of great husband or wife they have. You just don't know about everyone else's stress. Instead of looking at a couple and assuming they're happier than you, realize that if they are, it's because they work at it and make themselves happy, not because God blessed them with everything and you with nothing.

"But at least they have each other, a good relationship. I can't be happy being single and alone." Au contraire. You can be happy, no matter what relationship stage you're in: single, coupled, broken up, married, divorced, starting over. Happiness is not tied to a particular relationship stage. You can be happy married, but you can also be happy divorced. It isn't the events that happen to you that lead you to be unhappy. It's how you think about those events. That's why one person can be happy with very little, and another can have many possessions and love interests and never be happy.

"But having a relationship makes me happy. My boyfriend makes me happy." OK, I believe that you feel happy when you're with your boyfriend. But the truth is that you make yourself happy when you are in a relationship because at that time, you tell yourself that life is good. If you tell yourself that life is good at other times and focus on the good that is all around you every day of your life; you *can* make yourself happy whether you have a relationship or not.

And that brings us to the most important secret of finding happiness in relationships:

No one can make you happy— except you.

If you really think about it, you'll realize that **NO** one has the power to *make* anyone feel anything. Someone can certainly act in ways that are conducive, but whether or not we end up feeling happy has more to do with us and how we think than it does with our loved one's behavior. The same is true for our partner. We can't *make* our significant other feel anything, any more than he can make us feel anything.

Once you find a compatible relationship, you must make your own happiness. It is *not* your partner's responsibility to *make* you happy.

Now, this doesn't mean that you should stay in a physically or emotionally abusive relationship and try to convince yourself that you are happy. Not at all. However, in most normal situations, people could be much happier and content than they are.

Happiness is not being delusional or an airhead

Now, I'm not talking about living in a fantasy world or being an airhead, blithely oblivious to the world around you. For example, I don't like the adage, "When life deals you lemons, make lemonade." The reality is that it's not always possible to do that. If someone close to you dies, it would NOT be healthy if you felt overjoyed. For example, if you love your husband, but are happy when he dies, I would wonder if you are psychotic. Your emotions are out of sync with reality. If someone close to you dies, it IS very sad. You don't have to tell yourself that there was some positive reason why he died. However, you also don't need to get depressed and let your life fall apart either. Accept that you are disappointed, grieve and then move on to happier times. So when life deals you lemons, admit that you are disappointed with the lemons, but don't go off the deep end in lemon rot either.

A hidden motive for being happy

The first payoff for realistic, positive thinking is that you'll enjoy your life more. However, there's also a less obvious payoff: When you think and act happy, you draw happy, healthy people to you. So in essence, it's a continuous circle. If you think happy, you feel happy. When you feel happy, you're more likely to act in an outgoing, healthy, happy manner. When you do that, people will want to be around you; they'll be drawn to you, confirming your belief that the world is indeed a wonderful place. It's a self-fulfilling prophecy.

In contrast, when you think negatively, you feel negatively. When you feel negatively, it's much more difficult to act in a positive way. Instead, you're more likely to criticize others, to take things personally, to seem sad or angry or irritable or impatient. You essentially drive others away, confirming your view of the world as a nasty, stressful place.

So exactly how do you make yourself happy?

To make yourself happy, you have to think happy thoughts. How can you do that? Well, if you're like the majority of us and learned to think negative at a very early age, you have to consciously retrain the way you think and speak.

Change your negative statements to positive ones

We think so quickly, it may be a little difficult to catch yourself when you're thinking negatively. So start by monitoring your speech. Most people find it easier to change their verbal remarks than their thoughts in the beginning. So listen to what you say when you say it. When you hear yourself making a statement that is overly negative, stop yourself in mid-sentence: *"I'm sorry, I exaggerated. It's not the worst experience I've ever had. It was just not the best one, so I was a little disappointed. But I'm sure that I'll have many more positive experiences in the future."*

Change your negative thoughts to positive ones

Once you have gotten the hang of thinking positive when you talk out loud, try doing the same for your private thoughts. When you catch yourself thinking something negative, particularly if that negative is an exaggeration, stop the thought and change it for a more positive, but realistic statement. For example, let's say you catch yourself thinking, "Today is the worst day of my life. I just spilled coffee and ruined my best silk suit!" Take a deep breath, say, *"Stop it!"* to yourself in your head, and then replace the thought with, *"It has been a little stressful today, but it's only a suit. I'll take it to the cleaner, and if he can get the spot out, great. If not, there's more to life than worrying about a suit."*

If you change your thinking in this way, you'll be surprised at how much energy you have. Instead of feeling like you're bogged down with problems, you'll feel energized by your challenges.

"OK, Dr. Kate, I can see how thinking more positively about getting a coffee stain out of a suit could be helpful. But what do I do when a big stress occurs?"

When someone leaves or dies—the biggest stressors of all

Let's say your boyfriend/husband just broke up with you and you just found out he's been cheating. Many women would tell themselves, "I can't believe he did that to me. I'll never be the same again! My life is over! No one will ever love me again!" But instead of thinking those traumatic thoughts, try telling yourself the most positive, realistic thing you can honestly say: *"I wish he hadn't cheated and we hadn't broken up. I would have preferred to stay together. But in time, this hurt will heal, and I'll move on to someone more compatible. This is only a relationship stage, and it will be over before long. In the meantime, I'll take it a day at a time, cope with it and be happy in spite of it."*

The same kind of thinking can be used when someone close to you dies: *"I wish he hadn't died. This hurts, but in time, I will heal, and when I'm ready, I can move on. I don't like where I am right now, but this is only a relationship stage and it will be over before long. In the meantime, I'll take it a day at a time, cope with it and be happy in spite of it."*

Grieve when necessary, but then go back to thinking more positively.

Of course, you must grieve. Crying helps relieve stress, and sometimes it can be better to think about irrational ideas for a short while to help you vent (see **The Dr. Kate Quick & Dirty Grieving Technique** in the Appendix). However, that doesn't have to stop you from looking at the bright side of life in between. Yes, you lost someone dear to you, but the birds still sing, the flowers still bloom, and kids still say the darndest things.

Try to surround yourself with comfortable, emotionally supportive people and happy experiences (no sad movies!), and you can learn to enjoy your life again, even though you are alone. You just need to pay attention to the positives and notice them. (For more on coping with very stressful situations, see **Chapter 11—Loss & Letting Go.**)

Sell yourself on life!

I once had a client who was an expert sales woman. She picked up an empty styrofoam coffee cup on my desk, and said, "See this cup? If I want to sell you this, I'm going to get *very* excited about it. I'm going to tell you all about what's wonderful about this cup, and I'm going to tell you how much better your life would be with this cup in your life. I'm going to get so excited about it and describe everything in such glowing and enthusiastic words that you are going to get very excited about it, too, and you're going to buy this cup right away! And that's how I sell!"

I have often reflected on her words and can see a really good use for her technique: Use the same strategy to sell yourself on life!

Take charge of your destiny: make every day count

Years ago, when I saw critically ill medical patients in the hospital, I noticed that no one talked about how they wished they had gotten their MBA or bought that new house or great car. Rather, as they were preparing to die, they thought about other people who had passed through their life and wished they had appreciated them more. They regretted never apologizing to that person, never opening up to this one, never taking a risk on that one.

Well, today **IS** the beginning of the rest of your life. So make it count. Ask yourself: If you were dying tomorrow, what would you appreciate about today? The way your husband hugs, the way your children mess their rooms, the way the postman goes out of his way to ring your doorbell and hand you a package?

People who have died and come back—after their heart stops and is started again—often find a sense of peace they didn't have before. Death puts things in perspective again. It's hard to worry about stupid things when you've just gotten a new lease on life.

We all need to be smart and reawaken ourselves without going through the rough part of dying. Just as you need to remind yourself about what's good about other people, you need to remind yourself about what's good about your life.

We in the United States have the best standard of living in the world. Yet people in other countries seem to be happier with much less. The difference comes from expectations and demands and how we view the outcome. Americans expect and demand more. When we don't get it, we feel sorry for ourselves. It's a little like a spoiled child who expects to get everything he wants, then throws a tantrum when he doesn't. We take our advantages and standard of living for granted.

However, if we train ourselves to appreciate what we have, to focus on the positive in life (and everyone's life has some positive elements), if we teach ourselves to be content with those positives and not always looking and demanding more—then we can always make our happiness, no matter what life or relationship stage we find ourselves in.

The ultimate secret

And that is the ultimate secret of happiness: If you focus on the joy and what you like about your life, think about it often, remember it and smile:

> *You can be happy single, married, divorced, widowed—in whatever relationship stage you find yourself.*

You only have to choose to be that way, change your thoughts, and before long, the feelings will come. Acting **AS IF** you are happy can indeed help you become happy.

And remember, when you do that, other healthy and happy people will be drawn to you as well. It all becomes a self-fulfilling prophecy.

Exercises to fill your heart with joy

1. **Self-Review:** In your Relationship Notebook, write down adjectives that describe you. Put the positives in one column and the negatives in another. Now look closely at the list of negatives. Do you see words like *critical, negative, cynical* or *sarcastic*? If so, you need to work on making your thinking more positive. Is the negative column longer? Chances are you're also thinking too negatively about

yourself. See the exercises at the end of *Chapter 11—Loss & Letting Go*, for ways to raise your self-esteem.

In an ambiguous situation, do you tend to think that the situation is positive or negative? If a date doesn't call you on time, do you think that he has lost interest? Do you begin to worry about what you might have done to turn him off? If your husband is late coming home, do you worry about him cheating when he's never cheated before?

If so, then you know you have a tendency to think negatively in ambiguous situations. Be alert for that and when it happens, change those thoughts. Write the negative thoughts down in your notebook and next to each, put a more rational, realistic thought. Writing them will help you figure out what is positive, yet realistic. Eventually, with enough practice, you'll be able to change the thoughts quickly and easily in your head.

2. **Stop Soap Opera Thinking.** Watch a soap opera on TV. As you do, write down the over-dramatic negative statements made by the characters. For example, "He ruined my life!" is practically a standard. See how many irrational statements you can catch in a half-hour show.

Then listen to yourself when you are speaking. When you catch yourself making a soap opera statement or catastrophizing, stop yourself in mid-sentence and change your remark to be more positive and realistic. For example, if you catch yourself saying, "He meant everything to me. Now he's gone, and I'll never be the same again," say, *"I'm sorry, that's not really true. What I mean to say is, 'I'll miss him and I'll have some trouble living without him. But I will cope with this and be happy in spite of it.'"*

3. **Monitor Your Negative Thoughts.** Monitor how many negative thoughts you think in one day. Stick an index card in your pocket or purse, and each time you find yourself thinking or saying something catastrophic, make a tally on the card. Do this for one or two days. Then start changing your thoughts and statements to more positive ones. Use thought-stopping (see the *Appendix*) to control your negative thoughts. In about two months, try monitoring yourself again with your index card, and see if you have improved. You should see a dramatic improvement. If you don't, reread this chapter again and examine the positive thoughts you are using; make sure they're really positive.

Chapter 7

Communication
An essential ingredient

C ommunication is the key to our interaction with others, but it's far more involved than just opening your mouth to speak. *How* you communicate makes the difference between being understood or misunderstood and depends as much on voice inflection, speed, volume and pitch as it does on the actual words. Just by altering your intonation, you can turn a simple question such as, *"Why did you do that?"* into a sarcastic remark, a tease, a happy statement or a surprised expression.

Nonverbal cues such as gestures, body position, facial expressions and eye contact can change the meaning even further. If your partner is standing over you, hands on hips and glaring, the body language and facial expressions are just as important as the words. The same statement spoken in a gentle voice while the person puts an arm around you has a completely different meaning and effect.

We learn to say our first sentence around age two and then spend the rest of our lives learning to perfect it. So learning to talk is just the first step. Learning to *communicate* is where the real work begins.

The first step in learning to communicate more effectively is to find out how well you do it now. Take **The Dr. Kate Communication Quiz** in the Appendix to find out. Then read this chapter to learn valuable communication secrets.

Communication is the key to the success of our relationships

In out intimate relationships, we experience many opportunities to communicate—opportunities to either move emotionally closer to our partner or further away. Communication is dynamic—never static—and it is the key to the success or failure of our relationships. Since no two human beings can ever totally agree on all subjects, and all relationships experience problems at one time or another, how you communicate makes the difference between the joy of a happy, thriving partnership or the alienation that can lead to separation and divorce. Half of all U.S. marriages end in divorce and many more unofficial relationships also break up, suggesting just how much we need to improve our communication skills.

A learned skill

Communication and relationship skills are not inherited, but learned. Most of us are born to less-than-perfect communicator parents and consequently learn to think in depressed, angry, critical or negative ways.

Beth and Rita, for example, are the intelligent daughters of intelligent parents. Although the girls' parents loved each other dearly, they fought often and with great venom. They rarely voiced positive feelings, but focused instead on negative feelings that they expressed with great volume and intensity.

The fights usually started with the mother, who was a controlling person, telling the father to do or not do something. The father would not respond, so the mother did not feel heard and would repeat her directive. She frequently nagged and phrased her requests in a demanding, negative manner. She felt frustrated that she could not have her world the way she wanted it on her schedule. The father rebelled by drinking and getting surly.

One of their ongoing conflicts was the father's hobby of collecting and fixing old radios and other appliances. He was fond of combing the alleys and bringing home all kinds of broken, but fixable, *finds* that the mother considered *junk*. Of course, the father did his repairing in his off-time, so his treasures tended to sit where he put them for months on end. Radios and clocks littered the kitchen table, the porch, the counters and the basement. There was even a broken washing machine in the basement waiting to be fixed.

One day, particularly vexed that the available cooking space in the kitchen was rapidly shrinking, the mother snapped.

"Are you ever going to move those radios?"

"I'll move them," the father growled.

Ten minutes went by, but he made no effort to move the radios.

"So, hey, like I said, are you ever going to move those radios?" the mother persisted.

"**I told you, I'll move them**," the father replied in an angrier, louder tone of voice.

Another 20 minutes went by. Finally, in exasperation, the mother exclaimed:

"I guess you're not going to get those radios out of my kitchen, are you?"

"**G-dammit, I told you. When I'm g-d, sob-ing ready, I'll move 'em!**" the father roared at the top of his lungs.

He then shoved the kitchen table, knocking over the chair and sending one of the radios flying. "Now, look what you made me do!" he yelled.

From there, the argument disintegrated even further into graphic obscenities as the father told the mother exactly what she could do with her kitchen, and the mother told him precisely what he could do with his radios.

Each time they had a verbal exchange, the conversation got louder and louder until they were both shouting. Most arguments ended with the father going to the corner bar to drink, while the mother cried herself to sleep in the bedroom. Then the issue was dropped until the next time.

Beth and Rita's mother and father learned their style of communicating from their parents. Their parents also criticized them often, and the mother was raised to believe that a good mother tells her children how to live, how to act, and when they are doing wrong. While providing such direction is important when children are young, as children age, the parents must gradually allow them to make more of their own decisions. But Beth and Rita's mother did not change her degree of control. She continued to tell the girls and her husband what they should and should not do or say, expecting them to do exactly what she told them to do. She felt frustrated, hurt and maligned when they did not.

Love is not enough

Unfortunately, many people grow up in environments like Beth and Rita. The girls did not understand that their parents really loved each another. Instead, they lived with the constant fear that their parents might get divorced at any moment and their whole world might crumble. They felt helpless, like they had absolutely no control over the situation. Both girls grew up to be insecure and critical of themselves and others, with low self-esteem.

There is no end to how negative a verbal exchange can get. People who grow up in critical homes learn to be very good at throwing zingers at one another, but all that does is increase the negativity of any interchange. Underlying issues never get resolved, and both parties feel awful—hurt, angry, frustrated, maligned, put down, disrespected, lonely and helpless. Over time, bitterness and resentment build.

And so the cycle continues unless the adults and/or kids deliberately work on changing the pattern. If they try hard, they can change their behavior and break the cycle. They can learn how to think and speak positively and assertively, rather than negatively and aggressively. Then they can teach their children to do the same through their example.

Men and women come from different places

Along with the bad habits we pick up from our families, there's another big stumbling block to effective communication between couples: Men and women communicate differently. And before you dismiss that assertion as so obvious that it doesn't even need articulation, think about John Gray, Ph.D., the author of *Men Are from Mars, Women Are from Venus*, who uses this statement as the basis for a very successful writing and public-speaking enterprise. Although we may intellectually understand that men and women aren't the same, clearly we have a lot to learn about the hows and whys, and some work to do to overcome our emotional expectations.

Even though we know we aren't clones of one another, we frequently expect our partners to think and act just like we do, and we feel that our relationships would be perfect
if they did. "Why can't a woman be more like a man?" Professor Henry Higgins lament-
ed in *My Fair Lady*. More recently, in the movie *As Good As It Gets*, a young female fan
asks Jack Nicholson's character how he can write so well for women, and he responds, "I
think of a man and take away reason and accountability."

But it's not that simple. A woman's communication is not devoid of reason and
accountability, even though a man may sometimes think it is. Men and women just
express themselves differently, particularly when they feel vulnerable and confused.

It all starts with feelings

When women are under stress, they generally like to talk about their problems and
feelings. In contrast, men often withdraw and don't want to talk to anyone. So you have
a woman trying to talk through a problem, while the man doesn't want to discuss it.

Men have a more difficult time talking about their feelings because they have less
practice. Little girls surpass little boys in verbal abilities, but boys catch up over time.
However, while their verbal abilities and reading scores catch up, their ability to talk
about their feelings generally lags behind that of women. That's partly because women
talk so much about their feelings—they get a lot of practice. And we do that because as
women, we're taught that it's fine to emote and show sadness, happiness, joy, sorrow and
some anger. Men, on the other hand, are not given the same kind of latitude. They're
allowed to show anger and competition, but not the "gentler" emotions like sadness,
hurt or vulnerability.

It's gotten a lot better since the John-Waynesque-cowboy-of-few-monosyllables
days, but it's still not equal. Remember the scene from *The Prince Of Tides* where the
Nick Nolte character reaches out and tells his once abusive father that he loves him? It's
really hard for him, but he does it. His father looks at him and replies, "So, did ya catch
the score in the game last night, Son?" The son also reveals to the psychiatrist that in the
South, a gentleman learns to laugh, not cry. The "Southern Way" is to hide your feelings
and be polite and charming instead.

Even today, when gender attitudes have changed so much, men still learn that they
must always be in control and have power; showing your feelings makes you vulnerable
and is a sign of weakness.

Vulnerable men

So when men feel vulnerable, they tend to hide it, making it difficult for women to
realize how vulnerable they really are. When women feel vulnerable, they *do* talk about
it. Since the man isn't talking about it, the woman often underestimates how vulnerable
the man feels.

*A woman often underestimates
how vulnerable her man feels.*

Women strive to identify and label their feelings with words, then express those feelings in very clear English to their friends and loved ones. Men, on the other hand, have not had the same practice women have in identifying and labeling their feelings with words. They often feel confused about what they are feeling, and they don't like that. No one really enjoys feeling confused, but it's worse for a man. When a man feels confused, he also feels rather powerless, and since he's always supposed to be in control and have power, that's very uncomfortable. So a man feels less manly when he can't figure it out or fix it, and he's more prone to bury the feeling than try to deal with it.

Similarly, many men would rather react angrily than admit to feeling hurt. Why? Because hurt is another sign of weakness and vulnerability, and he's been trained—as a kid on the playground and as an adult working in business—that he must never show weakness or vulnerability The message is clear: To be a man means being on top in any situation. And that's a demarcation line that's difficult to overcome in any relationship.

Verbal men

Even a verbal man often feels like he can't hold his own in an argument because his mate can talk circles around him. The woman, of course, is not aware of his insecurity because he doesn't admit it to her. Instead, he's busy yelling to convince her—and himself—that he is powerful and in control.

The man who yells and stomps off in a huff may be acting this way because he doesn't know what else to do. He isn't trying to be mean or intentionally hurt his partner's feelings; he's just trying to do what he thinks he's supposed to do to hold his own. He feels confused about the situation and he hates feeling confused. So he is irritated with himself, too.

But feelings are only part of the problem

Another common difference between men and women is that women are more inclined to ask for help. Typically, a woman will ask for directions, while a man will wander around for hours trying to figure it out on his own.

Men also have trouble apologizing, because they consider it another sign of weakness. Women, on the other hand, are trained to be polite and apologize. In *Talking 9 to 5,* Deborah Tannen, Ph.D., noted that a woman will even apologize to a chair she has accidentally walked into and then feel foolish when she realizes it's not a person. Women often apologize too often at work, men not enough.

The bottom line is that women greatly appreciate a man who can apologize. They see it as a sign of strength, not weakness, when you can admit that you're not perfect and you've made a mistake. Since many men don't apologize, women really notice and appreciate those who do.

Men and women and conflict

Another key difference is the way men and women approach a difficult situation or a problem. A man often thinks in terms of fixing a problem, while a woman's first need is for emotional support. Frequently, when a woman talks about a problem, she isn't asking for advice—she's asking for understanding and empathy.

And then there's crying. Every woman alive understands that crying relieves stress. Yet many men don't have any idea what to do when a woman cries because they don't have much experience with it themselves. Some men say they cry, sure, but mostly it's a sniffle here and there. Men rarely sob like women. They tend to hold it in instead, because they aren't comfortable with crying. It's like walking around with their pants down in public.

As a result, men frequently react insensitively to a woman who is crying. They don't mean to be insensitive or inappropriate; they just don't know what to do or how to fix the problem, so they feel helpless and inept. One common response is to physically leave the room. Another common response is to simply ignore the fact that the woman is crying. A woman can be crying in her bedroom over something the man has just said, and the man won't go talk to her, apologize or just sit with her. Instead, he'll ignore her and act like nothing unusual is happening.

It's not an unbridgeable gap

A woman who understands the differences in the ways men and women communicate can be more patient when she tries to talk to her man. In general, a woman will have to extend herself a little more, perhaps suggest a compromise first, or lead the discussion in a calm and modulated way, being assertive, not aggressive.

When I work with couples, we talk about what to do when communication breaks down. If I ask the woman how she would like the man to respond when she's upset or crying, most of the time she responds that she'd just like him to say, *"Is there anything I can do to help?"* Or if she's crying over something he has said or done, she'd like to hear, *"I'm really sorry I hurt your feelings."*

Men typically think in terms of fixing problems and giving advice, not giving emotional support. So they need to be aware that most of the time when a woman talks about a problem or cries, she isn't asking for advice. She's asking for emotional support. Men also have to work to overcome their built-in resistance to asking for help and apologizing. They need to realize that both behaviors are neither threatening nor diminishing within a safe, trusting, intimate relationship.

Here's a chart that can help you conceptualize the differences between men and women and how they communicate:

DIFFERENCES BETWEEN MALE-FEMALE COMMUNICATION

Men, as a group, tend to:

Have a difficult time admitting when they don't know something.

Ask for help less often.

Won't ask for directions, feeling the need to figure it out for themselves.

Find it difficult to admit mistakes and apologize.

Have a more difficult time identifying what they are feeling, and once they do, have more difficulty trying to express it.

Have had a lot less practice expressing feelings. Often DO things with their friends, rather than really talking to them.

When confused, upset or feeling vulnerable, tend to withdraw into themselves rather than talk it out with friends.

Speak more aggressively than assertively

More likely to act angry than hurt and vulnerable.

Yell more than women and cry much less.

Use language more globally, less literally. "I'll call you when I get back from my trip," means, "I'll call you when I feel like it after I get home"—a few days or weeks or months later.

Like to fantasize out loud, but don't necessarily mean that they're going to do what they're fantasizing about.

Put more emphasis on actions, often underestimating how important it is to use words.

Women, as a group:

Have a much easier time admitting that they don't know.

Ask for help more easily.

Will ask for directions, and wonder why their partner's ego is tied into finding it himself.

Are more prone to admit mistakes and apologize too often sometimes.

Identify and express their feelings much more readily and easily.

Have been talking about their feelings since childhood! Talk about intimate topics with their girlfriends.

When upset, prefer to talk it out with their most trusted friends.

Tend to err on the passive, rather than aggressive side.

Often afraid to admit anger. Avoid confrontation, concerned about "being nice."

Cry more often and more vigorously than men.

Use language more literally. If the man says he's going to call when he gets home from a trip, the woman expects him to call within a few hours— days of his return.

Tend to take the man's verbal fantasies serious and literally. "I would really love to go skiing with you this winter at my favorite lodge," means, "He intends to see me at least until winter." She then feels betrayed when he doesn't do as he promised.

Really want a man to say, "I love you," not just show it through his actions.

Good communication

Now that you know how your childhood affects your communication and how differently men and women communicate, how can you use that knowledge to improve the communication in your relationship? Good communication involves sharing your feelings assertively (not aggressively) with each other, listening to your partner's feelings, and making reflective and supportive statements so he feels heard and understood. If you need to reach some agreement, then one person suggests a compromise and you negotiate until you agree on a compromise. You then try out that compromise, and if one or the other person isn't satisfied with it, you renegotiate a new compromise. You keep going in this fashion until you finally find a compromise that is acceptable to you both.

The biggest problem in most relationships is not that the couple can't agree, but that they don't know how to speak to one another in a manner that allows them to show respect and love while they disagree. Instead, they become insulting, critical and even sarcastic. They take each other for granted, forget what they love about each other, and focus on each other's flaws. They speak to each other disrespectfully and rehash old disagreements in antagonistic fashion.

So how should you communicate to keep your relationship thriving? Let's talk about helpful attitudes and expectations first. Then I'll share some secrets with you about technique.

Attitudes and expectations
Optimism

Always try to think positively about your partner and any disagreements you have. Partners can disagree on many things and still get along great together. If both of you are motivated, you can amicably resolve most disputes. At the very least, you can agree to disagree on an issue until both of you have had time to reflect further on the problem; then you can try again. Plus, optimism tends to be a self-fulfilling prophecy. If you think an interaction will end well, you can unconsciously structure it so it does.

Respect

Your partner has equal rights in the relationship, including the right to think differently from you on any topic, to express opinions, and to be heard respectfully. Show your partner as much respect and courtesy as you would give a stranger—or more.

When you and your partner disagree, respect your differences and don't assume that either position is necessarily right or wrong—they're just different. If your partner disagrees with you, it doesn't reflect a lack of feeling, so don't take disagreements personally. It also doesn't mean your partner is crazy. Assume that he has a valid point of view, even though it's different from yours; try to get into his shoes and understand his perspective. And even if you don't, support his right to hold a viewpoint that is drastically different from yours.

Openness—willingness to share feelings and thoughts

Don't expect your partner to know what you are thinking. You really don't want your partner to assume anything about your thoughts or feelings, because if the assumptions are incorrect, he might then draw inappropriate conclusions based on those unfounded assumptions, and then take action based on that misunderstanding. If you then assume you know what your partner's thinking and feeling, and basically react based on your assumptions and conclusions, before long, you will have quite the mess. Both of you may end up feeling hurt or angry about what you think the other person did and why, and in the end, it could all be extremely wasted energy.

So save yourself all the grief and don't expect your partner to read your mind. It's your responsibility to explain in an assertive way how you feel about a situation, and to ask your partner to express his feelings assertively in turn. If you both do this, you'll be amazed at how much your communication will improve.

And don't fall into the trap of thinking that you've known each other so long, your partner "just knows" how you feel.

Michael & Sue's Story

Michael and Sue fell into that trap. People often remarked on how "in tune" they seemed; they seemed to know what the other was thinking without having to say it out loud. When they cooked, they moved in sync around the kitchen, getting dinner together in a fluid kind of dance, passing things back and forth with ease. They assumed that they understood what the other was thinking as well. Life was good for them except for one thing: They had been trying to start a family for years, but had not been able to get pregnant. Tests revealed no physical cause.

Then one day, Michael and Sue began to talk. They were astonished to find that they hadn't really understood what the other was thinking or feeling at all. Instead, they had presumed and acted on those presumptions, triggering reactions in each other, which in turn led to further presumptions and unfounded reactions. The layers of mis-assumption, mis-communication and misunderstanding in their relationship were quite deep and complex, and straightening it all out was like peeling off the layers of an onion. Each misunderstanding and miscommunication was built on a false assumption of the previous layer of misassumption, misunderstanding and miscommunication. Permeating through it all was a lot of anger, hurt, and hostility—enough psychological chaos to prevent Sue from getting pregnant, even though there was nothing physically wrong and they were having sex.

So, the bottom line is: No matter how long you've been together or how well you think you know your partner, the process of open, verbal communication is critical to the health of your relationship.

Express your feelings openly and assertively and ask your partner to do the same.

There's just no way getting around it.

Care and attention

Don't take your love for granted. If today was the last day of your life, how would treat your partner? To build a good relationship, you must spend in-person time together, and show each other how much you care through both words and actions. Long-distance relationships are very stressful. Make quality time in your busy schedule to see one another, and put energy and effort into keeping your relationship fresh and exciting.

Karen & Mark's Story

Karen and Mark's relationship suffered from a lack of care and attention, as well as Mark's reluctance to share his feelings and thoughts with Karen. After Karen and Mark retired from teaching, Karen began having a number of accidents. Most were inconsequential, but one evening while she was preparing dinner, Karen cut herself quite seriously with a knife. Although Karen knew that her accidents were not intentional, she recognized that they were too numerous to be coincidental. So she came to me to figure out what was happening.

As we talked, Karen discovered that she was very frustrated with her marriage. She didn't know if her husband still loved her; she didn't feel important. He was a man of very few words, and now that she was retired and didn't have her teaching job to distract her, Karen felt like she was living with a stranger.

When I talked to Mark, I asked him if he loved his wife. "Of course," he replied. "She knows I love her." When I asked him the last time he told Karen he loved her, he couldn't remember. But he brushed it off by saying, "After all, I make pies for her. I clean the kitchen for her. Why else would I stay with her and do those things if I didn't love her?"

Mark was very surprised to learn that in fact, his wife did NOT know that he loved her. It took Mark a long time to work through his resentment that he had to learn to talk to his wife. He was raised to believe that men didn't need to talk to their wives or children— that only actions were important and that others should be able to discern thoughts and feelings from those actions. I reassured him that actions are indeed important, but they are not enough. His wife, like most partners in an intimate relationship, needed to hear the verbal, *"I love you,"* as well.

Good faith

Always try to communicate with your partner as clearly as you can, but recognize that no matter how much you each try, there will always be some misinterpretations due to the sheer number of communications, demands and hectic pace of everyday life. We don't always have the time to be specific about exactly how we're feeling at that exact moment. So always assume that your partner has your best interests at heart—even when you find yourself in an ambiguous situation (e.g., your husband is late coming home).

In return, your show of good faith helps your partner trust you and feel and act more intimate and loving toward you. When you realize that you have misunderstood one another (he told you he would be home late Tuesday, but you thought he meant next Tuesday), discuss the misinterpretation calmly, and clear up the confusion with a positive attitude.

Trust, honesty, loyalty and confidentiality

Every intimate relationship requires trust, honesty and loyalty to survive. You must also respect your partner's confidentiality and privacy and keep your business between the two of you. Don't complain about your partner to friends or relatives or reveal his secrets. Intimacy involves enjoying a relationship with your mate that you don't share with anyone else. To strengthen your relationship, work on improving the communication between the two of you. Work on being best friends, as well as lovers and companions.

Maturity and taking responsibility for your own feelings

Couples who communicate well don't blame their partners for making them feel or do something. They take responsibility for their own feelings and actions. As we discussed in **Chapter 6—Happiness & Relationships**, no one can **make** you happy. People who communicate well take responsibility for their own happiness.

That's it. Those are the secret attitudes and expectations of couples who communicate successfully. Now let's talk about the behavior involved in good communication.

Communication skills secrets

You may already be engaging in some of these behaviors, and if you are, great! These skills are vital to good communication. If you learn to do all these behaviors most of the time, you should notice a marked improvement in your communication with others, especially your significant other.

Practice reflective listening

(Since this skill tends to be more difficult for men than women, I'll talk directly to the men here.) Reflective listening is repeating some of what the other person has just said—paraphrasing it—to show that you're listening and that you also understand. For example, if your wife comes home and tells you what a rotten day she had at work and how stressed she was, and how she hit the fender of another car and was late picking up your son, and now she doesn't have time to prepare the dinner she had planned, she doesn't want you to give her advice on which body shop to take the car to or what she can make for dinner instead. She isn't asking for practical solutions. She's asking you to

let her talk through her frustrations and get them out. She's not blaming you for them, she's not asking you what to do, she just wants to talk it out, maybe cry a little and release some of the stress. The appropriate reflective listening response would be something like, *"You've had a really stressful day, haven't you, Honey?"*

Reflective listening statements encourage your partner to continue talking. After you respond in an understanding way, she will say something like, *"Yes, it was so awful... and then just when I..."* She will continue her story, feeling somewhat relieved that you are her good friend and listener, someone who really understands.

If she doesn't describe her feelings, just the events that took place, you can reflect back the emotions she might be feeling: *"Sounds like you're feeling very frustrated..."* She will probably agree and then talk more about her feelings. If she doesn't, *ask* her how she's feeling.

If she sounds confused, you can start your reflective listening statements with, *"So, what you're saying is...,"* or, *"It sounds like you're saying...Is that correct?"* That way, if she is trying to say something different, she will correct you by re-explaining herself.

You can also ask information-gathering questions between paraphrasing. But be careful to ask questions that are relevant to understanding the story, not those involving insignificant details. For example, *"Where did you break down?"* is relevant, but *"So, did Jack (the gas station tow guy) ever buy that new truck he wanted?"* is not.

Make supportive statements

After she has finished telling her story—and probably repeated herself a few times— then you can offer more emotional support through supportive statements such as, *"I'm so sorry that happened to you, Sweetie. You certainly don't deserve it."*

Supportive statements are remarks that show emotional support and empathy for the other person. Supportive statements are not expressions of sympathy. Sympathy is feeling sorry for someone, whereas empathy is feeling as if you were that person in that situation. After your partner tells you about a troubling event, supportive statements could include, *"I'm so sorry that happened to you!"* or, *"Oh, I can see how that would be very difficult to handle!"* But supportive statements aren't just appropriate for bad times. Make supportive statements when good things happen, too: *"Oh, I'm so happy for you!"* Supportive statements help us feel understood and valued.

Supportive statements do not contain criticism—either stated or implied. "Did you have enough gas in the tank? You know how you always try to wait until the car is on its last drop before you fill it," is not likely to help your partner continue talking. Remember, being "emotionally supportive" is showing support for her emotions—not criticizing her for having those emotions or for putting herself in a situation where she would feel that way.

Similarly, a statement such as, "I'll take the car and give it a good overhaul," may seem supportive, but by attempting to fix the problem, you effectively stop your partner's discourse. One common misperception about communication is that people tell us their problems to get helpful ideas about how to solve them. The truth is that most people talk about problems to vent and de-stress. They want emotional support, not practical ideas on how to fix everything. If a mate wants advice or solutions, she'll ask for them.

If your partner does ask for advice or help, couch it in tentative terms: *"Well, of course, you need to do what's best for you, and that may not be the same as what's best for me."* If your partner presses for your opinion, you can continue with, *"Well, you could try…if you want to."* Such a response gives your partner the freedom to accept or reject your advice, without feeling that you'll be hurt if she doesn't want to follow it.

With reflective listening and supportive statements, you are staying in the moment with your partner. You aren't changing the topic, glossing over feelings, or avoiding them because they're painful. You are allowing your partner to express her feelings and get them off her chest. This is one of the best ways to relieve stress— talking to someone we trust about our problems. When we verbalize our fears and frustrations and get them out into the open, they don't seem so bad anymore.

Positive reinforcement

Most people think a lot more positive thoughts about their partner than they ever verbalize. But all the positive thoughts in the world won't help your relationship unless you verbalize them to your partner! We tend to tell our partners when we don't like something, rather than when we do. If we don't also share our positive thoughts, the result can be very negative. Men often complaint that their wives nag. When women comment on negative details, but don't praise the man for what he's doing well, the over- all effect is negative.

So make a concerted effort to tell your partner when he's doing a good job or when he's trying really hard at something, even if he can't do it perfectly yet and maybe never will. People need to hear much more positive reinforcement than criticism. Recognizing your partner's efforts by verbally commenting on them (*"I can see you are working very hard at trying to listen, rather than giving advice"*) can motivate him to try even harder. It lets him know that you noticed and appreciate the effort. It also makes him feel good about himself, and that can be very energizing.

When you discuss disagreements, be sure to mention related points that you agree on. After your partner gives an opinion, voice your agreement with whatever part of his re- marks you can agree with, rather than immediately disagreeing and voicing your point.

Practice assertiveness

You've probably noticed that I have used the word *assertive* throughout this chapter. What is being assertive? Most people assume that *assertive* means the same as *aggres- sive*. They think of a sentence like, "She asserted herself," and believe that it means the equivalent of, "She had to be pushy to get her point across."

It would take a whole book to teach you all the important aspects of speaking asser- tively. But here's a crash course that will suffice in the meantime.

Assertiveness is expressing your feelings in a way that shows respect for the other person. It is a very intimate form of communication that you'll want to use with your mate, your friends and anyone close to you with whom you share equal status. It is very direct and clear, and tells your partner exactly how you feel in a certain situation. It sometimes involves standing up for your rights in a way that shows respect for the other person's rights.

Assertiveness is different from aggressiveness, which is basically attacking another person and standing up for your rights in a way that violates the other person's rights. And it's also very different from passive behavior or non-assertiveness, which is basically letting everyone walk on you. It's also different from being "passive-aggressive," which is being aggressive in a passive way and stabbing someone in the back. And it's different from being "political," which is picking and choosing what you say to accomplish what you regard as a positive outcome.

THERE ARE TWO BASIC SENTENCES INVOLVED IN ASSERTIVENESS:

1. ***To tell someone how you feel, say:***

   "I feel _____ (angry, hurt, sad, happy, etc.) *when* _____ (what happens or when you do _____)."*

   For example, you might say, *"I feel* disappointed *when* that happens," or, *"I feel* sad *when you* say that."

2. ***To ask for something, say:***

   "I would appreciate it if you would _____," or,

   "I would like it if you would _____,"

   "Would you please _____?"

   or possibly even, *"I want you to* _____."

Notice that you are basically *asking* or *requesting* that the other person do something; you are not telling him to do it or demanding it.

Also note that when you're telling someone your feelings, you take responsibility for your own feelings by starting the sentence with the word, *"I"* and say, *"I feel…"*

Do ***not*** say, *"You made me feel* _____" or, *"I feel* ___ *because you* _____ (did what)."* Both of those sentences blame the other person for your feelings, and as we have discussed before, no one can make you feel anything any more than you can make them feel anything.

When you don't know how you feel about something, say, *"I feel confused right now,"* or, *"I have mixed feelings about that."* If you know what is causing your confusion, you can express it: *"I feel happy and excited that we're going to see the family for the Fourth Of July holiday, but I feel a little disappointed that we won't be in town to go to Jean's party."*

Don't attack your partner, no matter how angry or frustrated you feel. For example, ***don't*** say, *"You are the most ignorant SOB I have ever known!"* or, *"You are so conceited,"* or, *"You think you're always right."* In general, never start a sentence with the word, "you." We have all been criticized enough in our lives to know that when a sentence starts that way, it usually ends with a put down. *"You're so stupid; you always get it wrong!"*

For the same reason, avoid all-or-nothing words like *everyone, everything, nobody, nothing, always, never, good, bad, best, worst, right* or *wrong.* They are generally inaccurate. For example, if we can come up with one instance where something did occur, then using the word *never* to describe it (saying it *never* occurred) is inaccurate. The same is true for words like *nobody, no one* and *nothing*. Similarly, if we can cite one instance where someone or something didn't occur, then words like always, everyone and everybody are inaccurate.

In addition, *right* and *wrong* and *good* and *bad* are moral, religious terms. They belong in discussions of religion, not everyday conversations with your mate. Instead, use more accurate, less power-laden words like *appropriate* or *inappropriate, helpful* or *not helpful, wise* or *unwise*. Try to steer clear of superlative words—those ending in *est* (e.g., *dumbest, messiest*) or preceded by the word *most ("You are the most self-centered...")*, and avoid power words such as *stupid* and *dumb*.

Never attack your partner's character or paint vividly exaggerated caricatures of his behavior. ***Don't*** say, *"You're so stupid, you wouldn't know a ___ from a ___,"* or, *"You couldn't see an opportunity coming if it came up and knocked you upside the head."* Instead, when you have a problem with something he's doing, describe the behavior you want changed, rather than blasting him as a person: *"I would really appreciate it if you would ___."* And that brings us to ***The Dr. Kate 20-1 Rule,*** a helpful way to ask for a behavioral change.

The Dr. Kate 20-To-1 Rule

Although healthy couples recognize and respect their differences, there are times in every relationship when partners want to ask each other to change some behavior they find problematic. Before your partner can hear your request for change, however, he has to feel appreciated and valued. We all tend to protect ourselves under siege. So if you're constantly nagging at your partner, expect him to tune you out, rather than being receptive to your requests.

Think about it. How eager would you be to grant your partner's request if it was couched in demeaning, critical sentences like, "You're so slow, a corpse would move faster! So, are you going to finish fixing that bicycle for me while I'm still young enough to use it, or what?" If you consistently rely on blame, insults and name-calling, all you're doing is ensuring that your partner won't hear you. Nagging and whining don't work. Constant criticisms and demands for change fall on deaf ears, while a polite request for a small behavioral change that follows many positive compliments is likely to be heard.

For that reason, I always recommend using ***The Dr. Kate 20-1 Rule*** when asking your partner for a behavioral change. First, give twenty sincere, positive reinforcements such as praise, hugs and kisses. Try to give generous positive reinforcement on a regular basis, not just the day before you're going to make your request. But be sure to also give him several positive reinforcements right before you make your request. Pick a time when you are both relaxed and rested and in a good mood. Then make your positive reinforcements.

"You know, Honey, I love you and I always love being with you, no matter what we're doing. I always enjoy going out with the kids on Friday family nights, and spending Sunday at your Mom's, with your brothers and their wives, and you know I love mingling with

your relatives at our family picnics and barbecues. I love your family and our family, and I love how we stay close with them."

Now make your request in assertive, not aggressive, terms. **Ask** for what you want, rather than demanding it or making your partner guess at it. *"But I was wondering— could we start having Saturday night as our special date night, just the two of us together? I would really appreciate it if you would make that time for us. Then we could spend quality time together, just like we did when we were first dating."*

Now end with some positive reinforcement. *"Just think, we could go out and have fun and leave our problems behind. I just think you're the best husband a woman could possibly have, and I'd like to have you all to myself one night a week."*

If he agrees, give a few more positive reinforcements to show your love and appreciation. *"Thanks, Honey, I really appreciate it. You are so good to me! I love being with you!"*

Now, there's nothing sacred about the number 20. I just use 20 to emphasize that the number of positive comments has to be **significantly** higher than the number of negative comments if you want someone to hear you and care about your request.

Now, it's your right to ask your partner for a behavioral change if his or her behavior is directed at you or has an impact on your life. But he still has the right to say, "No." If he does, you can say, *"I'm sorry you feel that way."* Or, *"I'm sorry you feel that way, and I wish you would take some time to think about it again and possibly reconsider."* Convey through your words and behavior that your partner has a right to have needs and preferences that may be very different from yours, and he also has the right to make his own choices regarding them.

Learn to correct yourself

If you hear yourself saying something harsh or critical, stop in the middle of the sentence, correct yourself, and don't be afraid to apologize. Steve had to learn that comments he thought were playful actually felt like criticism to his girlfriend.

Chris & Steve's Story

Chris and Steve were a committed couple who loved to have fun. They flirted with one another, played together, and generally had a good time. But Steve loved to tease. He had a tendency toward depression, so he tried not to take life too seriously. As a result, he often teased Chris, as well as his other family and friends. In Steve's eyes, teasing was an expression of love. But the more pressured Steve felt, the more he teased; it was also an outlet for his anxiety. To make matters worse, he was adept at zeroing in on sensitive issues.

While Steve was basically good-hearted and loving, his method of showing love and dealing with his own anxiety eventually took its toll on Chris. Chris also had a tendency toward depression and low self-esteem. Instead of recognizing why Steve teased and seeing it as a demonstration of his love for her, Chris began to feel criticized and put down. She frequently felt hurt and devalued when Steve teased her. The problem was that Steve teased so much that even though he occasionally told Chris he loved her, the ratio of negative teases to positive reinforcements was very high, and Chris felt criticized on a regular basis.

In time, Steve learned that his teasing could be misinterpreted as criticism. He started praising Chris more and teasing less, particularly about sensitive topics. Chris, in turn, learned to reinterpret the teasing. When Steve teased, instead of thinking, "He's picking on me again!", Chris would stop herself and say, "He's teasing me because he loves me and that's what he does when he cares about someone."

Steve learned to watch Chris' face more closely, to realize when something he said had a negative affect and to apologize and give more positives instead. By both Steve and Chris meeting in the middle this way to fix the communication between them, their relationship improved immensely.

Remember, you only have a right to ask for a behavioral change if your partner's behavior has a direct impact on you. If your partner yells at you or treats you in an aggressive manner, you can say, *"I feel hurt when you speak that way to me. I would appreciate it if you would talk about this issue in a calm, respectful way."* However, if you don't approve of the way your husband's mother treats him, you would be overstepping your boundaries to tell his mother how you feel about it. It is your husband's responsibility to ask her to change her behavior toward him, if he so chooses.

Learn the art of compromise

To compromise, according to the Word Thesaurus, means "finding a middle ground, striking a balance, making concessions, meeting halfway, finding a happy medium." It means, "to come to an agreement, adjust or settle by mutual concession(s), to find or follow a way between extremes, and to bind by mutual agreement." According to Mirriam-Webster Collegiate Dictionary, compromise is, "a settlement of differences by arbitration, a consent reached by mutual concessions, or something intermediate between and/or blending qualities of two different things."

So basically, when two people compromise, it means they both give concessions to reach an intermediate, balanced middle ground. No relationship can exist without a healthy amount of compromise, because no two people are ever so compatible that they always agree. Everyone has different opinions, desires and wants.

Successful resolution of differences includes telling each other how you feel, listening to the other's feelings with an open mind, calmly discussing potential compromises, negotiating, and agreeing to try a compromise. If the compromise you try doesn't work, either party calls a return to the drawing board. Then you calmly discuss the issue again and agree on a different compromise. You try that compromise out for a few weeks and see how it works. If either of you finds it unsatisfactory, then you return to the drawing board again. You keep going in this fashion until you find a compromise that works for both of you.

This calm method of discussion and negotiation shows respect for both you and your partner. No matter how much you disagree, you both have a right to your perspective, and it is only by showing respect for your partner's right to disagree that you can overcome the inevitable problems that occur in any relationship.

Giving in too much

But you are compromising too much when you totally give in on most things. The amount and degree of concessions over time should be roughly equal between the two parties. If some issues are not important to you, it's OK if you make all the concessions. It's not much of a sacrifice to give in about issues you don't care much about. Other issues may be very important to you, but not to your partner, and he can make all the concessions then. For issues you both care about equally, find a middle ground.

Problems begin when one partner is easygoing and used to giving, and the other is a taker who is used to getting exactly what he wants. The taker may feel that he is giving a lot when the other partner is actually doing the lion's share of giving. The taker feels like he's conceding because he wants it *all*, all of the time.

So you must not expect to always get your way. You should help your partner get some of what he wants, just as overall, he should help you get some of what you want.

The most important thing to remember when you're trying to resolve a dispute is that to settle it well, both parties have to feel that they got something from the result. An effective compromise is a win-win, not a win-lose, resolution. If one person feels that he lost out, the resentment is likely to carry forward and cause more problems. If the issue remains unsettled, the resentment grows, and eventually your mate can begin to feel that his needs are not being met at all. In time, and especially if other discussions meet similar deaths, your mate can decide living with you just isn't worth it and look for someone who does seem to meet his needs. In the end, neither of you wins.

Communication timeline

At the beginning of this chapter, I told you that communication is a skill we work our entire lives to perfect. We've already discussed many of the skills you'll need to be a more effective communicator. Now you need to learn the order in which to use your newfound skills. So here's a time-line and more pointers on how to use communication skills to settle disagreements between you and your mate.

1. Pick your battles

Pick your battles carefully, especially if you tend to notice a lot of little details and often disagree with your partner. The positive experiences in your relationship history must considerably outweigh the negative experiences. So don't sweat the small stuff.

2. Choose the time and place

Bring up the topic at an appropriate time—when you are relaxed, well-rested and in a relatively good mood, not when you and your mate are rushing to get to work in the morning or are otherwise stressed and distracted. Choose a place where you can talk privately without being interrupted. Turn off the television and eliminate all other distractions. Sit perpendicular to each other so you can make good eye contact. Don't try to have a meaningful conversation in a car. If you go to a restaurant to have your conversation, choose one where the music is soft enough for you to hear each other without straining, but where no one else will overhear your conversation.

3. Lay the groundwork

Introduce the topic gently: *"You know, ___ (your mate's name), I want to talk to you about something very important."* Pause and wait until you have your partner's full attention.

If that is not possible at this time because he has something else that has to be done right then, ask, "When would be a good time? It's really important that we have some uninterrupted time together."

4. Ask about your partner's feelings first, use reflective listening and agree with whatever you can agree with

If you believe that the two of you will disagree on the issue, ask about your partner's feelings first. *"How do you think we should spend the holidays this year?"* Use reflective listening and agree with whatever you honestly can agree with to help diffuse the situation. *"I agree with you that your mother is a very lonely woman and she loves it when we come to visit her. I know that you would like to do as much for her as you can while you can, and I understand that completely."*

Continue to let your partner state his feelings, while you agree with whatever you can, until he is finished explaining his position. Whatever you do, never tell your partner what he is thinking or feeling or presume to know. Always ask.

5. Give supportive statements when appropriate

"I'm sorry you feel stressed around Christmas. I can understand how difficult it is to be torn between two parents. I love you very much and hope we can figure out a solution so you can see both of them."

6. Then express your feelings

Then gently and assertively express your feelings regarding the issue. *"I would also like to spend part of the holidays with your parents. However, they're still not speaking to each other 10 years after their divorce, so that makes it harder. Plus my family is having a big Christmas Eve reunion this year in Chicago, and since they're not in the same state as your parents, seeing them all is going to be a bit difficult. I would like us to make at least part of my family's reunion."*

7. Take turns expressing yourselves assertively

Take turns expressing yourselves until you've both made your positions clear. Don't talk over one another. No matter how much you disagree, let your partner finish his thought before you speak.

8. Stay on track

Keep to one topic per conversation and don't bring up any other issues unless they are truly relevant to that one topic. This is the time to positively resolve your differences on one particular issue, not to digress into a litany of what you hate about each other. Also, be careful not to bring up past behavior that someone has amended or is working on through one of your other compromises. If your partner brings up past issues that have not been settled, set a date and time to discuss them. But stay in the present and resolve the primary issue.

9. Speak slowly and calmly

Keep your voice modulated. Pause before speaking and think about what you are saying while you say it. Don't cut your partner off in mid-sentence, raise your voice, or talk faster and faster. If you find yourself speeding up or getting louder, stop. Pause. Take a deep breath. Then start over again in a calm, slow, modulated voice.

10. Avoid power struggles

Steer clear of power struggles, which often take the form of accusation, denial, accusation, denial, accompanied by a rapid escalation of anger.

"You did _____ (some action)."
"No, *I didn't."*
"YES, *you did."*
"NO, I DIDN'T!"
or
"You are_____ (some adjective)."
"No, *I'm not."*
"YES, *you are."*
"NO, I'm NOT!"

No discussion or relationship ever benefits from such an exchange. When people become locked in a power struggle, they often make negative, exaggerated, inaccurate accusations that they don't even mean. Instead, take a deep breath and keep the discussion calm and respectful. Agree with whatever your mate has said that you can agree with: *"I understand that you feel I get my way more than you do. So let's talk about this calmly and try to come up with a solution we both find acceptable..."*

11. Brainstorm compromises

Once you have both discussed your feelings assertively and understand how you each feel, brainstorm compromises that might work. Make a list of the possibilities.

Discuss the plusses and minuses of each possibility, and pick a trial compromise. *"OK, what if we fly to see your parents a few days before Christmas? We can visit both of them on Christmas Eve, too, one for lunch and the other for dinner. Then we can fly to Chicago early on Christmas Day and spend the day at my family's reunion."* Or, *"Well, instead of rushing and worrying about getting snowed in, why don't we see your parents over Thanksgiving weekend this year, and mine over Christmas? Then next year we can switch, and see mine for Thanksgiving and yours for Christmas. How does that sound?"*

12. Set a time to reevaluate your compromises

Once you have decided on a compromise, set a time in the future to discuss how it worked. If either of you isn't satisfied with the compromise at that time, that person should offer another compromise. With any problem that involves ongoing behaviors (going out more often, changing the way you discipline your children, changing the way the two of you spend money), try the compromise for a brief period, such as two to four weeks. Set a time two to four weeks from then to discuss the issue again. If the two of you are happy with the solution, keep it. If not, the displeased partner suggests another compromise, and you renegotiate until you've identified the next trial compromise. Keep going in this way until you finally find a compromise that is acceptable to you both.

13. Agreeing to disagree

If you can't reach any agreement or compromise, agree to disagree and revisit the issue after you've both had time to reflect. *"It sounds like we're too far apart on this to solve it tonight. So let's just agree to disagree for now, and discuss this again next week after we've had time to relax and think about it on our own a bit. How does that sound to you?"*

Sometimes couples need professional counseling

You and your partner should consider seeing a psychologist if you find yourselves in any of the following situations:

- ❤ You try to resolve an important problem and can't, but feel that you must reach some compromise on that issue soon.
- ❤ You have so many issues that you don't know where to begin, so you don't talk about them at all.
- ❤ You have so many issues that whenever you try to talk to them, you end up in a fight instead, so nothing gets resolved.
- ❤ Your partner holds a different and more stringent set of rules and standards for your behavior than his, and will not recognize or respect your rights in the relationship.
- ❤ You or your partner simply don't have the verbal skills to be able to discuss problems assertively and reach satisfactory compromises.

In marital therapy, the psychologist will teach you to communicate respectfully and assertively while he referees the discussion and helps it go in a positive direction. As you practice and learn, you will probably feel more positive and loving toward your mate. And when you feel more positive and loving, you may be surprised to find that you and your mate are now willing to accept certain compromises that were previously out of the question.

But even if you and your mate come to the conclusion that you cannot live with the compromises and need to split up, you will be better friends afterward because you have discussed your problems in a respectful manner and renewed some of your positive feelings toward one another. You'll also feel better psychologically, because you'll understand better why the two of you split up, and that closure will allow you to heal faster and move on to a more fulfilling relationship. At that point, you can then apply all that therapy experience to your next relationship, so it stays more healthy and communicative all the way through.

Real-life Love@AOL letters about communication

I receive many letters from AOL members on the topic of communication, and I've included some of my favorites here.

We say things we don't mean...or nothing at all! MY AGE: 28 MY GENDER: MALE

Dear Dr. Kate,

I have been seeing a wonderful woman for three months now and it's generally been great. The problem is that whenever we fight, we are both so stubborn, we either say things we don't mean, or we don't say anything at all. We could literally spend two days not talking over a small issue until one of us breaks the ice and explodes. She says we fight like it's a contest or something. I agree and don't want it to harm our relationship; we have so much potential. Please help us.

Dear "Stubborn and Feeling Stupid,"

Put a post-it note on your bathroom mirror with the following sayings:

No one ever wins a power struggle.

Too much pride is a terrible thing.

Don't win the battle and lose the war.

Value what you have before you lose it.

When you brush your teeth in the morning, read over each saying. Then reflect on one of them and all it implies while you are in the shower.

In addition, take **The Dr. Kate Communication Quiz** (in the *Appendix*) to learn more about how the two of you communicate. It sounds like you and your girlfriend communicate in aggressive ways (overstepping your boundaries and taking advantage of the other person's rights while standing up for your own) and passive-aggressive ways (being indirectly aggressive, like using the silent treatment to get what you want). Instead, it's really important to learn to be assertive with one another—to stand up for your rights, but in a way that shows respect for each other's rights.

Start reading books on assertiveness and communication skills. (Do the exercises at the end of this chapter.) See a psychologist together to put the finishing touches on your assertiveness skills and learn how to apply them better.

Bring a tape recorder and record your sessions, especially when the two of you are roleplaying assertiveness with one another. Then a couple of months later, replay the first session, and you'll be surprised and very pleased at how much you've improved.

Best Wishes! And please keep me posted on your progress,

Dr. Kate

Who's wrong on 1st?
a/k/a can I really be wrong all the time? MY AGE: 40 MY GENDER: FEMALE

Dear Dr. Kate,

I have been living with a man (and my daughter) for about three years. He is very hard to handle, as **HE** is always **right**. And you guessed it, **I** am always **wrong**. I don't know how to do anything the **right** way **(his** way). It is really starting to bother me. It is his house, and I don't feel comfortable not doing things the **right** way **(his** way). Plus our conversation is horrible; he is not much of a talker. I need your help.

Dear "Ready To Leave,"
It sounds like you are living in a very punitive situation. Is he constantly telling you what you are doing **"wrong?"** Does he give you any positive reinforcement, or is it largely all negative? Did he talk more during an earlier stage of your relationship, or has he always been nonverbal?

A lot of people use inappropriate words such as **right** and **wrong** to describe behavior, when other more descriptive, less judgmental words such as **appropriate/inappropriate** and **helpful/not helpful** would not only be more accurate, but would also stimulate conversation, rather than putting it six feet under. Describing things as right or wrong just makes people more likely to resist, and the discussion can quickly lead to a power struggle in which neither party is willing to give in.

Ask your friend to accompany you to a psychologist for couples' therapy. Follow the suggestions outlined in **How To Invite Your Mate to Couples Counseling** in the Appendix. However, if he refuses to accompany you to therapy after six months or so, it may be better if you leave. It's very important that your daughter learn good communication skills, and that isn't likely in your current situation. In addition, everyone, including you, deserves to be in a relationship where both partners are willing to make compromises and work on improving the communication.

Be sure you don't make going to therapy a power struggle. Try talking about it like the two of you need to work on your relationship; don't tell him he has a problem. Even if he has to think the problem is your fault in order to go, it would be worth it just get him in. The issue isn't who's **right** or **wrong,** but whether or not the two of you can learn to communicate and build a fulfilling and rewarding life together.

All the Best, and please let me know how it works out,

Dr. Kate

Communication really works!

Dear Dr. Kate,
I wanted to give you a positive letter today. I was very hurt by my husband's apparent lack of sexual interest in me, and decided that the only way we could resolve it was to talk. We had the discussion, and together, we found ways to solve the problems. I was feeling that I was not attractive, or that perhaps he wanted someone else. He told me that he is

ually attracted to me—more than I would have guessed, but after work, housework, and putting our 3-year-old to bed, he's tired. But now that we've talked, he understands how I feel, and things are going much better!! :) It goes to show that communication can solve problems.

Dear Communicating and Loving It,
Congratulations! I'm glad it's working out for you.

There are many times when it seems the way we're thinking about an issue is the only possible way to consider it. But I can guarantee you that there are always many possible perspectives. The key is to ask your partner about his feelings, assertively state your own, then negotiate and try to find an acceptable compromise. Try it out and if it doesn't work, go back to the drawing board and brainstorm another compromise. Keep doing this until a reasonable compromise is found that is acceptable to both of you.

I am very happy that your marriage is going better. Remember, relationships and marriages always take work. However, the result of your labor can be extremely rewarding!

Best Wishes, and Enjoy! Keep in touch, and thanks for your letter,

Dr. Kate

Am I a fool to take him back?

MY AGE: 41 MY GENDER: FEMALE

Dear Dr. Kate,
I left my husband two years ago, because we had stopped communicating. We were overwhelmed with so many family crises and financial problems, we just weren't able to communicate through all the stress. The end result was that we lost each other to the point that I didn't think he loved me anymore, and I didn't feel I was in love with him.

We made four attempts to reconcile during those two years, but each time, one of us backed away because we still weren't able to communicate our fears and concerns. When I finally decided time had come to get off our on-again/off-again merry-go-round of a relationship and file for divorce, my husband immediately became involved with another woman. I was devastated by his infidelity and the cruel method he used to end our relationship. The children felt hurt as well.

I filed for divorce six weeks ago and have used many of the techniques your describe for stopping negative thoughts and grieving my loss. I'm surviving pretty well at this point, and trying to move forward. Then last week my husband called to let me know he had reflected on what I'd said about him hurting the kids, and had stopped seeing this other woman.

Prior to our most recent serious attempt to reconcile, I had finally figured out that I still loved him; everything that I had accomplished on my own didn't mean as much because he wasn't there to share it with. After he told me about ending his affair, I saw a new window of opportunity to try to put our family back together, and I finally told him what I had discovered about myself and my feelings. He confided that he still loves me, too, and our conversation then blossomed into the most sharing, open communication we'd had in years.

Is it possible that we could still work things out at this late date? So much has happened and so much time has passed. Are we once again repeating a bad pattern? Or is there a chance that we could learn to communicate and compromise, and finally give each other what we really need?

Dear "Am I A Fool?",
No, you're not.

Your letter tells me that you both share a lot of history together, and that you definitely love each other and have compatibility in a lot of areas. What you need is help with your communication skills.

I strongly urge both of you to see a psychologist together for marital therapy. Right now—while you are both motivated, talking, and trying, and it's a top priority.

Because before too long, more stress and life are bound to happen. And before you experience another major stress, you'll want to make sure that you have both learned to be assertive and open with one another, and that you are able to express your feelings and reach satisfactory compromises. It's important to learn these skills when times are better, so that you'll be able to demonstrate them when life gets tough.

There is absolutely no couple that doesn't experience life stresses, and the longer you live and stay together, the more stresses you'll have to weather. You can do so successfully and grow closer to one another through it all—IF you continue to communicate and give each other emotional support.

All the best, and please keep me posted on your progress,

Dr. Kate

Exercises to hone your communication skills

1. **Improve Your Communication Step By Step.** During these next few weeks, listen to how you say things and pay attention to your body language. What tone of voice are you using? How are you standing? Where are your hands? What does your facial expression say? What words are you using? How does the context of your words change them? How loudly are you speaking? Take notes in your Relationship Notebook, and ask your partner for feedback. Identify areas where you need to improve, and try to add one new positive behavior (e.g., reflective listening, supportive statements, *The Dr. Kate 20-1 Rule*) every week. Chart your progress in your notebook. Doing so will also help you stay organized.

2. **Reward Your Partner.** In your Relationship Notebook, make a list of all the things you love about your partner. Then give him at least 10 positive reinforcements/rewards every day. It isn't that difficult—kisses, hugs and praise all count! Remember to kiss hello, goodbye and goodnight each day, and give your partner lots of hugs and smiles.

3. **Do More Reading.** Go to my site on *Love@AOL* (AOL Keyword: Dr. Kate) and use the search function to find more advice I have written on communication. Read as many of those letters and articles as you can. You can also buy some books on assertiveness training and communication skills (see the list of recommended books in the Appendix for some suggestions). Share what you learn with your partner, and suggest that he read the articles you liked best.

Chapter 8

Sex too!

Sex in a long-term relationship

*I*n Chapter 4, we discussed sex as part of a beginning relationship. In this chapter, we'll look at sex from a different, but still very important, angle—how to make sex thrive in a long-term relationship.

Common challenges for long-term couples

At my AOL site, I have received thousands of letters about sex from committed couples. It is perfectly clear that "living happily ever after" doesn't happen unless you pay attention to your love life as you go along.

If you haven't yet read Chapter 4, do so now. Many of the problems, myths and solutions mentioned for new relationships have relevance for committed couples as well. Then come back to this chapter to learn more about specific challenges that affect long-term couples.

When, where, how, how much and with whom?

Sound familiar? Let's consider each of these issues and special considerations for long-term couples.

When

What time of day do you want to have sex? Does your mate agree? If so, great. However, if your partner is a morning person and you're a night owl, your partner may enjoy sex first thing in the morning when you are thinking about sleep and nothing else. Conversely, at night when you feel sensual, amorous and ready to rock and roll, your partner may be grumpy, irritable or fast asleep on the couch. These things may not have mattered much on the honeymoon and during the early stages of your marriage, but over time, such differences in rhythm can become quite problematic.

How much

Another issue is how often to have sex. Many couples start ou
every day of the week and sometimes more than once a day. Howe
come along, it gets progressively harder to find the time. Women oft
ing exhausted by the end of the day. They gradually begin to feel m
"mother," and less and less like a sensual woman. As the kids get ol
it harder to have spontaneous sex—what if the kids hear them? Unless the couple
makes a concerted effort, they may find that sex gradually decreases to a standstill.

Ironically, the committed or married couple often finds themselves in a situation quite opposite the one they dealt with when they were just beginning to have sex. Then they never knew when they would be able to see one another, and they often took advantage of the time they had by having sex. Now that they can have sex any time they want it, many couples find that they don't really want it as often. They get into a pattern of saying, "We'll do it tomorrow." Other priorities seem more important at the moment. Unless they're careful, the couple can gradually have less and less sex until "tomorrow" doesn't come very often at all.

Still other couples learn that although one person is interested in sex, the other has almost no sex drive. Perhaps the woman pretended to like sex a lot more in the early days when she was still trying to win the man's affection. Now that it's a done deal, she turns her attention to other areas of her life, and the man feels cheated.

Or perhaps the man assumed his wife's lack of interest in sex prior to marriage was due to her religious convictions and restrictions. However, the marriage night proves to be a let down, and the rest of the years are filled with little-to-no sexual activity. He learns that one reason his wife was able to abide by those religious restrictions was that she had a very low sex drive to begin with.

Or perhaps the wife finds that the man was so respectful of her wishes to refrain from sex before marriage because he has a very low drive or an unusual sexual problem. Now she's crawling the walls, wondering where it all went wrong.

Or perhaps their sexual differences are part of a larger problem. The man talked to the woman when they were courting. But now that they are married, he's gone back to his nonverbal ways, and she is lonely. Yes, he's still willing to have sex, but she has no desire to have sex with a man she doesn't feel close to. She needs to hear, *"I love you"* as much or more as she needs the physical affection and sexual stimulation.

Where

Then there is the question of where to have sex. The partner who likes to wait until they are safely in their conjugal bed for the night may be appalled by the lover who wants to take her right on the couch before the Late Show signs off! If the couple enjoyed "christening" every room of the house, they may find themselves stifled when the children arrive.

How

And of course, committed couples often end up disagreeing about *how* they have sex. One might prefer intercourse while the other thinks oral sex is just fine, thank you. Older or more conservative women sometimes find oral sex psychologically distasteful, while the man is eager to indulge. Unfortunately, these women often don't allow the man to give them oral sex, or if they do, their mindsets are so strongly against it that they don't enjoy it anyway. Or perhaps the woman is frustrated because although the man wants her to give him oral sex, he isn't willing to reciprocate. It's surprising the number of partners who don't realize when they are asking their mate to abide by what amounts to a strong double standard that puts the other at a disadvantage.

The same man who used to give his wife a half hour of foreplay now wants to have quickie sex and fall off into a deep sleep in 15 minutes or less. Just when his wife is getting in the mood, he's finishing and ready for zzz's. Or even worse, he allows his wife to give him oral sex, giving her the impression that he will reciprocate with oral sex or intercourse. Then just as she is getting psyched about it, he orgasms and falls asleep, promising to take care of her "the next morning," which of course does nothing for the woman that night.

Sometimes one partner is much more experimental than the other. A man might decide he wants to try anal sex, and his wife is not willing to oblige because she finds it painful. He might want to roleplay getting spanked or playful sadomasochism and bondage, and she feels uncomfortable about it.

In a surprising number of marriages, one or the other partner discovers something disturbing about their mate after the wedding. The woman may return home unexpectedly one day to find her husband dressed in her clothes. Or maybe she finds a stash of porno magazines or films under the bed—a stash he promised to throw out when they got married. She may be working on the computer, and see an unusual file. When she opens it, she finds to her dismay that her husband has downloaded porno from the net. Worse yet, it might contain child porn or sex with animals. Or perhaps she learns that he has a foot fetish, or a whole box of sex toys that repulse her. Or he loves to wear the baby's diapers...

I have received letters about all these problems and more.

With whom

This issue would seem to be obvious. You have sex with your committed partner, right? Well, you would be surprised how often I get letters from people wanting my opinion on group sex, open marriage and swinging. Porno films are widely available now, and people often get lots of ideas from watching them. So when their marital sex gets a little humdrum, they start thinking about adding a little "spark" to the mix.

Well, spark is fine, of course. But inviting another person into your marital bed is not. Part of what keeps you and your mate close is the fact that you share secrets and intimacies only with each other. As we noted before, sex is one of the most intimate acts anyone can do with another person physically. So when a third person enters the equation, all kinds of problems can result.

One or the other partner may decide that they enjoy this type of sex so much that they really don't want to return to straight one-on-one sex. Or one spouse may become jealous and suspicious watching his mate have sex with the third person. Even when it goes off without a hitch, there are often repercussions. The husband may come down with a whopping case of jealousy after the fact. The wife may have difficulty getting the images out of her mind. It can bother her so much that she prefers not to have sex for awhile. What may have seemed erotic at the time, accompanied by lots of alcohol, now seems more like Pandora's nightmare.

Even though the couple is not cheating on one another, the fact that they each saw their partner having sex with another person can be just as detrimental to the marriage as having that partner cheat on them. The betrayal factor in threesomes and swinging is a lot lower, but the visual image of the partner with another person is much more vivid.

Open marriages don't work because one spouse seems to be getting more outside sex than the other. The couple may establish rules, like they have to be in bed with one another when they wake up in the morning, or they have to have an equal number of partners. But often there are arguments when one partner breaks the rules, or when the husband goes on a mission to find more partners for his wife so he can sleep with that new woman he's just met. In addition, there are outside problems. People love to gossip about other people, and nothing is more interesting than someone else's sex life. So it's not uncommon to find that someone has been talking, and now the neighborhood knows about the unusual sexual couplings that have been taking place at your house. In Chicago, there was a scandal a few years back where teachers lost their jobs after being seen at a swinging party.

And if some enterprising person has taken pictures, there may be more Pandora to pay. Even in a large city, word has a way of getting around and it can become very uncomfortable. In a small town, it can become unbearable and necessitate moving. I once had a client who was actually blackmailed after someone drugged him and shot pictures of him in compromising positions with other people. When you start soliciting strangers to come into your bedroom, expect that anything might happen. And when it does, to whom will you complain?

Solving the sexual challenges
So how can these problems be solved?

How much? Have sex often to keep your relationship thriving
Sex can be the glue that helps a couple, compatible in many other ways, *stay* a couple by keeping the physical intimacy—and the emotional intimacy—strong. When a couple doesn't have sex for awhile, they are more likely to drift apart. They start picking little fights over ridiculous things, and generally start treating one another more and more like their "best enemy" than their best friend. All things considered, making love on a regular basis keeps the couple closer.

It's very hard for a woman to have sex with her mate when she's angry with him. So if the couple has a pattern of having sex every night, they are far more likely to end up talking about what's bothering them. In contrast, if they rarely have sex, an argument or disagreement can fester, unresolved, for weeks, months or years.

Making love keeps a couple talking and interacting, and the sexual/physical interaction and intimacy strengthens the emotional intimacy. It also helps lower their sexual craving, relaxes them—and generally keeps them saner!

So what should you do if you want sex and your partner doesn't, or vice versa? Many couples fall into the pattern where if one wants it and the other doesn't, they just don't have sex. If you follow this guideline, however, you won't have much sex, and that can cause you to drift apart. Instead, it's preferable to say: *"If one person is in the mood for sex, we'll have sex. That person does his best to get the other into the mood."*

After all, that's what you did before you were married, right?

Older can mean better

In **Chapter 4—Sex!**, we talked about secrets to great sex and dispelled some of the myths that have caused grief for centuries. Another dangerous myth we should talk about here is unfortunately accepted as truth by many older people. That myth says that when you reach a certain age, you lose interest in sex, as well as your ability to have it. This belief can be problematic if you have reached that certain age without finding your life partner, or if you stop having sex with your spouse as a result.

In fact, if you believe this myth, it might actually cause you to have sexual problems. For example, if you think you can't have sex, you may not even try—which then means that you don't have sex when you're older and the myth was correct after all! Similarly, if you think the fact that you continue to be interested in sex means you're a pervert because no one else your age is interested, you can become very self-conscious about your natural drive, which can then cause you to have erectile difficulties when you do try. So believing in this myth can become a self-fulfilling prophecy!

Fortunately, the truth is that interest in sex and ability to have sex can be enjoyed your whole life through. As a man ages, his sexual responses slow down, just as his other physical abilities (e.g., the speed at which he can run around the block) slow down. It takes longer to achieve an erection, but he can also maintain the erection longer. That can be very enjoyable for the woman, who generally needs more time to orgasm than a man. When the man's responses slow even more, he does not need to ejaculate each time. As long as both partners realize this and don't push him to ejaculate, the man can continue to enjoy sex his entire life, and so can his wife! So—it's never too late to have wonderful sex with your spouse or long-term partner.

Sometimes older people feel embarrassed that they still have a sex drive. What a waste of emotion! As we said earlier, sex is a normal, healthy drive. Just as you never outgrow your other drives, like eating and sleeping, you never outgrow your drive for sex.

The gym for your libido

Just as the heart is a muscle that stays strong with regular exercise, so, too, the libido. The best way to stay in good sexual shape is to continue having sex! It exercises your heart and keeps you interested in having more sex. And if you and your mate have been without it for a while, just ease back into lovemaking slowly—relax and enjoy. After all, you wouldn't begin an aerobics program by running a marathon, would you? If you have had any physical problems, especially involving the heart, check with your physician first. Then break yourself in slowly. Start with gradually pleasuring one another, take it slow, and in time, your stamina, interest and pleasure in sex will return.

When to have sex? Compromise!

If you disagree about the time of day to have sex, try to work out a compromise. Try alternating, having sex one morning and then the next night. Or you can compromise and have sex at night during the week and in the morning on weekends.

You can also look for other ways to resolve the problem. If the wife is too exhausted at night, the husband can hire a maid or babysitter to allow his wife to get more time to herself. Many a woman has been surprised to find that when she has time to sleep and personal time to relax and take care of her own needs, that sex drive she thought was long gone suddenly returns! And the man walks away thinking the maid and babysitter money was very well spent indeed.

The husband might also help his wife out by taking care of the children after dinner and putting them to bed while his wife grabs a quick nap. Then she's ready for some intimate playtime with her husband.

How to have sex? Great sex, good sex and maintenance sex

Sometimes women believe that every sexual encounter with their partner should be romantic. The truth is that no one can have great romantic sex every time—unless you're not having sex very often, and it's better to have sex more often. We live in a busy world and have multiple demands on our time. "Maintenance sex" on a regular basis, before or after a busy day is fine, as long as you periodically have "great sex," spending more time and attention pleasuring your partner (and vice versa) in a more sensual, less orgasm-directed way.

A good sex life for long-term couples typically involves a lot of good sex, some great/ peak experience sex, and maintenance or quickie sex in between to relieve tension.

On the other hand, husbands also need to realize that just as men tend to be bio-physical—focused on the biological and physical parts of the act, women need the psychosocial—or psychological and social aspects of lovemaking just as much. In fact, the most common question women ask me is, "How can I get him to be more romantic?"

It's a wise man who gives his wife what she wants so that he can benefit from the after-effects. Buying her cologne, lingerie and pretty things may help her feel more like a woman. Taking her to datelike restaurants and indulging in flowers, bubble baths, candlelight, champagne and strawberries may net you an evening of incredible sex. In fact, you just might want to splurge on that house with the fireplace and 2-person Jacuzzi!

There are also many old bed and breakfasts in the countryside, and they are frequently empty during the week off-season. What could be more fun than having a whole romantic mansion to yourself?

You may think you can't afford some of these things. But when you consider that keeping your sex life thriving is the glue that holds your marriage together, can you afford not to? And if money is really tight, you can still find romance in other ways. Try packing a picnic basket with flowers, candles, homemade sandwiches and a bottle of wine. Then head to the country and find a cozy spot by the lake. On a summer night, it just might suffice! You can also find cute little strip motels off the highway that cost about $25 for two. They don't have phones or cable TV, but that can be beneficial for a couple stealing some private time together.

Be sure to read *Chapter 9—Marriage*, for more ideas on how to keep the spark and romance in your marriage.

On the other hand, if you do everything you can to get in the mood for your spouse, but he still has a higher drive than you can accommodate, it's OK if he indulges in masturbation in between lovemaking sessions with you. Some women find this insulting. However, as long as your husband is not taking anything away from your lovemaking by pleasuring himself in between, there's no harm done. It can actually help by relaxing him and making it possible for him to give you the kind of romantic sex you want when you are able to have sex with him. On the other hand, if he prefers masturbating himself to having sex with you, your marriage is in serious trouble.

Where to have sex? Take turns compromising!

Similarly, you and your partner can usually compromise on where to have sex. Alternate who chooses the location every night. One night, you can choose the bedroom, and the next night, your spouse can pick the living room floor. If children are a problem, or if one of you is too inhibited, try taking a vacation together to some exotic locale, where you can both unwind and get in touch with your bodies and each other. Or hire a babysitter one night a week so that you and your husband can go to a hotel or a cabin in the woods and have mad, passionate, LOUD sex without worrying about anyone you know overhearing.

It's often easier to change behavior in a foreign locale, where you have never practiced your old inhibited behaviors. Then once you have gotten more in touch with your sensuality and feel freer, you can transfer those feelings and behaviors back home.

How to have sex? When to compromise

Compromising on how you have sex can be easier or more difficult. The rule here should be that if the desired activity is painful or not healthy, the couple does not indulge. Otherwise, one partner will try to cooperate with the other. For example, I highly recommend that both parties try to oblige the other with oral sex when that is part of the lovemaking one partner desires. And if your partner is giving you oral sex, do your best to return the favor. The spouses should also oblige with regard to intercourse and trying various positions.

On the other hand, many women find anal sex painful, and obviously, it is not reciprocated in kind with a heterosexual couple. So if the woman finds it painful and does not want to participate, the husband should not push it.

Where other activities are desired, consider whether or not they are healthy. For example, if one wants to try a little playful bondage, the other should try to oblige. On the other hand, that's different from serious sadomasochistic sex, which is abnormal and to be avoided. Sex should never be used to associate pain with pleasure.

That brings us to another sex secret:

Orgasm is one of the most powerful positive reinforcers/rewards known to man. Whatever you put in front of it is likely to increase.

This is extremely important to remember. Any fantasies or actions that precede orgasm are likely to increase, so it's vitally important to keep those fantasies and actions 1-1 and healthy.

So serious sadomasochistic sex is out, along with sexual preferences that are always pathological and to be avoided. For example, sex with children, animals, forced sex and serious sadomasochistic sex is **NEVER** appropriate. And sex with a third party is generally always a bad idea for the ideas we cited earlier. Similarly, pornography depicting these acts is always to be avoided.

However, behaviors that aren't pathological in moderation can occasionally be indulged. For example, making love to someone's feet or allowing the reverse is not harmful, but doing that and only that is to be avoided. Using a vibrator once in awhile can be fun, but using it all the time can lead to the person not being able to appreciate the less intense sensations of a tongue or fingers. If one person occasionally likes to be tied up or *playfully* spanked (as opposed to serious sadomasochistic sex) by the other, that's OK to roleplay once in awhile. You can even roleplay various situations and film them once in awhile, as long as you're careful to lock up the tape or destroy it after viewing it together. If both parties are amenable, watching an occasional porno flick (just 1-1 heterosexual consenting sex) together is OK. However, always needing to have a porno film going while having sex is NOT a good idea.

And watching porno that depicts anything other than 1-1 male-female heterosexual sex can also lead to problems. You may begin to fantasize about group sex or homosexual sex, and when reinforced with orgasm, those fantasies may increase until you eventually find yourself longing to act out the fantasies in real life.

In general, it's OK to occasionally do some playful roleplaying. Just be careful to limit the amount, so you that you still indulge mainly in "regular sex." Otherwise, you may eventually find that you're not able to enjoy sex the "regular way."

And be careful with any fetishes that seem difficult to control. For example, if the man wants to wear his wife's clothes or diapers, we're getting into dangerous territory here, in that people who hold those fetishes seem to have trouble controlling them once they are rewarded with orgasm.

Real life love@AOL letters about sex!

As you may imagine, AOL members write me frequently to ask about sex. Here are some of my favorites:

You have to say, "yes!"

MY AGE: 44 MY GENDER: FEMALE

Dear Dr. Kate,

I have just read your column for the first time. I want to say to all the married men and women who don't want to have sex with their wives/husbands: There is always someone out there who will. I am single and although I do not get involved with married men, I have been approached many times by married men from age 20-50. I am very fit, attractive and outgoing. Women, men are always looking at other women, not just the young ones. Please don't make it easy for them to cheat. Take care of your affairs at home, so they won't happen outside. I will always say, "No," but, remember, you have to say, "Yes!" And if you don't love it, get counseling and learn to love it!

Dear Observant,

I agree with you entirely, except I want to make it absolutely clear: The same goes for the husbands. While women of the past stayed home full-time and weren't exposed to as many temptations, they certainly have opportunities now. And while women may not be as pointed as men in searching for extracurricular activities, in my observation, they are frequently more romantic and more inclined to act on an affair by getting divorced.

The bottom line is that we all need to appreciate our loved ones and show them we care. Too often, we are busy taking out our anger, hurt and anxiety on them. Not because they are responsible, but because we're comfortable with them and can't tell the people we're really angry, hurt or anxious with. We're nicer to strangers than our own families sometimes. And that's just not cool.

It's also a great way to ruin a marriage and a family.

Sex/making love is one way to express our caring in a positive way. It bonds us together physically, and helps us feel emotionally closer. And even if we're not in the mood to start, we can certainly try to get in the mood.

If one person wants to have sex and the other doesn't, and the couple then opts not to make love, they'll end up having very little sex and will eventually drift apart. In contrast, if they opt to have sex even when they're in different moods, they will spend more time bonding and becoming close.

Also, it's very difficult to make love to someone when you're angry with him, so if you try to have sex, you may very well end up talking about something rather than allowing it to fester beneath the surface. It's kind of hard to get naked with someone you hate, so rather than giving up the act and moving further and further away from each other, try resolving the antagonistic feelings instead.

Remember to be nicer to your mate than anyone else, rather than the other way around. After all, you promised to love and cherish each other 'til death do you part, and that includes being your spouse's best friend and partner. If everyone did this, the divorce rate would certainly drop, and everyone would be a lot happier.

Thanks for your comments. Please keep in touch,

Dr. Kate

Clitoral stimulator melt-down: am I getting immune?

MY AGE: 41 MY GENDER: FEMALE

Dear Dr. Kate,
I was never able to achieve orgasm during sex until I married in my 30's. My husband stimulated me with his fingers, but never wanted to experiment with marital aids. After his death, I met a terrific boyfriend who likes to experiment. We purchased a clitoral stimulator from the local adult toy store. At first it worked tremendously. Now it doesn't work as well or as quickly. Changing batteries doesn't work. Do you think something is wrong with me? Or am I getting immune to it? It's not like I can go to Sears and buy a Craftsman Clitoral Stimulator with a guarantee.

Dear No Energizer Bunny Here,
Yes, you can become immune to sex toys. That's why it's best if you don't always rely on them for orgasm. If the unit works (and you can tell by looking at it ahead of time), then assume that the difference is in how you respond to the stimulation.

The first time you experience an orgasm, it's very exciting, especially because you haven't had one before. However, the more you experience one, it becomes a little less exciting. Something new is always more exciting. So the first time you used the stimulator and enjoyed it, it was more exciting than the last few times.

Have you tried oral sex? Many women find that they are able to experience orgasms better that way than through intercourse, since the stimulation is more direct (as it is with the vibrator). It's also a bit more intimate, since it's your boyfriend doing it, not a machine.

I would recommend that you vary the stimulation from one lovemaking session to the next, so that you have some variety and avoid becoming desensitized (immune) to the sensations.

All the Best and Enjoy! And please keep in touch and let me know how you're doing from time to time,

Dr. Kate

Super sex at 66!

MY AGE: 66 MY GENDER: MALE

Dear Dr. Kate,
I have read through many of your letters and find them quite interesting.

Yes, men and women do have sex—intercourse, oral, all kinds of sex, after 50, 60 and upwards. My "girl" friend will be 73 in a month. We don't live together or even in the same city, but when we do get together, we have sex for several—yes, several—hours. We both reach many, many orgasms, can't keep count, and really enjoy each other. So, guys and gals, keep trying. If you get tired of the "missionary" position, try something else.

This gets me every time: She sits on me while I am lying down. No movement from either of us, but her muscles inside her do all the action. It takes a while, but she will bring me to a climax that is "out of this world."

Dear Super Sex At 66!,

Thanks for a great letter. It sounds like your girlfriend knows how to use her pubococcygeal (PC) muscles very well. It also sounds like the distance may add to your delight when you are together. The pent-up sexual energy and desire keep you motivated. The fact that you schedule quality time together, travel specifically for that purpose, and then spend that time intensely focused on each other also helps.

And last but definitely not least, your positive attitude about sex and staying in condition really contribute as well.

All the Best, and Enjoy! Please let me know how you're doing from time to time,

Dr. Kate

HoT sEx exercices for added sPaRk! ZiNg!! SiZzLe!!! ;)

See the Appendix for these exercises. If you haven't read *Chapter 4—Sex!* yet, read it now to learn even more.

Sex: the barometer of your relationship

While sex should not be the main focus of your relationship, it is usually a very important part of it. In the context of a healthy relationship, sex helps to keep you and your partner physically and emotionally close. It helps you and your partner feel an intimacy between you, since lovemaking is something you share only with each other and no one else. When you and your partner drift apart sexually, it is easy to lose the emotional intimacy as well.

Many people are embarrassed to admit to one another how important sex is to them; sometimes they don't even know it themselves. They frequently ignore the warning signs until the relationship has fallen apart. So, use your sex life as a barometer—a warning light. If your sex life isn't flowing smoothly, chances are your relationship isn't either.

The good news is that sexual problems are usually very easy to treat, once they are actually acknowledged and worked on. So—if you are not satisfied with the sexual part of your love life, now's the time to work on it. And of course, the reward is absolutely enjoyable!

Chapter 9

Marriage
Taking the big step

*I*n *Chapter 5—Making A Commitment,* we talked about deepening your attachment to someone and making a commitment. We talked about when to live with someone and when to hold out for marriage. We explored what happens when someone is afraid to make a commitment, and how to work through that problem. In this chapter, we'll concentrate on marriage and how to make it work. To better understand the challenges, let's look at some data first.

The data is in—happily married people are the happiest of all

Studies report that happily married people are the happiest of all. The next happiest are happy singles, and the bottom group are unhappily married folks. It's clear that people prefer to have a companion and love interest, and when they have someone to share their thoughts, feelings and hopes and dreams, they feel less stressed and happier over all. As I mentioned in the Introduction, having a good companion to talk to and share your problems significantly lowers your stress level, the chances of developing stress-related illnesses, and it can even extend your life. So a good marriage can provide you with all these benefits.

But a bad marriage does just the opposite—increases stress, makes it more likely that you will develop stress-related problems, influences you to feel more unhappy, and can shorten your life. So the challenge is to find a highly compatible mate, then work on the relationship to keep it thriving for as long as possible.

Are you ready?

So how do you know when you and your mate are ready for marriage? Ask yourself if the two of you show the following signs of emotional maturity, stability and personal competence that can greatly increase your chance of staying happily married.

Education and career

Ideally, it's better if you marry after you have finished your education and started a career that will support you and your family for the rest of your life. If you have legitimate reason to believe that you can finish your education during the early days of your marriage, you could get married before graduation. However, as we mentioned in **Chapter 5—Making a Commitment**, the pressures of going to school, working and supporting a family have ruined many a marriage. So whenever possible, it's best to finish school first, while you are free of other responsibilities and able to focus on getting the job done.

A woman should not rely on the man to support her. Once she has finished her education and has established a career, it's fine if she wants to stay home full- or part-time to raise the children. But life is a series of relationship stages, and a woman needs the security of knowing that she can support herself in the event of her husband's death or divorce.

Besides needing a healthy income, the more you bring to the marriage, the more stimulating you will be for yourself and your partner. If the woman hasn't experienced school or work and the man begins to rise in his career, he may feel that she is holding him back. He is being challenged on a daily basis and learning and growing, and she has nothing to discuss with him at the end of the day except what the kids did that day. If you instead remain an interesting and interested person in your own right, without becoming dependent and clingy, your spouse will be more likely to appreciate you.

Maturity and age

In my opinion, people tend to mature in their late 20's to early 30's. Maturity involves first having experiences, then assimilating what you have learned from them into your awareness, so that you can live wisely and avoid serious mistakes in the future.

In my opinion, women should try to marry between ages 28 to 35. Before 28, you need to date around and gain experience with people, especially men. You then use that experience to mature emotionally and to select an appropriate mate. Marrying too soon cuts you off from that experience. Men usually mature a little later than women and don't have to worry about getting pregnant, so it's good if a man marries between age 28-40.

You will change a great deal before age 28. If you marry before that time, it increases the chance that you and your partner will grow in different directions. In addition, most people in their teens and early 20s don't have very good communication skills. They have not yet been tested in their careers. They have not had much education or the kind of work experience in which they learned to communicate, negotiate and compromise. As a result, they make more mistakes in their marriages. If you marry at age 18, you're basically going to grow up in your marriage. That means that anyone you marry has to be especially understanding and forgiving of mistakes. You will also have to be especially understanding, tolerant and forgiving of your spouse's mistakes.

In addition, you may live to your 80's, 90's and beyond. If you marry at age 18, can your marriage last that long? How can you know that the person who is compatible with you at age 18 will still be compatible with you when you're 68?

Will you be satisfied with that lifestyle your whole life? Or will you wake up at age 40, wonder what you missed and long to experiment? Will that happen to your mate? The time to sow your wild oats is when you're an adolescent and young adult. When you are 40 and married, with 2.2 children, it's inappropriate—and extremely damaging to many people—to do so. Yet often people who marry young try to reclaim their lost youth when they undergo their mid-life crisis 20 years later. It's common for people who marry in their late teens and early 20's to divorce and marry again in their late 30's or early 40's.

Self-sufficiency

Another factor that contributes to marital success is living as a single person for at least a few years prior to marriage. One of society's common marriage myths is that your spouse will complete you and make you whole; after all, you're marrying *your better half*. The truth is that you have to be happy and whole in order to attract a healthy mate for marriage. You can't rely on your partner to make you happy. You have to be emotionally mature—a fully functioning person and fully present marital partner—to make the marriage work. Your everyday life has to be stable, and you need to be able to work, pay your bills on time and live a balanced lifestyle. It's important that you have good self-esteem, and like yourself for who you are, not because your partner, your family or your friends love you. It's important that before marriage, you do all you can to solve any emotional, behavioral, family, career, education or personal problems you have. Don't rely on your mate to take over your life and make your problems go away. Don't look to a mate to save you, but rather, to add the icing on an already fulfilling and happy life.

Is your relationship ready for marriage?

Once you feel you're ready for marriage, then you need to take a good, hard, clear-headed look at your relationship. The time for assessment is not after the honeymoon, but well before you send out the wedding invitations.

Discuss your relationship goals and life goals with your partner to ensure that the two of you are in sync. The more you can prepare yourself with realistic expectations for marriage, the better. Do not assume love conquers all. Confront and discuss the five most common marital problems—*before* you get married:

- 💜 **Money**—How to spend it, how much to save, and how much time and energy to put into getting ahead versus enjoying the present.
- 💜 **Sex**—When, where, how and how often.
- 💜 **In-laws**—How often to see them, how much information to share with them, how intrusive to let them be in your lives, how to handle problems with them, and how to maintain a united front (seeing the marriage unit as primary), even when a parent doesn't recognize it as such.
- 💜 **Children**—How many, when to have them, when/how/how much to discipline them, how much time to stay home with them versus working outside the home,

how to handle everyday problems, who's responsible for what child-rearing tasks, and how to present a united front even when you initially disagree.

- 💜 **Spare Time**—With whom to spend it, how much time for play versus work, how much time together versus how much time apart, how much time with other friends and family, how much time alone together versus how much time with the kids.

Premarital counseling can help you cover all these bases and explore any differences that exist.

Take *The Dr. Kate Compatibility Quiz* (located in the Appendix) to help you decide if you are compatible with your partner, and have him do the same. In addition, you can both take *The Dr. Kate Communication Quiz* (also located in the Appendix) to assess your communication skills, identify any problem areas and learn how to improve them.

Never discount or dismiss certain signs of emotional maturity or personal problems so serious that they will ruin any relationship, especially marriage: alcoholism; drug abuse; physical, sexual or emotional abuse; psychosis; repeated lying or cheating. Any of these problems should immediately raise red warning flags and send you off in the opposite direction. Don't think you can save anyone in the grip of such serious problems. Remember, you each have to be whole people in your own right before you can make a relationship work.

The realities of marriage

The truth is that no matter how compatible you are and how well you communicate, living with someone is never easy. The more compatible you are, the easier it is, but no two people are ever perfectly in sync. What keeps a marriage going is the ability to communicate and resolve conflicts through respectful negotiation and compromise.

But people often hold false expectations for marriage—they think it will be easy and just flow. Women get extremely excited about planning the wedding and all the fun activities leading up to the event. They're caught up in the excitement of *being in love*. Then after the wedding, it's not uncommon for the new husband and wife to feel a bit of a letdown. The real work of getting along with someone on a day-to-day basis steps in and can be a lot less fun.

Life doesn't glow every day simply because you're married. The problems you brought into the marriage still remain, as do the problems your spouse introduced. If you married quickly, you now find out what your mate is really like.

After the wedding, it's common for both parties to relax. Relaxing with your mate is good—provided you still try to give your partner your best effort. If relaxing means that you stop caring about what you look like around the house or how you talk to your spouse, or if you no longer try to be your best in all ways, the net effect of letting yourself go—psychologically, personally and interpersonally—can be marital strife.

Feeling secure in their love, couples take a little of the energy that they focused so intently on one another during their courtship and turn it toward other interests. There is room in a marriage for separate interests, but it's a careful balancing act. There isn't any magic to a marriage, and if you don't continue to treat your mate like the most important priority in your life, eventually your intimacy will suffer.

Many married people continue to consider their mate their highest priority, but they don't talk and act that way. People fall in love because of how they feel about themselves when they are with someone; if that person starts to act like their worst enemy, the love will fade. At the very least, the spouses will stop feeling excited and happy about each other, and instead, the love will get buried under anger, resentment and hostility. That's what happened to Elena and Todd.

Elena & Todd's Story

Elena and Todd had been married for several years. In the beginning, they shared everything and made an effort to show each other how important they were to one another. As time went on, however, they started getting busier with their own projects and careers. One day, Todd noticed that when he came home, Elena didn't stop what she was doing to greet him. Busy in another part of the house, she would not even call down to say, "Hello." When asked why he got divorced, Todd cited this example as a symbol of what happened in the marriage. Elena got so busy with other aspects of her life that Todd no longer felt like a priority. Elena did not agree with his perception, of course. She had become more involved in her career and was very busy, but she still thought about Todd and considered him a priority. However, her actions did not convey those feelings and over time, Todd felt less and less desired.

Many couples experience similar problems. Your spouse can't feel like a priority if your behavior suggests that he isn't. You can tell him you care, but it's very important that your actions support your statements. The demands of everyday life make everyone's life hectic at times and it's easy to get caught up in your individual needs and daily plans. However, if you don't work hard at intersecting schedules with your mate, you'll rarely intersect. And when you do, it's more likely to be when you're sound asleep, not during quality time.

Everyone wants to feel special; it's a normal human trait. And most people want to feel particularly special to their spouse. When both partners feel and behave like the other is their best friend and top priority, THEN the union stays strong.

Marriage secret #1: Marriage does not equal ownership

Marriage in no way confers *ownership*. Marriage does not mean that you own your spouse or that she has to do what you want.

Healthy marriages require respect. Respect implies freedom, allowing the other person to be her own person. A man who controls his wife or a wife who controls her husband is not showing respect. Respect is treating your spouse as a fully functioning adult, capable of making decisions that show good judgment. When there is a disagreement, assume that your mate has a valid opinion and good sense, and that both points of view are valid. They try to understand your spouse's point of view—even if you don't completely agree with it, and make some kind of compromise. Of course, your spouse has to be a responsible, fairly functional adult, without serious personal problems, or this communication process can become very skewed.

Marriage secret #2: Love does not conquer all

You can love someone dearly, yet still have trouble getting along. It's easy to love someone; love is an emotion. Living with someone is significantly more difficult; it requires a series of behaviors over years. A healthy marriage requires that both parties be emotionally mature and in love. The romantic attraction and caring have to be there, but also the emotional maturity.

Marriage isn't a miracle. It requires hard work, energy, communication, togetherness, intimacy and compromises on a daily basis. Partners must make the time to continually work on their relationship or their marriage will fall apart.

Marriage secret #3: Your partner is your best friend

In a study of long-term marriages, husband and wives who had been married 15 years or longer were asked why they thought their marriages lasted so long. Even though they answered independent of each other, the answers given by the men and women were more similar than different. The most common response was that they were each other's best friend. They believed that marriage was forever; they believed in the sanctity of marriage. They also believed that if they held on long enough when things got bad, their lives would eventually get better again.

Best friends are honest, loyal and confidential; they trust one another. These qualities are the cornerstones of any committed relationship, especially marriage. Trust is a leap of faith. No one can prove to you that he is trustworthy; he can only prove that he's not. When you're best friends, you trust that your partner will look out for you and protect your best interests.

Intimacy is also extremely important. Intimacy develops when you share secrets, behaviors and feelings between the two of you that you don't share with anyone else. Since sex is such an intimate act, it must be shared only with your mate. Without this exclusivity, the marital bond is weakened. That's why threesomes and open marriages don't work well, and why affairs are so damaging.

It's vitally important to be honest with your mate at all times and to keep your word once you give it, no matter how tough it may be. If you become involved in a situation where you feel some other action would be better, you raise the issue with your spouse and discuss it openly, looking for a better solution. When problems arise that affect both you and your mate, you discuss how to handle them, decide on a course of action, and present a united front to the world. You turn down extramarital affairs immediately out of loyalty to your partner.

As best friends, when you disagree, you listen to your partner's point of view with respect and try to work out the problems amicably. Believing that marriage is forever carries you through difficult situations and encourages you to continue working on your problems in a constructive way until you find satisfactory solutions.

Marriage secret #4: Pay attention to the critical times of day

To stay happily married, your partner has to *feel* important to you. One of the best ways to nurture this feeling is to pay attention to three critical times of the day when the two of you should come together:

💜 When you first wake up
💜 When you first see one another after being apart for work or other activities
💜 Right before bedtime

At these three critical times, give your spouse a smile, a hug and a warm kiss, and make him feel special. Stop what you are doing and give your mate your undivided attention. Spend 10 to 15 minutes talking to one another in an upbeat, friendly way. Then even if the kids come into the room demanding attention or you have to go back to writing that critical report, at least you and your mate have bonded in a special way. The good vibes produced between you can help avoid a myriad of other problems.

For example, what often causes problems between two people is how they interpret the other's remarks or actions when they are ambiguous. When two people live together, so many interactions occur that it's impossible to be totally clear in all those communications. Clarity is certainly the goal, but you'll never hit it 100 percent. In addition, sometimes a remark can be interpreted in two entirely different ways. You'll mean it one way, never realizing that your partner is taking it the other way. At times of such ambiguity or seeming negativity, it's extremely important that you both understand that you always have each other's best interest at heart.

Of course, it's easier for your mate to do this if you remain close emotionally, and show your mate that he's a top priority. The more you drift apart and act as if other people or tasks are more important, the less support your spouse will feel and the more likely he will be to interpret whatever you say in a negative way.

Spending 10 to 15 minutes of positive, upbeat, warm, caring, quality time together three times a day—at those critical times—sets the tone for the entire day and night. Neither Cindy nor Kara was aware of this simple secret.

Cindy's Problem

Cindy was a conscientious professional who had hundreds of little details running through her head all day long. She usually woke up before her husband, but liked to lie in bed planning her day. When the alarm went off and her husband woke up, she greeted him with some negative comment that came from the plans she was making in her head: "I forgot to take care of that printer problem. I hate working with that guy. He never does what I ask him to do the first time, and I have to keep bugging him to get it done right. Oh well, I guess I'll talk to my boss about it today." Meanwhile, her husband Doug had just come back from a lovely dream. The last thing he wanted was to be greeted with Cindy's agenda for handling that day's problems. It would have been far better for their marriage if Cindy had greeted her waking husband with a kiss, hug, smile and a positive, *"Good morning, Honey!"*

Kara's Problem

Kara stayed at home with her children because she and her husband Ken felt it would be best for the kids. But staying home with three toddlers started to take its toll. Sometimes Kara missed adult conversation so much that she felt like she could start screaming at any minute.

Kara telephoned her friends and family during the day, but still eagerly awaited her husband's return every evening. As soon as Ken came through the door, Kara would launch into tales of what each child had done wrong that day and which appliances were on the fritz and needed repairing. Ken started feeling anxiety at the end of the workday, dreading to walk in and be hit with a deluge of complaints from Kara. Whenever he had a chance to go hunting or fishing with his buddies, he eagerly took the opportunity, because it allowed him to relax and get away from all the problems. Kara then took Ken's weekend trips as a sign of rejection—that Ken was not interested in spending what free time he had with her. She felt even worse about herself and her life, and even more compelled to complain to Ken whenever he walked in the door.

Both Cindy and Kara needed to step back and look at the big picture—the effect that their negative verbal statements had on their husbands at that time of day. Kara also needed to get out of the house on a regular basis so that she could find herself again. Besides her mother role, she needed to be intellectually challenged and feel her competence as a person in her own right. Kara found part-time work, transportation and a babysitter. Even though the money evened out, she felt better just mixing with adults for part of the day. She had more to discuss with Ken than the everyday problems at home. Because she wasn't in the kitchen all day, she ate less, lost weight and began to take more care with her appearance. Ken was pleased, and gradually their sex life also improved.

Be positive and enjoy one another

As important as it is to share positive time early in the morning and after work, the most critical time may be right before bedtime. Remember, you and your spouse are going to sleep for 6 to 8 hours afterward, and that sleep may include reactions to whatever you both say and do. If you spend your last waking moments talking about stressful events, it's more likely that you will have trouble falling asleep. You may wake up during the night or have nightmares. These disruptions, in turn, can make you more cranky the next day, and so the stress continues day after day.

In general, for two people to stay together, they have to enjoy each other's company. You can still talk about problems and receive emotional support from your spouse. However, it's important to pick the *appropriate time* to discuss those problems. It's also important to reach a resolution of sorts before the end of the day. Try not to discuss problems first thing in the morning, first thing when your mate arrives home, or the last thing before bedtime. Instead, make your interactions warm, upbeat, personal and intimate at those times. This simple practice will help cement the bond between you, and help your mate give you the emotional support you need during the other times.

Marriage secret #5: Hold regular roundtables

Build a mechanism for discussing problems into your weekly routine. For example, the Mormons have a very good practice. Once a week, they hold family roundtables. Family members are invited to say whatever they want about whatever they like. They are allowed to express their feelings openly—both positive and negative. Mom and Dad still make the decisions, since they are the adults, but the kids are allowed to say what they feel and respectfully express their opinions, even if they're different from the feelings and opinions held by their parents.

In my opinion, every couple should adopt such a practice, whether they have children or not. If they have kids, they can still hold special roundtables just for Mom and Dad. It's important to make time to discuss your disagreements in a respectful fashion. If you build in a regular time—for example, Sundays after lunch, you will end up discussing issues before they mutate into marriage-threatening problems. Following this practice regularly and openly and designating a special day and time for it will make it far less threatening. You'll be less tempted to bring issues up at inappropriate times when you're riding in the car, getting dressed or talking on the phone). Plus, if you talk about your disagreements on a regular basis, you will probably resolve them more quickly and have more time to express your positive feelings. If some problem occurs that you can't resolve between you, you will have ample time to see it coming and take effective measures to get the help you need to solve the problem—before your marriage falls apart.

And when you do talk about problems or disagreements with your mate, make sure that your positive interactions far outnumber the negative ones, and that you resolve your disagreements assertively and respectfully. See *Chapter 7—Communication* for more on how to do this.

Marriage secret #6: Have children for appropriate reasons

One sad myth that couples buy into too often is the belief that a child will save their marriage. The truth is that children put extraordinary stress on a marriage. They take up an enormous amount of time and energy and cost a great deal of money. If you and your spouse are already having personal problems, if you're financially strapped, or if you are stressed out because you don't have enough time together as it is, adding a child to the mix can overwhelm you and drive you even farther apart.

A child should always be planned. You should carefully consider how adding that child would affect your marriage, finances, workload, career, relationships with family and friends, retirement plans and every other part of your life. You should also consider whether or not you would be a good parent and what you would bring to that child.

It's imperative to take a realistic view of parenting. Although parenting can be a richly rewarding experience, it's very difficult and frequently frustrating work. Children are amazingly selfish and self-absorbed. Your child may not appreciate you until he is a young adult, if at all. Along the way, the cuddly baby and cute toddler will have many difficult moments and may end up acting out as a teen. Do you have the emotional maturity to be the adult and handle these situations in a positive manner? Do you have the resources to be able to give that child the security and emotional and intellectual stimulation he'll need? Are you willing to accept the drain on your personal time and finances, and all the other sacrifices you'll need to make over the years?

Remember, too, that a child is not a temporary responsibility. You are committing yourself to at least 21 years of primary care, and the rest of your life to being responsible to some degree.

Too many women expect that they will be able to have it all, but that's an unrealistic expectation, impossible to accomplish. You can't give 100% to your career, 100% to your husband, 100% to your family and friends, have 100% of all your personal needs fulfilled, and still be a 100% parent to your child. It simply can't be done. Something has to give somewhere.

There are no rules or one right way for apportioning your time and energies. Each person has to figure out what mix of responsibilities she can handle and how. Then each couple has to decide how to compromise so that both spouses can achieve what they need in the relationship. So, think parenting through carefully in advance and make wise choices.

Marriage secret #7: Be proactive in your life together

Make your life choices consciously; don't just fall into them. Many people allow life to happen to them because that way, they don't have to take responsibility for what happens. They can always blame the situation and their unhappiness on someone or something else.

It's OK to take risks in life—just think them through carefully, understand what the possible pros and cons are, figure out how you will handle any repercussions, and if you choose to proceed, do so with your eyes wide open. That way, if something doesn't work out, you'll be prepared. You'll be quicker to take action to rectify any problems since you've already anticipated them. You'll also be more satisfied with the outcome than you would have been had you not anticipated it or taken the possibility into consideration.

Together with your spouse, make a plan—a 1-year plan, a 5-year plan and a 10-year plan. Feel free to discuss the plans and as a couple, change them from time to time as your needs and feelings change. It's far better to think about your life, plan it and make choices than to wake up at 40 and realize you're been living someone else's life, doing what someone else wanted you to do, or just dangling in the wind changing course with your every mood and whim.

Marriage secret #8: Be flexible and have a sense of humor

Just like trees, truly resilient people are those who bend in the wind. Stress—the wind of life—is a permanent part of everyone's life. You can reduce it, but you can't fully get rid of it. Flexibility really helps a couple weather the storms and stay together. Conversely, if you're rigid and demanding of life and your partner, your union is bound to be short-lived and miserable. And finally, to keep everything in perspective when things do go wrong, it really helps to have a healthy sense of humor. See the joy and humor in life and share it with your partner. Read *Chapter 6—Happiness & Relationships*, and practice those principles to make your own life, as well as marriage to your partner, the best it can possibly be.

Real-life Love@AOL letters about marriage

AOL members write me frequently on the topic of marriage. Here are some of my favorites:

We want a baby

Dear Dr. Kate,
I've been reading a lot of your advice and it seems like you really know what you're talking about. I'd like to talk to my mother about this, but I wouldn't get very far without her yelling, screaming and carrying on. My boyfriend, 19, and I love each other, and we've started making long-term plans. I asked him, "In ten years or so, if neither of us is married, would you consider me?" He said definitely. Recently, we've been discussing having a child. He thinks it will be a big responsibility, but he has his heart set on it, and he's emotionally and financially ready to take care of it. I want a child, too; I've had lots of experience taking care of other people's children, and I want one of my own. What should I do?

Dear Longing To Be Mom,
I'm glad you like my advice, because what I'm going to say may be hard for you to hear. However, please listen with an open mind.

I know you feel very adult right now, and the law says you are legal age. However, you will change enormously in the next 10 years, as you become more and more emotionally mature. Before anyone can mature, that person first has to experience life. Maturity then develops by building on those experiences, learning to make wise life choices and avoid mistakes. In my opinion, most women do not mature until their late 20's and men not until after that.

Please don't have a child before you're married, and please don't get married so young. Marrying anyone at 18 is a huge risk. You and your husband may change so much in the coming years that you grow apart and find yourself divorced at age 37. Then you'll be a single mom, with no career and four kids. I have worked with many women who had children when they were young. Looking back, most of them wish they had delayed motherhood.

Get your life in order first. Are you going to college? What profession do you want to pursue? How much education will it take, and how will you pay for that? Make a career plan for yourself. How will you become a responsible, independent person with a good house and enough money to support yourself—without the help of your parents or boyfriend? Your boyfriend should be making similar plans.

If you still love your boyfriend when you are 25 or 26, and you have your career on track, then you can make plans for marriage and babies. While your body is fine for making babies right now, your emotions are not. A child is not IT, but a real person with needs that cannot be fulfilled by teenagers. It's time to live your life, learn and grow, so you can eventually pass that wisdom on to your child. If you're stuck at home with a baby, you shorten your emotional growth, as well as that of your child.

Best Wishes. Please let me know what you decide to do and how it works out,

Dr. Kate

The thrill is gone...learning to love reality

Dear Dr. Kate,
I have been married for two years and have a beautiful 13-month-old daughter. My problem is that I no longer love my husband. I try and try to "rekindle" our marriage, but I still end up feeling empty and alone. I feel like we're roommates. I have even lost the desire for sex altogether. I shudder when he kisses me. And when we do have sex, I end up in the bathroom crying after it's over. Please help. I'm too young to live an unhappy life. What advice can you give me?

Dear Lonely and Confused In Cleveland,
It sounds like you are moving at break-neck speed in this relationship. If you've only been married two years and have a 13-month old daughter already, then you must have gotten pregnant when you were only married two months. If you loved your husband when you got married, you probably still love him. But your feelings of love are buried in the day-to-day fatigue and frustration of being a new mom.

You may have also had unrealistic ideas about what marriage and children were supposed to be like. You rushed into them only to find that the reality was quite different from the fantasy. That's OK. It just means that you now need to learn to find the good in the reality. You may also be somewhat angry with your husband, as though he is to blame for those fantasies not coming true. That's not OK. It's important not to blame him for things that are not his fault. If he does exhibit some behavior that bothers you, learn to discuss it and negotiate compromises. Accept responsibility for whatever problematic behaviors you are contributing and work to build a satisfying life together.

It's also very normal that you would be experiencing some adjustment problems in the first two years of marriage. Having your child so soon just added to that, because you had to adjust to the three of you before you and your husband had finished adjusting to being a "two."

Consult a psychologist with your husband to work on your marriage. Be sure to... (try the exercises at the end of this chapter) to rekindle the intimacy and romance. In therapy, ask your husband to help you plan the dates and let him know how important this is to you.

All the Best. Please keep me posted on your progress and feel free to write again if you need additional assistance,

Dr. Kate

Dear Dr. Kate,
My husband and I have been married for 10 years. We have two beautiful children, whom we both love dearly. My husband is a very good person and we get along well. However, I find him boring, and don't feel "in love" with him. I try to find ways to put "spice" into our relationship, but frankly, can't seem to succeed. I don't really want to divorce him because it would be devastating to our children and also hurt us financially. What do you think?

Dear Spiceless,
Have you talked with him about this problem? It sounds like you're trying to carry the load for adding the seasoning to your marriage. Any 10-year marriage is going to need some periodic revving, with help from both parties, or it will become very stale.

Don't tell him you find him boring—and don't tell him you're not "in love" with him. Those kinds of phrases can come back to haunt you. They hurt, and people have trouble forgetting them. Just tell him in an assertive way that you need more. *("I love you, and I feel we need to put more spice in our relationship. I've been trying to do that, but I need your help and participation, too. Let's think about this together and brainstorm some ideas. What can we do to add spark and romance to our life together?")* Let him suggest some solutions, and you might be pleasantly surprised. (Try the exercises at the end of this chapter as well.)

If you still can't get anywhere after talking with your husband and trying these suggestions, then ask him to consult a psychologist with you for marital therapy. If he won't go with you, go to therapy by yourself to learn more about what you can do, given the conditions, to improve your relationship. Only when you have tried everything and nothing has worked, and you still find the situation intolerable, should you divorce. Presently, there are still many things you can try.

All the Best, and please let me know how you're doing from time to time,

Dr. Kate

Exercises to enhance your marriage

1. **Put the spark back!**

   A. Remember what worked before. Think back to the early days of your romance. What worked well then? What did your spouse like? What made him respond especially well to you (a certain outfit, cologne, something you used to do)? Make a list in your Relationship Notebook.

   B. Set a weekly date night just for the two of you. Ask your spouse if you can try a little experiment. Every Saturday, have a "date" just with each other. Take turns planning the evening. When it's your turn, your spouse does exactly what you want (pick something he also likes the first time to entice him to try this exercise). The next time, he plans and you comply. Alternating in this way allows for change and added fun, and reminds you to put special effort into your time together, just as you did in the early days.

C. Talk about dreams and positive feelings on your date. Don't criticize or bring up everyday emotional stresses and strains. Rediscover what brought you together when you were courting.

D. Plan one weekend a month together after you've been dating weekly for awhile. That extra time should add to the possible activities you can do together. Alternate the planning every month.

E. Increase your daily activities together. If your spouse has any interests you've been avoiding, try some of them with him. Ask him to take a fun class with you—dancing, massage for couples, tennis, cross-country skiing. If you haven't been having much sex, getting physical together through sports, dancing and other non-sexual activities should help you reawaken your physical body and make it easier to continue that "mutual body awareness" into the bedroom.

F. Make new love traditions. Traditions and ceremonies help us bond with spouse, family and friends. We feel closer and more intimate with those sharing our special customs and traditions.

Make a list of the traditions and customs you and your spouse currently share. Then brainstorm a list of other things you could do. For example, on January 1, you'll go ice-skating together to welcome the new year. On the first day of summer, you'll celebrate with a picnic in the park. On your birthdays, you'll exchange books filled with homemade coupons that can be redeemed for certain favors (e.g., one full body massage, candlelit dinner or an hour of babysitting). If you enjoy the traditions, keep them. If not, draft new ones. Before long, you will have significantly increased your fun interactions together, and feel more confident and hopeful about the future of your marriage.

2. **Strengthen Your Bond Through Positive Communication.** Tell each other ten things you really like about each other every day. Remember to kiss and hug good morning, hello, goodbye and goodnight and spend 10-15 minutes in upbeat conversation at the three critical times each day. Establish a weekly round table for you and your spouse.

3. **Take a marital enrichment workshop** with your spouse to work on communication and jumpstart your marriage.

Stage 3 of The Love Cycle—

Letting go

Chapter 10

Tough times
When your relationship is in trouble

Y ou're standing at the cleaners, getting ready to hand your husband's jacket to the clerk, when you suddenly remember to check the pockets to make sure he hasn't forgotten anything. You're startled to find a crisp new business card. Looking at it, you see it's from a woman, probably from that trip he took to New York City last week. You're about to put the card in your wallet to give it to your husband, when you flip it over and see a note on the other side: "Really enjoyed the laughs. See you soon! Carol." A wave of fear washes over you, and you feel a foreboding sense of dread in the pit of your stomach. What does this mean? Who is this woman and what kind of laughs did they have? And why is he going to see her soon?

The hardest part of any relationship is when you finally realize it's in serious trouble, and begin to confront the possibility that it may be time to let go. Lying, cheating, emotional abuse, jealousy, physical abuse—the situation may have finally become intolerable. Or maybe you're just getting tired of all the fights and mishagosh (craziness) at home.

Sooner or later you find yourself asking, "Have I chosen the wrong person?" That's when it's time for a serious assessment of your relationship. Are the problems insurmountable? Or are they difficult, but fixable?

With this chapter, we begin discussion of *Stage 3 of the Love Cycle—Letting Go.* We've already talked about finding love in Stage 1 and making that love work for you in Stage 2. In *Chapter 7—Communication,* we discussed how to use good communication skills to resolve differences. In *Chapter 9—Marriage,* we discussed how to make your marriage thrive. Now in this chapter, we'll look at what happens when that process breaks down and you face serious trouble.

No couple gets along all the time, and in fact, studies show that the two of you can disagree on many things and stay happily married, as long as you discuss problems amicably and negotiate fair, reasonable compromises that are satisfactory to you both. But being able to communicate in that fashion requires a great deal of respect, and your relationship faces real trouble when the respect and emotional support between you starts to erode.

How to tell if your relationship is in trouble

If your relationship or marriage isn't satisfying and happy, you'll probably sense it, although some people become very adept at blocking that awareness out of their consciousness. If you notice that any of the behaviors listed below are beginning to appear in your relationship or marriage, **TAKE ACTION IMMEDIATELY:**

When you or your partner:
CHANGED FEELINGS
1. Don't find one another to be fun and stimulating.
2. Don't enjoy each other's company as much as before.
3. Feel good at work, but dread going home; don't look forward to seeing one another.
4. Feel tense around each other, and other people often feel tense around the two of you.
5. Feel numb around each other.
6. Frequently feel angry, hostile, resentful, frustrated, hurt, neglected, put down, disrespected, maligned, insignificant, unimportant or some other overwhelmingly negative feeling when you think about each other or are around one another.
7. Hold resentments that continue past any disagreements.
8. Start to feel like enemies, not friends.
9. Don't feel like you are in love or love one another any more.
10. Frequently fantasize about other people in a romantic or sexual way.
11. Prefer to be with other people more than each other.

COMMUNICATION BREAKDOWN
12. Don't really talk any more, or maybe you never did.
13. Don't share ideas, feelings and dreams together any more.
14. Tend to talk about problems, not good times and positive ideas.
15. Don't laugh together much any more.
16. Confide in others more than each other.
17. Find it difficult to discuss issues without bringing up past disagreements or getting into an argument.
18. Blame each other for many things, even when you're clearly not responsible.
19. Don't ask for the other's opinion on issues that concern you or your life together.
20. Have interactions that are more negative than positive.
21. Don't try to compromise when you disagree, but instead, insist on your point of view and become rigid and inflexible.
22. Rarely say, *"I love you."*

ATTITUDE CHANGES
23. Are less considerate, thoughtful and tolerant.
24. Feel more impatient, rude, sarcastic and disrespectful toward each other.
25. Strive to control the other.
26. Are jealous of one another.
27. Treat the other with a double standard.

BEHAVIORAL CHANGES
28. Touch each other less.
29. Have sex much less often or not at all.
30. Are physically, sexually or emotionally abusing each other or someone else.

LACK OF TRUST AND LOYALTY
31. Talk about each other to other people.
32. Criticize and belittle one another in front of other people.
33. Tease at the other's expense, often in front of other people.
34. Don't trust the other to protect your best interests.
35. Are cheating or believe the other is cheating on you.
36. Are lying or think the other is lying to you.

LACK OF SOLIDARITY
37. Don't present a united front to your children.
38. Allow others (e.g., friends, family) to intrude into your relationship.

Your interactions with each other should be positive and happy most of the time. As soon as that begins to change, don't procrastinate. Take steps to improve your marriage.

Secrets for saving a troubled marriage/relationship

The first step for saving a troubled relationship or marriage is to recognize the signs that something is wrong. If you noticed any of the above signs occurring in your relationship, write them down in your Relationship Notebook. Then make a list of your biggest problems and disagreements. If you don't know what's wrong, just start writing whatever comes into your head. What are you thinking and feeling?

Now go back and write down what seems to be causing each problem. If you have written something negative about your spouse, is it really your partner who is causing that problem? Is it the poor communication between the two of you? Or is it due to someone else and you are just conveniently blaming your partner? People often blame their partner when they're angry at someone else, but don't feel they can express their anger to that person.

People often blame their partner when they're angry with someone else.

For example, if you are angry at your boss and know that you can't vent at him, you may come home and blast your spouse instead. This is really a backhanded compliment to the spouse, because we tend to express negative emotions only to people with whom we feel comfortable— usually the people we love who love us back. The spouse is a very likely target because we trust that the spouse loves us and won't leave us. In contrast, we know that the boss might fire us if we vented our angry feelings at work.

However, continually taking out your anger, hurt, frustration and other negative emotions on your partner or spouse can eventually drive that person away.

Similarly, people often blame their partner when they are angry at themselves, but don't want to admit it. They can become very angry at their partner for having a personality flaw that they themselves have.

In my opinion, the single most important behavior that breaks up relationships is acting negatively toward your partner, and second most important behavior that breaks up relationships is not acting positively enough.

> *Acting negatively toward your partner and not acting positively enough make it likely your relationship will fail.*

Every person needs to feel special, particularly in a close relationship. You fall in love partly because of how you feel about yourself when you are with that person. If your partner then turns on you and starts to act like your worst enemy, it's easy to feel out-of-love instead.

The word *feel* in the last sentence is correct. You may *feel* out of love, but actually still love your partner. You have *not* really *fallen* out of love. However, the anger and hurt are so strong that they can mask the love, so that you can't feel it for awhile. On the other hand, if the problems were corrected, you might be surprised to find that the love is still there; it was just hidden for awhile.

Passive-aggressive behavior ruins marriages

Couples frequently become passive-aggressive as a relationship deteriorates. Instead of addressing the problems in a straightforward, assertive, respectful way (as outlined in **Chapter 7—Communication),** they start to attack one another in an indirect, behind-your-back way. For example, let's say you and your spouse disagree about sex, but you feel uncomfortable about discussing sex due to your upbringing. You would like more sex, but you don't feel you can say that. So you try to be cheerful about the lack of sex, but find yourself growing physically frustrated and mentally on edge.

Eventually, you start to feel a bit neglected, rejected, insulted, demeaned and hurt, as though there must be something wrong with you because you want so much sex and your husband doesn't. He must not love you as much as you love him, or he would want sex more. So one night, you find the courage to raise this issue. But you feel awkward asking for sex, so you hint instead of conveying how important it is to you. Your husband hears your words as critical to him, so he blocks out a lot of what you're saying and eventually turns his attention to something else. You feel even more rejected and hurt, and he feels criticized.

The next day, you're using his car and have a fender bender. He gets angry that you damaged his car, but instead of discussing everything in a straightforward way, he stays out with the guys that night and doesn't phone home to tell you he's OK. You are frantic, pacing the floors, but when he comes home, you don't talk about it. Instead, you go to bed. But the next time you have the opportunity to stay out and not call home, you do. Eventually, you and your husband may end up in a screaming match about which one of you is cheating or being most inconsiderate to the other. But the real issue underlying the whole interaction—the fact that you want more sex than he seems prepared to give—is never addressed.

The real issue must be discussed or the disagreement will not get resolved.

That is the most damaging part of any passive-aggressive (indirectly aggressive) interaction: The real issue never gets addressed and resolved. Meanwhile, the behind-your-back aggression causes hostility to mount, until you are the best of enemies instead of best friends. And unfortunately, because you know each other so well, you can also wound each other very well. You know your partner's Achilles' heel, and you can go right for it. You can take information that was revealed to you in a tender moment, and use it to wound your partner in an angry moment. And he can do the same.

Couples who are reluctant to address a particular problem frequently end up in interactions like these. In time, these interactions make it more and more difficult to have a fair, respectful discussion. Resentment is covered up and covered up. Finally, just like the fabled carpet under which all the dirt is swept, the ugliness begins to leak out the sides.

Along the way, your self-esteem erodes. Perhaps you start eating or drinking more to compensate, or find other destructive behaviors, which only serve to further obscure and complicate the problem.

Finally, another person comes along who treats you with respect and gives you praise, and it is very difficult to resist. If you give in and cheat, your relationship with your mate erodes even further.

Be assertive, negotiate and compromise instead

The key to avoiding this kind of grief and the unhappiness and breakups that usually follow is to regularly discuss your problems in a positive, upbeat, respectful way. Use the communication skills outlined in **Chapter 7—Communication** to express feelings and find reasonable compromises.

Some people believe that if two people are compatible, they should not disagree with one another. The truth is that you need to be stimulated by your partner, and if he always agreed with you, you'd be pretty bored.

> ### *Some disagreement can be stimulating, if handled respectfully.*

If you have a tendency to run from problems rather than facing them head on, you need to be especially alert to this pattern in your marriage. Realize that the sooner you face your problems, think them through and try to fix them, the better.

Problems that can be fixed

Almost all problems can be fixed, provided you and your partner:

- ❤ Are really motivated to fix them;
- ❤ Are motivated to live psychologically and physically healthy lives;
- ❤ Respect one another;
- ❤ Are willing to compromise;
- ❤ Are willing to get help, including learning to communicate better, if you're not able to fix the problems yourselves.

Compromise means that you are willing to accept a solution that is a little different from the one you wanted. There are very few issues for which a reasonable compromise cannot be found. In contrast, there are many issues that have lots of room for compromise, including the most common problems couples fight about: their sex life, how to spend their money, how to raise the kids, how to spend their time and how to handle in-laws.

Sometimes you may not be able to resolve the problems between you and your partner; you may need professional help.

When to get help for your relationship

Consult a psychologist:

- ❤ When you're having trouble figuring out your own feelings and needs.
- ❤ When you need to jumpstart the old excitement and spark you once had in your relationship. Life is hard; it takes a toll. Just as you have to wash the salt off the car after the winter snows, you have to renew your marriage excitement from time to time.
- ❤ Whenever you notice that you or your partner are beginning to think, feel or act in ways noted in the list at the beginning of this chapter.
- ❤ When you and your partner have tried to work out a problem, but can't seem to do so. The more serious the problem or the greater number of problems, the more important it is to seek help and the quicker you should do so. Chances are

the problem could be resolved if the two of you communicated better, and you can learn to do that in therapy.

🖤 When you or your partner are being rigid and inflexible on some issue due to unresolved conflicts from your past.

It is very important to understand that **YOU** can't be your spouse's therapist. You have to relate to your partner on an even, equal level. If you try to be your partner's shrink, your mate will resent you and it won't work anyway.

On the other hand, if you consult a psychologist together, your partner may be able to hear what the doctor is saying. Your partner isn't fighting with the doctor the way he's fighting with you, so the psychologist may be able to tell him things that you never could without a blowup. When you and your partner discuss the issues, your partner may be defensive as a result of your past interactions. He hasn't shared that history with the doctor. So he may be able to admit things he couldn't admit before, to see the problems more clearly and try to work on them. In addition, the psychologist has the skills to work with your partner and help him change his troubling thoughts, feelings and behavior to more healthy ones.

Even psychologists can't be therapists to their mates. It just doesn't work. In a disagreement, your spouse will generally think that you are looking out for your own interests more than his, no matter how objective you're trying to be.

The sooner you get help, the sooner therapy can end and the less expensive it will be. If you are basically still getting along, but come to therapy when you can't resolve a problem about how often you have sex, therapy will be shorter-term and less stressful. If you wait until you are both so angry you could spit, where you are not only fighting about your sex life, but also how you spend your money, your time, how you respond to your in-laws, where you should put that ugly orange chair and everything else under the sun, therapy will take longer and cost more money and emotional stress. It's like peeling an onion. The more layers you find, the longer and more costly the treatment. And often, if there is enough resentment and bitterness built up, the relationship will die anyway, despite last minute efforts to save it.

Problems that can't be fixed

Of course, there are some problems that can't be fixed. These include when one person refuses to compromise, when your relationship or life goals are diametrically opposed, or when your partner has severe psychological problems or immaturity that make it impossible for the two of you to live together happily, and he refuses to get help. Let's consider each of these in more detail.

Refusal to compromise

If one partner refuses to compromise, the opposite partner has to decide if she can always give in to save the marriage. That isn't a healthy situation, and eventually, if the overly compromising partner rebels, it effectively ends the relationship.

Chelsea & Joe's Story

Chelsea met Joe when she was in her mid-20's. He was a wealthy, handsome businessman 20 years older, and she admired his intelligence, sense of style and power. Joe liked Chelsea because she was so young, pretty and innocent. They got along very well. However, as Chelsea started to age and mature, she became surer of herself as a person. She developed her own opinions, some of which were not the same as Joe's. They started to experience friction in their relationship. Joe was used to people following his orders, and he expected it from Chelsea, too.

I saw Chelsea and Joe together for a few sessions, but Joe had no intention of compromising. In his mind, his position was **right** and if his wife disagreed with him, then she was **wrong** and it was her problem. **She** needed to change, not him. Joe steadfastly refused to compromise, and Chelsea decided she would rather be healthy without Joe than to continue giving in on everything and being a convenient doormat.

Inability to compromise due to conflicting life goals

On rare occasions, spouses find that they have relationship or lifestyle goals that are so different, they can't compromise on them even though they basically believe in compromise and do compromise on routine day-to-day disagreements. For example, if one of you wants to give away all your earthly possessions and live out your life as a missionary in Africa, while the other wants to work on Madison Avenue, live in a high-rise and wear Gucci, it's highly unlikely that you'll be able to find a suitable compromise.

Sometimes couples don't openly discuss their life goals before they get married; they find out later that they greatly disagree. Or one spouse may have thought she could be happy with her compromise, then changes her mind. Or she may believe she can change her husband's mind after the wedding bells have rung. Or they may have been in agreement on these goals when they married, but some event happens that radically changes their goals and they later find themselves seriously disagreeing.

Jeff & Sherrie's Story

Jeff and Sherrie were smitten with one another. They were a loving, lively couple and enjoyed life together. They were extremely well-matched, except that Jeff was 15 years older than Sherrie and divorced with two sons, while Sherrie had never been married before and had no children. They discussed children, and Jeff told her he didn't want any more. Sherrie loved Jeff and wanted to marry him, so she happily compromised on that issue. But after they had been married 7 years, Sherrie started thinking more about having children. She was in her mid-30's now, and she began to realize that her child-bearing years would not last forever.

She raised the baby issue again, but Jeff remained adamantly opposed. Years earlier, one of his sons had gotten deathly ill and the physicians were at a loss to explain it. Jeff had prayed for God to give him the sickness instead. Jeff's son got well, and shortly afterward, Jeff developed cancer. He was eventually cured and remained cancer-free, but the experience left him feeling that having children was too traumatic. While he adored his sons and was extremely proud of them, he just didn't want any more children. Although they discussed their disagreement in a loving and amicable way several times, Jeff and Sherrie each remained committed to their own position. They divorced, remained friends, and Sherrie eventually married a younger man who shared her dream of starting a family.

Refusal to get professional help

When one or both of you need professional help and refuse to get it, the relationship is bound to fail. This would include cases where one or both spouses are emotionally immature, use inappropriate communication, have poor ethical codes or have psychological problems severe enough to cause stress in the relationships. Often women come to therapy first, and find it difficult to convince the man that they need therapy as a couple. (See **How To Invite Your Mate To Therapy** in the Appendix.)

Much of this difficulty goes back to the way men are raised, which we discussed in **Chapter 7—Communication.** Because men learn that they should be perfect—knowing everything and being able to fix everything, without asking for help—many find it difficult to come to therapy. Seeing a psychologist is akin to admitting that they are flawed and need help. Men hate to show vulnerability, and psychotherapy sessions can be very scary to someone who can never be vulnerable or show it.

Jill & Ethan's Story

Jill and Ethan were very much in love. They had a great time together and enjoyed each other immensely. However, in time, Jill began to notice that Ethan had some unusual behaviors. If he wanted to know something, he would jump in a car and quickly drive there, instead of making a phone call. He was interested in everything and everything seemed to compete for his attention. And he didn't seem to be able to handle frustration. He would start a business, be very excited about it, then abandon it quickly when problems developed. He had difficulty prioritizing and focusing, and had trouble finishing a project before getting distracted and turning his attention to something else. He spent money without thinking, running up huge debt.

Ethan was immensely charming; however, that charm covered up a lot of what Ethan was feeling. He actually felt like a failure, but he didn't tell Jill. When something didn't work out as he liked, he felt worse and worse about himself. He started drinking and acting depressed. The more tense and anxious he was, the more active he would become and the more he would drink. He began bringing characters home to get drunk at the kitchen table while Jill laid awake in the bedroom, trying to sleep so she could go to work the next day.

Ethan went to a doctor and was treated for depression. It helped some, but the medication just didn't seem to solve the problems enough to make the relationship stable. He continued to overspend and show faulty judgment.

Then one day, Jill was looking for information on the Internet and stumbled across a web site for people with adult ADHD (Attention Deficit Hyperactive Disorder). As she read the list of behaviors involved, Jill realized that it could have been Ethan they were describing. Jill was elated that the behaviors were treatable; there was help available! She quickly told Ethan about it and tried to convince him to see a professional who could help him. Ethan, however, could not accept the information. He was already feeling too awful about himself. He blamed Jill for his problems because he could not admit to himself or Jill how badly he felt about himself. He finally left town, leaving everything behind. Jill consulted an attorney, who explained that she would remain liable for some of her husband's future actions and debts. Since Ethan tended to be impulsive, overspend and show questionable judgment, that liability could cause her enormous grief. He urged her to divorce as quickly as possible.

Jill was very upset, because she still loved Ethan very much. But she couldn't stay married to someone who was out of control and not ready to face his problems and get appropriate medicine and therapy. Whatever Ethan did affected Jill, yet she had no control whatsoever over him. And Ethan had very little control over himself. Jill had no choice but to divorce him, but she was very sad. More than anything, she would have preferred to fix the problem and make their marriage a success. However, since Ethan refused to work on the marriage, there was nothing else she could do.

Robert & Darlene's Story

Robert had a problem similar to Jill's, except he had previously been happily married for 20 years. Then one day, his wife Darlene developed psychotic symptoms. He rushed her to the emergency room, where stroke and other neurological problems were ruled out. The diagnosis was paranoid schizophrenia. She was hallucinating and thought people were talking to her. She would wake up several times during the night and start screaming at the voices. Yet Darlene steadfastly refused to take the medication that could have controlled the hallucinations. Robert was heartbroken. He had lost his companion and partner. He didn't even know this new woman, and he had no ability to control her or force her to get help. He had difficulty getting to work each day, because he could not sleep with her screaming all night long. Robert consulted an attorney who told him it was highly unlikely that the state would intervene and hospitalize his wife against her wishes. She would have to demonstrate that she was dangerous to herself or others. He urged Robert to get a divorce, and after much deliberation, Robert agreed.

If your partner is ill and won't get help, you may need to end your marriage.

Sometimes you can't save your marriage, no matter how much you want to. If your partner is psychologically ill and refuses to get treatment, you either have to live a very unhealthy existence or leave the relationship.

If your partner is:

- ♥ An alcoholic, drug addict or sex addict; or has a serious gambling addiction;
- ♥ Psychotic or suffers from serious psychological problems or immaturity;

❤ Physically, sexually or emotionally abusive,

❤ A child molester or perpetrator of crimes,

❤ and refuses to get help,

you usually must leave the relationship to save yourself.

It's possible to live with an alcoholic if you use the services of Al-Anon and learn not to be codependent or enable your partner's disease. However, the situation will be extremely rocky. You will not be able to work out most problems between you until the main problem, the alcoholism, is treated. Addicts of any kind deny and blame others; they don't accept responsibility for their feelings and actions. They don't know how to communicate about feelings and effectively work through differences. As a result, it is almost impossible to have a healthy relationship even apart from the alcoholism.

Drug addicts and sex addicts have those same problems, and also demonstrate less socially acceptable behaviors. Drug addicts are so completely driven by their drugs that they just don't function well with or without them. Their whole life becomes a search for their drug of choice, and they are willing to forget any loved ones in that pursuit. Being around them also causes legal risk. Sex addicts are even less socially acceptable. Some of their behaviors are legal (frequenting strip bars), but many are not (exposing themselves, hiring hookers, peeping in windows).

Partners who are physically, emotionally or sexually abusive must not be tolerated. A woman who lives with an abusive man loses her self-esteem little by little. He cuts her off from her loved ones, preferring to dominate and control her himself. The woman needs to leave him before the stakes get too high. She cannot change him, and he will never go for treatment unless it is mandated by the state. Even if they do get treatment, these men have problems that are very difficult to change. Often they have been abused by their parents. The woman may need to use community services to avoid being murdered.

In my opinion, once a man has crossed the line and hit a woman, the woman needs to leave. Since most men have more muscular strength than women and are more aware of how to use it, the woman is frequently in real physical danger. Even if he gets treatment, the man may still be so angry that once he has convinced her to return, he takes his revenge out on her. If the woman is doing the abusing and can physically harm the man, then the same advice holds for the man—he needs to leave the situation as soon as he can safely do so. If someone has physically abused a child, the situation is similarly dim.

If the man has sexually abused a child and doesn't get help, there is no hope. Even if he gets treatment, the odds for a successful relationship are very poor. The man has shown impeccably poor judgment and has learned some very unusual sexual preferences. He is a sex addict of a very serious kind, and the woman has to decide if she wants to live with the fear of his recidivism hanging over her. I just don't think it's worth it.

You can't control anyone. You can't make your mate do anything or not do anything. If your partner has poor judgment, the aftereffects of his behavior will have an impact on you and your life together.

In cases of physical and sexual abuse, the victim must act to protect herself and her children. The sooner she acts, provided she does so in a manner that minimizes her danger by using social service agencies and shelters, the better. The more she stays despite the abuse, the more she rewards her partner's misbehavior, and the more likely he will be to physically or sexually abuse her or the children again.

The woman has to take into account that if she stays, she is not only hurting herself, but her children as well. The lessons kids observe in the home today will make them the adults they become tomorrow. If the woman doesn't leave, her children may end up abusing their spouses or becoming an abused spouse one day.

Emotional abuse is less serious because it doesn't involve physical danger. However, emotions are certainly important, too. Emotional abuse can hurt the spouse and severely impair the development of a child. The abuser needs to get treatment regularly or the victim should not stay.

Keep the therapy door open

In general, it's best not to pick a partner who doesn't believe in seeing a psychologist or other mental health professional if/when the need arises. If you marry someone like that, it greatly limits your ability to solve relationship problems. It means that if you can't solve them yourselves—if you don't know how to communicate well enough to work everything out amicably, or if you ever hit a disagreement so emotionally charged that you could use a referee—you'll just be out of luck. Your partner will not agree to go with you to get the help your relationship needs.

I once had a patient who avoided doctors because he was sure that when you went into the hospital, you never came out. As a result, an entirely treatable skin cancer ate through his lip, tongue and face, until the inevitable occurred—he was admitted into the hospital and never came out.

The same thing happens with psychological difficulties. If you try your best to ignore them, the problems build until eventually, they will not be solvable and you will suffer greatly. If you instead approach psychological problems in a calm, matter-of-fact manner, like the other problems you fix every day (need a roof fixed, hire a roofer; need your car fixed, hire a mechanic), you'll be able to resolve your interpersonal problems much more easily and with a lot less pain. The greatest thing to fear is fear itself, especially when it comes to psychological difficulties. Just face the problem, get the help you need, and do the work suggested to fix the problem—and things should improve considerably.

Exercises to help you through tough times

1. When you read this chapter, did any of the stories remind you of your relationship? Which ones? Do you and your mate engage in any of the problem items listed at the beginning of the chapter? Which ones? Mark those problem signs off in this book, and write them in your Relationship Notebook. Now, how will you try to correct each one? Take one behavior each day and try to correct it. At the end of the day, note your progress in your Relationship Notebook. If it didn't go as well as you'd like, ask yourself why. Continue practicing that behavior the

next day. If the problem is listed under the "can't be fixed" problems, schedule an appointment with a psychologist to discuss your options.

2. Did you find yourself becoming upset with your mate today? When you feel upset, start writing in your notebook. Don't censure your thoughts; just write as fast as you can and get as many down as possible, putting one thought per line and skipping a line in between. When you're finished, go back and review each one. Is your mate really responsible for that behavior? Or is he a convenient scapegoat—are you just blaming him because you can't tell the other person about your anger? Make a note stating the real situation next to that thought (e.g., *"Tom isn't responsible. I'm really not angry with him, I'm upset that my career isn't going the way I'd like it to go right now. Tomorrow I'll work out at the gym to release my anger, rather than taking it out on Tom."*).

3. If you decide your mate is responsible, how will you handle the problem? Review **Chapter 7—Communication** for ideas. Write your plan in your notebook next to or under the related thoughts.

4. Examine your thoughts for signs of irrationality and exaggeration. Perhaps your mate is responsible for that item, but you are blowing it out of proportion. If so, rewrite the sentence to be more accurate. For example, if you wrote, "Tom never picks up after himself and it's driving me crazy! He thinks I'm his personal slave!", rewrite the sentence: *"Tom doesn't clean up after himself the way I'd like him to, and I feel annoyed about it. But it's not driving me crazy. And I have no idea what Tom thinks about this topic, since we haven't really talked about it lately. I'll make a time to discuss it with him. One possible compromise would be to hire a maid to clean once a week, so I wouldn't feel so stressed. Other possible compromises could be…"*

Chapter 11

Loss & letting go
Divorce, breakup, death

*E*veryone hates loss, and there's simply no greater loss than losing a loved one. It hurts a lot. And it hurts for a long time. Whether you lose a spouse through divorce or death or end a long-term relationship by breaking up, the effects are virtually the same. You have the emotional pain and upheaval to survive. Piled on top of your extreme emotions are legal and other practical issues that require energy and focus at a time when you don't even want to get out of bed in the morning. You may even develop physical problems from the stress you're under. You may feel as if your life is over.

Although you have no control over the death of a spouse, in many cases you do have at least some control over your marriage and whether or not it ends in divorce. Many couples think and talk about divorce prematurely. The high divorce rate in this country reflects the unwillingness of many people to work on their relationships. In my experience, many people divorce for foolish reasons or turn to divorce too quickly as a solution to their problems. Too many people bail out when things get rough, even though they promised to stay through life's ups and downs. Far too few people go to therapy before throwing in the towel. Anything worth having is worth working on, and intimate relationships are no different. In many cases, you can save your marriage and make it stronger. But you have to be willing to make the effort.

Divorce is no quick fix or easy answer. Never underestimate the pain and loss of divorce. Its effects reach beyond you and your spouse. Your children, your families and even your friends will feel the fallout, some more acutely than others. So if you are not yet divorced, but are involved in an unsatisfying marriage, it's time for some self-evaluation.

When not to divorce

There are many inappropriate reasons to divorce, and the majority of them arise from emotional immaturity. If you are thinking of divorcing in a fit of anger, to show your spouse you're right and he's not, on impulse, or because your marriage isn't perfect, then your first task is to confront and deal with your own emotional immaturity.

Do not file for divorce when you're clinically depressed or your judgment is compromised in any way. Do **NOT** file for divorce to pursue a relationship with someone new or someone you're already cheating with. Your lover may suddenly disappear when you become available.

Instead take **The Dr. Kate Compatibility Quiz** and **The Dr. Kate Communication Quiz** (in the Appendix) to explore various factors that can make or break your relationship and home life. Set some goals, write them down, and talk to your mate about working together to make your marriage satisfying for both of you. Focus on communication. Reread **Chapter 7—Communication** and **Chapter 9—Marriage**, and learn to communicate and show your mate that he's a priority in your life. See a psychologist together for couples counseling, but do not file for divorce unless you've seen at least three different psychologists to try to fix your marriage and have not made any progress or achieved any breakthroughs.

When to divorce

Some relationships, however, cannot be salvaged, despite your best efforts. Reasons to call it quits include the following:

- 💜 Your mate is physically or sexually abusive to you or the children.
- 💜 Your mate is psychologically sick and refuses to get treatment, and the illness makes it difficult for you and the children to live happy, healthy lives.
- 💜 You have gone alone to therapy for more than a year, but your mate steadfastly refuses to accompany you or to work on your marital problems in any way.
- 💜 Despite therapy and exploring the issues and possible compromises, you and your mate can't compromise on an issue that is of urgent importance to one or both of you, such as when you want children and he doesn't.
- 💜 The problems you have with your mate are so severe that you don't want to be with him any more, no matter what happens in the future and even if you end up alone.

Consult a lawyer about your rights and what to expect in the divorce, and discuss that information with your psychologist before you file. Consider the pros and cons in detail on several occasions. Work through your anger and hurt as much as possible. Make sure you're not making this decision on impulse, but seeing the situation clearly and responding to it maturely.

What divorce really means emotionally

If you are contemplating divorce, you need to know what to expect. Divorce is a far-reaching loss that affects every aspect of your life. It is the number one stressor, and recovery can often take two years or more.

The emotional toll is significant. Both spouses normally experience a wide range of emotions, which may include: shock, confusion, hurt, sadness, depression, anger, rage, jealousy, feelings of revenge, hopelessness, denial, self-doubt, low self-esteem, bitterness and hostility. And your children suffer emotionally, too. It is extremely painful for children to watch the breakup of their nuclear family, and they often think that they somehow caused the divorce. Those concerns can magnify the pain for them.

In divorce, you lose your closest companion, your steady sex partner, the routine that has structured your life and the family traditions you built together. These are all very important parts of your life, even if you and your spouse were not getting along before you split. Marriage, routine and traditions are a source of stability; they give us a strong sense of being grounded. When that support is abruptly torn away, it shakes our very foundations.

As a result, many people internalize the rejection of divorce and question their self-worth and ability to attract others: *"He didn't love me enough. I wasn't thin or pretty enough." "I wasn't rich or powerful enough to keep her attention." "I didn't succeed in my business; she couldn't respect me." "No one will ever love me again!"*

What makes the situation worse is that often the spouses have said some pretty terrible things to each other before getting divorced. He has yelled at her about how fat she's become. How could she have let herself go like this? For the past 10 years, he's been embarrassed to take her to company dinners! She has screamed at him that he never made enough money for them to live comfortably, and that sex with him was always awful.

Worse yet, one of them may have said he never really loved the other—ever.

That's enough to send most people reeling. When partners fight, they often say extremely cruel things that they don't mean. During and after the divorce, those accusations and cruelties can rotate through your consciousness, causing emotional havoc. And even though there may be some truth behind those accusations (e.g., she did gain weight, and he wasn't the best lover), the way in which the criticism and blame are exaggerated and yelled at mega-decibels just serves to put more salt in the wound.

Another common reaction is embarrassment. Just as your marriage was public, your divorce is public. Your marital status is now "divorced" in conversation and on legal and government forms. Divorce is also the ultimate rejection. The person who knew you most intimately has decided not to live with you any more.

Divorced spouses also have to face the loss of their dreams. Many people, especially women, have spent their entire lives dreaming about romance and family. We wanted the man who could love us with passion and enthusiasm our whole life through, someone with whom we could be best friends, lovers and mates—intellectually, spiritually, physically, sexually. We wanted to be a team with Prince Charming, comforted that he was by our side; we wanted to grow old together.

And when we thought we had it after dreaming about it for so long and then we lose it, it can be very upsetting.

Let's face it, divorce shakes up the rhythm of everyone's life. People generally don't crave change of that magnitude. People send out wedding announcements and cards, not "Congratulations On Your Divorce!" cards. No matter how you cut it, divorce feels like failure to many people. And failure can be very difficult to take.

What divorce really means in a practical sense

Divorce involves financial changes. On the purely practical side, each spouse ends up with less money than they had together. If the woman did not maintain her career and marketability in the workplace, she may now find it difficult to make ends meet. Two households have to be maintained now, and living conditions often change for the worse. If children and joint custody are involved, both spouses have to rent/buy living spaces that can accommodate those children—an expensive proposition.

Along with the loss of your spouse, you will likely lose a significant part of your social network. Since you are no longer a member of your ex-spouse's family, you're now excluded from their family celebrations and get-togethers. Many of your joint friends may disappear as well when you are no longer a couple. Your own family may view divorce as a stigma and pressure or ostracize you because they don't believe in divorce.

Remember when I talked about women being judged more for their relationships than men? That adds to the stress women feel about divorce. A woman who has put her husband through school and later entertained for him as he rose in his career often loses her social status and feels like a castoff after the divorce.

I was appalled when I read the following notice in one of the downtown Chicago society papers: "Line up ladies! Mr. (Rich and Famous) has just filed for divorce!" What a double standard! What about Mrs. Rich and Famous? She didn't even get one line of print. Divorce made her a forgotten woman, while it made him a highly marketable commodity!

Divorce can also involve professional losses. Even though it is not the terrible stigma it used to be, divorce can be detrimental to people in certain professions (such as the clergy), or to those who work for old-fashioned bosses in family-oriented firms. And the professional aspect really gets tangled if you and your mate built a business together. Divorce often means selling off part or all of the company to split the profits.

How to tell your spouse

The bitterness and pain of divorce are magnified many times if you break the news in a thoughtless and unfeeling way. There is no easy way to tell your spouse that you want out of the relationship, but you can show empathy and respect.

Make a time to discuss it *in person* when no one else is around and you won't be interrupted. Tell your mate you have something important to discuss, so that you get him ready psychologically. Approach the subject gently by asking your partner how he feels about your relationship. Use reflective listening and supportive statements to show him that you understand how he feels. Let him vent. Agree with whatever you can: *"Yes, I agree, we haven't been getting along very well."*

Then bring up your feelings and thoughts in a calm, assertive way, always beginning the sentence with "I" rather than "you": *"I feel very disappointed that we seem to have different goals. I want to have children, and it seems like you don't. Is that correct?"* Use a soft, gentle tone of voice and be sincere, not sarcastic or critical. Address the problem, rather than attacking your partner.

Be honest, but respectful: *"I understand that you aren't ready to have children, but I am. I love you. But I don't think it's good for either of us to continue in a relationship where we are constantly frustrated because our goals are so divergent. As much as I love you and wish things could be different, I think it would be better if we split up. I think you're a wonderful person, but our needs just aren't in sync right now and I don't see how they will become so in the near future...How do you feel about it?"*

Show respect and empathy for your partner. Reverse positions in your head, and treat him the way you'd want him to treat you if the situation was reversed.

How to tell the kids

The sad fact is that many divorces involve children. It's extremely important to realize that children often blame themselves when something goes wrong between their parents. You know how irrational your thoughts can be. Take that, multiply it by 10, and then add magic to the mix and you'll understand better how kids think. Often children feel that Daddy/Mommy left because they were bad. It never occurs to them that the problems were between Mommy and Daddy. Kids are at the center of their universe. If something bad happens, it is happening chiefly to them. Since they've been told so often that they should "be good," it's easy to make the logical jump and think they're losing their family because they were "bad." At the same time, they might also strike out and blame one or the other parent unfairly to alleviate some of their guilt and uncertainty.

So when you tell your children about the divorce, be sure to make it clear that it was not their fault. Even if they don't seem to be internalizing blame, talk about it with them.

If at all possible, you and your spouse should talk to your children together to break the news. NEVER criticize your spouse to your children or put your kids in the middle. It is unfair and very traumatic for them. Even if your spouse attacks you, demonstrate respect and control by not counterattacking.

Young children don't usually know how they are feeling. But just as you feel overwhelming pain, sadness or anger, your child is also feeling similar emotions. The difference is that you have an adult's perspective and a sense that you can control your own world—at least somewhat. In contrast, the child has a profound sense that she cannot control what is happening at home. When children feel, they react. And those reactions can take many forms.

Some kids get physically ill from anxiety and suffer stomachaches or headaches. Other children may withdraw and escape through video games, the computer, music or TV. A child who was previously quiet and shy might become aggressive with other children or even destructive. Older girls might get seductive to try to win the approval of boys. Children will generally concentrate less and do more poorly in school. Pay attention when a child seems to be taking the divorce too well. She may be hiding feelings from you. Expect that your child should have some response to the loss. If she doesn't, chances are she's burying it and will react in the future. Talk to her about the divorce and encourage her to verbalize her feelings to you.

The bottom line is that you can expect just about anything. Keep your eyes open and don't be afraid to see the problems. Bringing them to light in a positive and productive way can save the life of your child. Don't criticize, blame or be short with your children. If you feel overwhelmed, or if a child is acting out or seems to need help, don't hesitate to consult a psychologist with your kids. The time and money you spend today can avoid a host of other problems in the future.

Breaking up is like divorce

Even if you're not married, breaking up is a mini-divorce. Depending on the length of time you've been together, your expectations for staying together, and the interconnection of your lives, breaking up can yield the same kind of suffering as divorce. A breakup usually involves fewer legal problems, but not always. Many couples combine checking accounts, and if you have bought a house or started a business together, you can have the same property-splitting difficulties as a married couple.

Breaking up is even more stressful if you thought you were working toward marriage and are running out of time to create your family.

The pain of being widowed

Losing your spouse to death does not carry the stigma of rejection, but the pain is no less intense. When your dearest companion dies, it leaves an incredible hole in your life. You have lost the person you trusted most to keep your confidences, the person with whom you shared years of traditions, memories, customs and routines. You have lost your sleeping partner, your sex partner, your co-parent, perhaps even your coworker. You have lost the laughter you used to share. You've lost the warm and fuzzy feelings—the security of knowing that someone looked out for you and cared about you every day.

If your spouse dies suddenly, the shock often adds to your suffering. If you have to face disorganized finances, death without a will, or other practical difficulties such as having to support yourself, the combination of pain, problems and responsibilities can be overwhelming.

Even if you don't have legal or financial problems to face, you still must arrange the funeral, notify everyone and send thank you notes. Then you must face the task of cleaning out your spouse's closets and drawers.

When the practical tasks are finished, you are left with an empty house and millions of memories. How can you forget him? Every chair, every picture, every object in your house reminds you of your life together. Your song comes on the radio, you catch the scent of his aftershave on a jacket, you find a note he wrote you stashed in your wallet—sights, sounds, smells and touch can all evoke memories of your life together.

The house is too quiet and perhaps even scary. It seems to have lost its soul. You may even feel like your life is over. After all, life as you have known it and dreamed it is over. You may have nightmares or be unable to fall sleep. You may wake up in the middle of the night and be unable to get back to sleep.

Your children will have their own grief, their own reactions and their own adjustment problems. Younger children may act out at home and at school. They may irrationally blame you, themselves or God for the death. You have to help them cope when you can hardly help yourself, and your anxiety about their welfare adds even more stress.

One common emotional response to the death of a spouse is anger, often aimed in many directions. You may be angry at you spouse for neglecting his health and financial affairs and leaving you with this mess. You may be angry at yourself for not acting sooner when he got sick.

You may be angry at God. You worked hard, you obeyed the Golden Rule, you did everything the right way. Yet your life has now seemingly come to a halt, while other not-so-good people are out there enjoying themselves. It isn't fair; you want it to be, and you are angry that it's not.

It's hard to be angry at God. It's even harder to be angry with someone who is dead. You can't scream at him and get it off your chest. And you feel guilty that you are mad at him, and that just confuses you more.

Living through the emotional pain

So how can you survive the pain of divorce, breaking up or being widowed? The most important survival technique is to work hard to banish irrational thoughts.

For example, when your divorcing spouse doesn't want you any more, it doesn't mean that you are a failure or the worst scum that ever walked the face of the earth. ;-) It doesn't even mean that you are undesirable or destined to be alone for the rest of your life.

It just means that the two of you were not really compatible—at least not at that time. If you had been, you'd still be together. You might have been compatible with the part of him you loved dearly, or with the person he might become in 20 years, or if he wasn't ill or if he got treatment. Or if he'd had a different family and upbringing. Or...Or...Or...

Perhaps things would have lasted longer if you had cherished your time together while you had it and not taken it for granted—if you had behaved a little differently. Perhaps you married young and the two of you grew into different people who no longer shared the same goals, interests and perspectives. At that point in your life, the two of you were not compatible enough to make the relationship work.

No matter what happened, it's very important not to blame yourself or your mate. You each did what you felt was best at that time. Even though you might completely question your mate's judgment (and even if we asked 100 people and they all agreed that your mate showed lousy judgment), the fact is that he did what he felt was best based on whatever he thought about at the time.

People don't generally go out of their way to make others miserable. They just make choices based on what they perceive to be best for their needs. Your mate may have acted selfishly, immaturely and unwisely, but then we all do at times. Nobody's perfect. We are all human and we all make mistakes. And that is why it doesn't make any sense to blame either yourself or your partner. Blaming doesn't change anything. It just makes you feel worse.

On the other hand, you can't expect to weather a divorce without any irrational thoughts and vacillating emotions. You are going through a time of great stress, and denying your feelings can be just as unhealthy as totally giving in to irrationality. But you can express your emotions without resorting to blame or exaggerations. If you tell yourself, *"I really don't like this. I wish I could have stayed married and kept our family intact. I will miss him and the good times we had, but eventually I will get through this, heal and start over,"* you will feel less stressed than if you think, "Life isn't fair! This shouldn't happen to me! He shouldn't have done this to me, that no-good ___! Everyone else gets what they want in life except me!"

Similarly, if you turn the blame on yourself and think, "I really messed up royally. I should have seen it coming. I should have worked harder on it and kept it all together," you will feel worse and it will take you longer to heal. If you instead think, *"I wish I had behaved differently at the time, but I'm going to learn from this and apply that knowledge to make my future better,"* you will feel disappointed, but hopeful.

When you assign blame, it's much more difficult to let go and move on. Blaming weights you down. It wears on you. It sucks the energy out of you. Instead, you can recognize that you and your spouse are both human, and you both did what you felt was best at the time or you wouldn't have done it.

Giving yourself the gift of forgiveness

Why should you forgive your mate? You don't have to. However, realize that if you don't forgive your mate, the person you hurt most is you. That's right, YOU. Because you are keeping the wounds open in the process. Oh, sure, you might hurt his feelings a little. But you will hurt your feelings a **lot** more.

Being angry takes a lot of energy, and you only have so much energy. If you squander it on negative thoughts and feelings, you're not going to have as much for positive thoughts and feelings. And that's a real waste!

When you are angry with someone and stay that way, you are allowing that person to remain important to you. You are choosing to keep the pain alive. If you wake up every day obsessing about what he did to you, you make your past your present and allow negative thoughts to consume you. And when you allow such negativity to take over your life, you draw other unhappy people to you. Basically, you create the pain you want to avoid. Suzanne had to overcome blaming both her husband and her children.

Suzanne & Dean's Story

Suzanne was married to Dean for 50 years. Almost from the beginning of their marriage, she felt that he wasn't being entirely faithful to her. But he kept her on the defensive by blaming her whenever anything wasn't done perfectly. Suzanne tried her best to please him. She kept her figure in shape, dressed up to greet him every evening, always had dinner on the table on time, and raised their three children. Meanwhile Dean built his successful business.

The first time Suzanne had proof of an affair, she confronted Dean. He vowed to stop the affair and do better. For awhile, their relationship improved, but gradually the situation deteriorated and Dean became increasingly critical of Suzanne. She later learned that this behavior signaled the start of an affair with a new woman. Dean's affairs were always long-term relationships.

When the kids were grown, Dean got less concerned about keeping up pretenses and Suzanne was no longer able to hide from the evidence. She noticed money missing from the checkbook, and a private detective confirmed the existence of a mistress. They separated. Dean continued his dalliances while living separately and staying married.

Suzanne was mortified when her kids met the mistress. She felt deeply hurt and betrayed when they seemed to support their father, even though his cheating had caused the marriage to dissolve. She had done her best to make the family unit stable. Yet her children didn't seem to appreciate that. They would come to town and not visit her. They invited Dean and his mistress over for holidays, while she spent the day alone. One of the sons even let the mistress throw him a special party. While money was not a problem, Suzanne had lost her status, a good portion of her family, and her dream of a lifelong marriage. Along the way, the stress also took its toll on her immune system and she developed cancer. She bitterly blamed her husband for taking so much away from her, and she blamed her children for not standing by her and appreciating all that she had done for them.

It took Suzanne awhile, but she gradually learned to accept that life isn't fair and that her children might never come to appreciate her. She learned to reinterpret the idea of a "successful marriage." Instead of viewing her marriage as a total failure because it didn't last until death, she learned that living with someone for almost a half century is an amazing accomplishment. She learned how to care more about what she thought and felt and less about what her husband or kids might be thinking and feeling. She learned how to forgive them.

Forgiving is important to Suzanne—emotionally and physically. Besides helping her heal and move on, it's also vitally important to keeping her cancer in remission. Suzanne forgives every day and tries to stay centered, appreciating the good things about her life and being thankful for them.

The past is over if you let it be over. When you hate, you keep the pain alive and risk making yourself physically ill. When you forgive, you let go. You allow the pain to be in the past.

Forgiving is not the same as forgetting. You will never completely forget; you're in touch with reality, and you know the marital problems happened. But you don't have to keep them in a constant replay pattern in your conscious mind. And when you do occasionally think about them, they do not have to evoke such incredibly strong negative feelings.

If you forgive your spouse and yourself, you can be happy in spite of your loss. You can't go back in time and change what happened. You can't re-do it. However, you can learn what you can from that experience and apply that knowledge to the future to make your next relationship better.

If you think in such a calm, forgiving way, you will feel better and it will be easier to live a positive life. You will heal and be able to move to another relationship stage that you'll enjoy more. And because you will be healthier, you'll also be far more likely to draw healthy people to you.

Techniques for dealing with irrational thoughts

So keeping your thoughts as rational as possible is the first order of business. Two techniques can help you.

Thought-stopping

Use **Thought-stopping** (described in the Appendix) to stop thoughts about your ex or your deceased spouse. With thought-stopping, you make a conscious effort to replace negative, exaggerated thoughts about yourself, other people and the world with positive, more realistic thoughts.

The Dr. Kate Quick and Dirty Crying/Grieving Technique

Use **The Dr. Kate Quick & Dirty Crying/Grieving Technique** (also described in the Appendix) when your irrational thoughts build to crisis levels. Use it when you feel a lump in your throat so big that it seems as if you're going to choke, when you feel an incredible heaviness on your chest, when something small like the cat spilling her milk brings tears to your eyes, or when you're so irritable, you feel like you're going to take someone's head off. This technique allows you to vent your emotions while controlling when and where, so you can minimize the fallout. It lets you completely indulge your irrationality for a limited period and express all the fears, anger, and sorrow that have been hanging over you—to cry and get them off your chest so you can return to being more rational again.

Taking care of yourself

Besides taking care of your mind and your feelings by keeping your thoughts as rational and positive as possible, you also have to keep your physical body going. You have to eat, sleep and get through the days. And if you have children, you also have to see that they eat, sleep and get through the days as well as possible.

So be kind to yourself. Acknowledge that you are undergoing one of life's biggest stresses, and don't add to your burden. Don't volunteer for projects you don't need to do. Don't try to cook Thanksgiving dinner for your extended family, for example. Let someone else do the cooking or take everyone out to a Thanksgiving brunch. Spend your time holding your kids and playing a game with them rather than fussing over dinner and entertaining guests.

Stay away from unhappy, critical or angry people and anyone who affects you adversely. Avoid watching sad movies on TV. Get up and get dressed every day, even when you'd rather stay in bed with the covers over you. Get fresh air and sunlight, both of which can really lift your spirits. Take your vitamins and don't drink too much alcohol. Instead, de-stress by taking warm baths and listening to soft music—or by doing whatever it is that helps you feel peaceful and relaxed. Alcohol is a depressant, and while it may initially help you forget your problems, after a certain point, you'll just start sobbing instead.

As much as possible, put away items that remind you of your loved one. Obviously you can't get rid of everything, but don't expect to heal while you have his shoes sitting by his side of the bed. If you can't do it yourself, call a loyal friend, explain the problem and have her help you.

Avoid making any major decisions. When people are under stress, they often find it difficult to prioritize, and judgment suffers.

Getting closure

Divorced spouses need to understand what happened. Closure is very important to healing, but often your ex doesn't give you that option. This is particularly true when a spouse deserts the family, leaves one marriage and almost immediately marries someone else, or just refuses to talk. The rejected spouse doesn't understand what happened. How could someone who swore to be faithful and wanted a family behave that way? When a spouse denies you the benefit of closure, the pain of divorce is even more intense.

Remember Jill and Ethan from the last chapter? When Ethan left suddenly, Jill had to deal with the legal issues of divorce and dispose of his clothes and personal possessions as if he had died, too. The situation was enormously stressful. Plus Ethan did not give her the satisfaction of talking through the marriage. She could neither fix the marriage nor get closure. She had to figure it out as much as possible on her own, with my help. To make matters more painful, Jill had put off having children until their lives and careers were stable. The divorce and the healing time she would need before she entered another relationship would make it extremely difficult for her to reach her goal of making a family. She mourned not only the loss of Ethan's company and the laughter they had shared, but also the loss of her dream.

When your marriage ends, try to get as much closure as you can. If you and your ex can talk about your relationship and your breakup, take full advantage of the opportunity. You don't have to agree; you probably won't. You just need to understand his thinking. If your spouse won't talk, you might want to consult your friends and get their impressions. Sometimes an ex will tell a friend something he wouldn't tell you.

In my opinion, everyone who goes through divorce or the death of a spouse should consult a psychologist to help them through this difficult time. At the very least, attend a few sessions to review your marriage and get some closure. Professional guidance can greatly shorten the amount of time you grieve. Friends can be very supportive and you should talk to them in confidence. However, they can't usually give an organized analysis of your situation, and they certainly don't have the time to talk to you week after week for as long as you need to vent. Your psychologist can help you cope with the stresses and strains of divorce and give you a balanced perspective of your situation.

In therapy, review your marriage with the psychologist. Bring up your fears and discuss them. If you have regrets, express them out loud and explore them, too. Do any of your thoughts, feelings, fears and regrets relate to your past and the way you were raised? Explore that connection. If your ex-spouse is unwilling to participate in these sessions, a psychologist with years of experience in handling divorce can help you figure it out and gain closure.

If you have any big decisions to make, discuss those with your psychologist first. Everyone's judgment suffers when they're under stress. Your psychologist can tell you when your thinking is irrational or unwise and help you avoid many mistakes. If you're having difficulty with your children, bring them along to a session and let them voice their feelings.

Your psychologist will also give you emotional support and guidance. When you're coming down on yourself too much, she'll point that out and help you forgive yourself. Conversely, when you're blaming your spouse too much, she'll help you take responsibility for your part of the marital problems. When you see your therapist, you *constructively* explore the marriage and divorce or death of your spouse and your feelings. In that setting, such exploration is helpful, since you can learn from it and get help for any irrational thoughts that are exaggerations of reality. By seeing your therapist once a week and using thought-stopping in between, you're limiting your thinking about your loss to times when it is productive. In time, your therapist can help you accept yourself, your spouse and life with a healthy, positive, down-to-earth attitude.

Sometimes a person will say, "I'm going to do some thinking and work on myself." What that usually means is, "I'm going to bury everything as much as possible and try not to think about it." But burying painful feelings is not the same as coping with them.

When you see a psychologist to work through your loss, it helps you face your pain and work through it in the most efficient, effective way. If you don't use a psychologist, you could wake up three years later in the same pain you felt the day you experienced your loss. By trying to bury the feelings, you keep them alive. Just because you throw a handful of ashes on top, the fire doesn't stop. It keeps burning inside. And those unresolved feelings can cause you to act out in unhealthy and detrimental ways.

When therapy isn't an option, but a necessity

While I always recommend therapy for anyone who has experienced a serious loss, therapy is absolutely imperative for dealing with certain associated problems or reactions.

You should definitely get professional help if you're having trouble keeping your job or taking care of your children. If you are consumed with hatred, envy, jealousy or revenge thoughts, if you can't stop crying, or if you are so irritable that you are taking your anger out on everyone you encounter, you need a psychologist to help you deal with your emotions. Similarly, if you use routinely use alcohol, drugs or sex to anesthetize yourself, if you take a lot of physical risks, or if you begin having accidents, you need to see a psychologist.

You should also see a psychologist if you are suffering from clinical depression. Depression is not the same as feeling sad. Sadness almost always accompanies loss and involves intense emotional pain, but the pain improves over time. Depression is a more serious problem because it goes past grieving and has a more pervasive and sustained impact on your entire life. When someone is depressed, many physical and psychological symptoms may persist. It's important to be able to recognize these signs.

Symptoms of depression

- ♥ Psychomotor retardation (thinking or moving very slowly)
- ♥ Changes in sleeping—either sleeping too much or not being able to fall asleep, or waking up in the early morning and not being able to go back to sleep
- ♥ Changes in eating—either no appetite or eating all the time
- ♥ Changes in sex drive—usually a decrease, but sometimes an increase
- ♥ Difficulty concentrating
- ♥ Difficulty remembering things
- ♥ Feelings of self-doubt and low self-esteem
- ♥ Thoughts of suicide
- ♥ Crying
- ♥ Disinterest in people or activities
- ♥ Flat affect—feeling empty
- ♥ Feeling unusually irritable, hostile and on edge

Most people associate depression with crying and suicidal thoughts. While those symptoms are one manifestation of depression, a depressed person can actually be quite irritable instead. It's easy to overlook anger and irritability as symptoms of depression, since other people generally get angry in return, rather than trying to pinpoint the cause of your problem. Depressed people can also feel apathetic, flat and empty. Or they may talk about killing themselves with a big smile on their face ("smiling depressants").

Always take depression seriously and get professional help. The best treatment for depression is cognitive-behavioral therapy. This type of therapy involves examining your thoughts, figuring out which are irrational/not helpful, and changing them for more rational/helpful thoughts.

Your depression may respond to cognitive-behavioral therapy alone. However, if you can't make progress in therapy because you don't have the energy to do the necessary homework, then an antidepressant may give you the energy to work on your problem. Ask your psychologist for a referral.

Under no circumstances should you use the medication as a substitute for therapy, however. The cognitive-behavioral therapy is what will, in the end, fix the problem, by helping you think positively and rationally. If you only take medication, it's more like drugging yourself and you may very well find that the depression returns when you stop taking the medication.

Understanding your relationship stage

The final step to recovering from loss is to realize that you are in a relationship stage that does not have to last forever. And that's one of the most important secrets of this book—that life is a series of relationship stages. Nothing lasts forever. When your marriage ends through death or divorce, you can move on, no matter what your age. You just have to work through the hurt, heal and get to the next stage.

If you want to recreate a family life, you can eventually do so. You can't rush it and make it start today, and you will have to live as a single person first. But in time, you can move on to another relationship stage. When you can tell yourself this secret and believe it, you will immediately feel better. Yes, you are hurting and you don't like the pain. But you can be happy and whole in spite of it. And eventually, you can find someone else to start over with—IF you so choose.

The six secrets of recovery

We've explored the six secrets of recovery in the preceding sections. Now let's recap them here.

To recover from a serious loss or trauma in the most efficient, effective manner:

- See a psychologist to vent, get closure and learn what you can from your loss.
- Avoid blame; forgive your spouse and yourself.
- In between therapy sessions, use thought-stopping to change negative, irrational thoughts to positive, realistic thoughts.
- Use the grieving technique when you occasionally need to give into irrationality and indulge your grief.
- Take care of yourself physically and emotionally.
- Understand that you are in a time-limited relationship stage and can eventually heal, move on and start over.

If you follow these secrets, not only will you heal faster and more thoroughly, but you'll also be less likely to end up in a rebound relationship or other predicament because you were upset and exercised faulty judgment. These techniques allow you to meet your stress head-on like a mature adult and heal yourself at the deepest level.

Real-life Love@AOL letters about loss and letting go

AOL members write me frequently to ask questions about divorce, breaking up, death of a spouse, forgiveness and closure. Here are some of my favorites.

When is marriage over? Fighting over nothing... MY AGE: 26 MY GENDER: MALE

Dear Dr. Kate,
How do you know when your marriage is over? We constantly fight—about nothing really. I am not physically attracted to her anymore, and she is constantly cursing at me for no reason! But I still find it hard to call it quits. Kinda strange, eh?

Dear Dazed and Confused,

No. It just sounds like you are at one of the more difficult spots in your marriage. You can work through this with motivation, your wife's cooperation and professional help.

The fact that you "find it hard to call it quits" suggests to me that you still love her. When people are angry with one another, that anger can effectively hide the feelings of love they have for each other. When they learn to communicate better and resolve their conflicts amicably, they suddenly discover that they are able to feel the love again.

Make an appointment with a psychologist for marital therapy and ask your wife to accompany you. You should consider divorce ONLY after you have attempted therapy for years with more than one psychologist, and find that you've made little progress and still can't get along. (I'm assuming here that your marriage does not involve physical, sexual or significant emotional abuse, or an unusual problem that cannot be resolved.)

All the Best! Please keep me posted on your progress, and write again if you need additional assistance,

Dr. Kate

He wants to move on!

Dear Dr. Kate,

My spouse of 30 years has had a long-term affair and now wants to end it. He has asked for forgiveness, and said he's sorry. He wants to pretend it never happened. He also refuses to go to counseling. I am deeply hurt, confused and angry, and I have mixed feelings about the marriage surviving. I am in counseling. Please advise. Thank you.

Dear Hurt and Angry Wife,

I feel for you. It's only normal to feel hurt, angry and confused at a time like this. It's also natural to have mixed feelings toward him and your marriage.

I'm glad you are in counseling. That should be your main focus right now. Try not to make any major decisions while you are under such stress, because your judgment may be off for awhile. If you need to decide something, run it by your therapist to get his opinion.

I have my doubts about anyone who professes to be sorry, then refuses to get help. To me, it's like denying the incident took place. Instead of denying that he made a mistake, as your husband is doing, it's important that he face it and do everything he can to learn not to repeat the same mistake again.

You don't say how long he has refused counseling. Try following the steps outlined in *How To Invite Your Mate To Counseling*, located in the Appendix. If he still refuses to go, there isn't much you can do. Regardless of what he does, continue therapy so that you can receive the emotional support you need and help in making your life choices.

Best Wishes, and please let me know how it works out,

Dr. Kate

Still traumatized by breakup 3 years ago!

Dear Dr. Kate,

Three years ago, I was totally traumatized when the girl I had been seeing for two years suddenly left me. Within two months, I was terminated from my job for lack of performance. Although I was immediately able to obtain employment, my work performance continues to suffer. I have tried all the methods outlined in your column, but here I am, three years later, almost as upset as the day we broke up.

I have recurring dreams about my ex several times a week. I feel like I've lost my best friend and the one person I loved more than anyone or anything in my life. I also feel that a part of me is missing. I do date, but my heart simply isn't in it. A year ago, I was asked out by a famous TV actress. Instead of having a great time, I used the date to try to make my ex jealous and perhaps lure her back. Where do I go from here?

Dear Totally Miserable,

I would suggest you see a psychologist who specializes in cognitive-behavioral therapy, as well as relationships. It's important to go beneath the surface and examine your ideas about this woman, what she meant to you and what it means to be without her. I would guess that you are holding some irrational ideas which are making it difficult for you to let go.

For example, when you write, "I have lost my best friend and the one person I loved more than anyone or anything in my life," of course you are going to feel upset. But is that statement rational? No. For one thing, your life has not ended. She may be the person you have loved most to date, but that doesn't mean that she has to be the one you will love best in your life—unless, of course, you choose to make it so by not moving on.

Similarly, when you write, "A part of me is missing," you allow yourself to feel incomplete and desolate. However, that statement is not really rational; it's exaggerated. A more accurate statement would be, "I lost someone I really cared about, and I feel very disappointed about it. I wish it hadn't happened. But if I let myself move on, I could very well find someone more compatible who loves me as much as I do her."

Your ex couldn't have been that compatible with you, or she would have loved you as much as you loved her and you'd still be together. You wanted her to be compatible and love you dearly, but it didn't happen. And when the person you're with doesn't want you as much as you want her, it just means that there is someone else out there who is more compatible.

Are you generally a fairly stubborn or rigid person? Those traits may be getting in the way here. Sometimes people don't move on because they are angry that they didn't get what they wanted. Explore this issue in therapy.

I assume that you are trying to use thought-stopping. Have you removed everything that reminds you of your ex from your house, car and office? If not, do so immediately. You can't expect thought-stopping to make you forget when you are looking at visual reminders of your ex on a regular basis.

If you have done that and thought-stopping still doesn't seem to be working, then you're probably not doing it correctly. When used correctly, thought-stopping always works—because you are changing your thoughts to more positive, healthy thoughts. If you stop every thought about your friend except when you are discussing her with your psychologist, you should find that in about two months, you are not thinking about her much at all. In about four months, you should be almost free of thoughts about her and feeling much better.

Cognitive-behavioral therapy and reframing your thoughts should help decrease your recurring dreams. When you begin to think and feel less upset about the breakup on a conscious level, you will have an accompanying decrease in upsetness on an unconscious dream level as well.

I'm sorry you're hurting. Call the psychologist now. Life is too short to live it in such a stressed out manner.

All the Best, and please let me know how you're doing from time to time,

Dr. Kate

Exercises to help you through this difficult time

1. **Raise Your Self-Esteem.** How is your self-esteem these days? In your Relationship Notebook, make a list of ten qualities you like about yourself. For example, "*I have a warm heart.*" Or, "*I'm a good teacher.*" When you're done, review your list to make sure it's completely positive (e.g., "I'm a good teacher sometimes" or "I try to be nice" is not acceptable). Make any changes so that your list is completely positive, then memorize the list. Put a piece of masking tape over the face of your watch. Whenever you want to see the time, tell yourself one item off your list before moving the tape. Try to vary the item. Do this for a week, then draft another list for the following week. Keep going until this habit is engrained. At that point, take the tape off and put a little green dot on your wrist next to your watch as a reminder instead. Every time you see that dot, smile and tell yourself, "*I like me!*" or say one of your list items.

2. **Make A General Schedule.** It's always easier to follow a schedule than to remember everything in your head, and that's particularly true when you're under stress and have extra difficulty remembering things. So make a general schedule, including activities that will help you de-stress (e.g., "Noon: Take a 20-minute walk to relax.... 9 p.m.: Take warm bath, do some deep breathing and listen to soothing music.").

   Review your schedule. Have you allowed yourself enough time to sleep well, eat right, socialize with others, get some sunshine and have personal time? If not, change the schedule to allow yourself that time. Then put your schedule in a central location and keep a copy with you at work. Look at it often to keep yourself focused, particularly if you find yourself staring off into space and worrying.

3. **Make A List of Things To Do.** To help you remember, list whatever has to be done that day on an index card. Put the card in your purse or pocket for easy reference. When you finish a task, cross it out and say, "Good job!" to yourself.

4. **Reward Yourself For Your Efforts.** At the end of every day, tell yourself five things you did well today. For example, "I spent 20 minutes taking a walk in the sunshine at lunch instead of racing to the store and back. I felt better this afternoon as a result." If you start to think about things you didn't do well, flip the thoughts over and tell yourself how you will do them differently tomorrow instead.

Stage 4 of The Love Cycle—

Starting over

Chapter 12

Starting over
Creating a new life

The odds that you'll stay with your partner for the rest of your life are not very high. Approximately half of all marriages end in divorce, and the breakup percentage for relationships is even higher. Even if you're in the stay-together 50 percent, you still might find yourself alone because, on average, women outlive men by seven years. Those facts mean that at any point in time, many people are starting over after divorce, the breakup of a long-term relationship or the death of a spouse. So if you find yourself in the Starting Over Stage, you can take some small comfort in the knowledge that you have plenty of company.

Most people don't jump happily into this stage. Divorces are painful and emotionally wrenching, particularly if you've been married for years and have children. No one wants to survive a beloved spouse, and the prospect of being single again after 40 years of marriage only adds to the grief. Even if you were only married or in a relationship for a few years, you may dread getting back out there again. You may even feel that your love life is over.

But you are never too old to have love in your life—to love someone and be loved back. My motto, which also happens to be the motto of my center in Chicago, is, "*Life's too short not to love someone.*" This chapter can help you make the transition from married to single and find a new love to share your life with.

Kid in the candy store behavior—*when you're liberated by divorce*

Although divorce is never easy, some people who have been married a long time—and especially people who have buried their sexuality and playfulness for years—often feel liberated when they divorce. They frequently go on a dating spree, going out practically nonstop. This can lead to some uncomfortable situations, as Mark discovered.

Mark's Story

Mark had been married for 30 years. For the last 12 of those years, he had not slept with his wife—or with anyone else. Mark and his wife did not have an antagonistic relationship; theirs was more a steady drifting away from each other over the years. Mark finally got motivated and divorced his wife, and then he began to explore his new life as a single person. When he came to see me, he was dating nine women—at the same time—and all of them worked at the same company. The company had offices spread over many floors of a large building, and Mark had carefully chosen the women from different departments so that they would not know about each other.

Mark was very excited to be free and dating again. However, in his exuberance, he had forgotten one thing: Despite the large size and office space of the company, it had only one cafeteria. More than once, Mark was lunching with one of his girlfriends when another one walked by!

My first suggestion to Mark was that he slow down. My second was that he not date anyone else from his company. And my third suggestion was that he avoid seeing anyone for lunch, especially in the cafeteria!

Mark was busy every night trying to make up for lost time. He had always been responsible and conscientious, and now he was nearing 50. He felt that he had missed a part of his youth, and he wanted to have some fun. If you're in the same situation, there's no harm in making up for lost time this way, provided you are honest with yourself and your dates and conduct yourself in a way that is sexually responsible.

Often, people who throw themselves into dating after a divorce are running, not healing. By going out every night or just about every night of the week, you are so busy that you don't have time to think about what's bothering you. It's OK to busy yourself with work and your new social life, provided you are also seeing your psychologist to face your problems head-on and process what happened in your divorce. Running and total avoidance are not healthy strategies for anyone. Eventually, when you stop running, your problems will still be there.

Sexual responsibility is also important. Always take precautions to keep sex as safe as possible. Use latex condoms every time, as well as another form of birth control to further help prevent pregnancy.

And finally, it is imperative that your dates understand your dating/sexual status. In other words, it's important that they know that you are not being exclusive with them. There's no need to tell them specifics about any other people you are seeing, as that would be cruel, but they need to know that you are seeing others. By being honest about your dating status, you give your dates the information they need to make an informed choice about whether to have sex with you or continue seeing you. Exclusivity is an important factor to many single people who are looking for marriage partners. Allowing your dates to assume that you're being exclusive when you're not is unfair to your dates and can lead to feelings of hurt and betrayal.

Waiting until the kids are grown—when you're trapped by divorce

The opposite of The Kid In The Candy Store Mistake is to hide out after your divorce or the death of a spouse and wait until the kids are grown before attending to your personal needs. Often the person doing this is concerned about the effect her behavior will have on the kids—and that's a legitimate concern. However, it's also important to realize that often this behavior frequently has another purpose: It allows you to hide and procrastinate. It allows you to deny a part of your life out of fear. Nora fell into this trap.

Nora's Story

Nora was a well-educated, hardworking mom with two children. She had been married for 14 years and thought her marriage would last forever. But her husband had other ideas. He had an affair and left Nora for another woman. Nora's two children were traumatized by the breakup of the family, particularly since their father wasn't conscientious about his visitation. Initially, Nora poured all her energy into spending time with her children and helping them through this difficult transition, all the while working long hours to make ends meet. Nora was 39.

Then Nora's mother became ill, and Nora had to work even harder to help her mother. Just about the time when she could have spent more energy on herself, Nora was busy tending to her mother's needs.

Many years later, after her mother had died and her two kids had entered college, Nora had time to think. Her children were caught up in their own lives, their own friends, their own goals. Nora was alone. She came to The Relationship Center™. She was 54.

While we did what we could to help Nora find a mate at 54, it would have been a much easier task when she was 41 or even 44. Nora had given her children and her mother her full attention by staying home and not dating. What she didn't realize at the time was that she could have given her family the necessary attention without ruling out dating completely. Instead, Nora put her life on hold for 15 years.

Take care of your needs, too

While many divorcing people find it difficult to juggle all their responsibilities, it's not a good idea to table your personal needs for several years.

You are a human being, not a machine, and you have needs, too. You need to live a balanced life. It's important for you to have some personal time, including four hours on a Friday or Saturday night to date. Think about it: Four hours out of a week is nothing. Make the time.

If you deny yourself and try to sacrifice too much, you may become irritable, depressed, lonely and angry. You may become sexually frustrated or bury your sexuality so much that when you finally do meet a potentially compatible person, you don't know how to interact with him. You may turn to food, alcohol or drugs to fill your needs, and experience all the negative repercussions that such addictions cause. But one thing you will not be able to do is fully escape your need to have an adult companion in your life. If you think you can, you're just kidding yourself.

Another problem that comes with denying your own life is living too much through your children. This dependence and its expectations put enormous pressure on your children. They can't live their lives for you. You have to create your own personal life.

You will eventually come to the point where you want someone in your life. However, if you are female, you may be very surprised to learn that with each passing year, it gets increasingly more difficult to find a compatible mate. If you divorce at 39, the odds are fairly high that you can find someone compatible before too long. When you are 45, it gets harder. At 50, it gets even harder.

Transitioning from attached to unattached

So between the two extremes of Mark and Nora, there is a middle road—the approach that works. The first step is to accept your new single status and learn to be alone. The next step is to establish a social life.

Before you step back out into the world, you need to become comfortable just being by yourself. If you are too needy or too unhappy, healthy people will feel uncomfortable around you and they'll run away. To attract healthy people, you have to first be and feel healthy and happy. Be sure you've read *Chapter 11—Loss & Letting Go* and are following those suggestions to speed your recovery. Review *Chapter 6—Happiness & Relationships* as well. Remember to see your psychologist to help you through the grieving process.

Stick your toe in the water first

When you feel up to it, start socializing with family and friends so you get out of the house. Don't worry about dating right now. Just renew acquaintances and friendships with your same-sex friends. People often lose touch with their friends when they're trying to save their marriage or care for an ailing spouse. Now's the time to revive those relationships.

Have lunch with a friend once a week or see supportive family members. Just remember to do what is good for your head. Don't see your most problematic friend and take on her problems right now. You need some inner peace and balance. Try to surround yourself with people who are positive and uplifting. If you don't feel good after seeing a particular friend, chances are this friend is not someone you should be seeing right now. Only see people you enjoy.

Then wade in a little

Once you're more comfortable with yourself and ready to establish a social life, start expanding the activities you do with your friends so you can meet new people. Develop a network of single friends who like to have a good time and are emotionally supportive. If you already have some single friends, they can help you ease into your new life by accompanying you to events and introducing you to their friends.

If you don't have any single friends, try some activities where you'll meet nice people of various ages, genders and marital status. You can develop new hobbies, take fun classes, do church and community events and activities for mixed groups. See **Chapter 2—Flirting & Dating** for more ideas. You're not really ready yet to start dating, so you don't need to restrict yourself to singles events. It's just important for you to get out of the house once a week and mix with people.

If you're still hurting a bit, explore any support groups that might help. Hospitals, churches and other community organizations often have groups to help those who have lost a loved one through death or divorce. You might also consider volunteering short-term; sometimes aiding others gets your mind off your troubles and helps you feel needed and appreciated.

Start swimming

When you've recuperated even more and feel ready to meet more single members of the opposite sex, start targeting your activities to that end.

Find out if your church has a singles group. If not, other churches in your community probably do, and you don't usually have to belong to the church to attend parties and socials for singles. Some churches even have groups divided by ages. If the nearby churches don't have singles events, find out what kind of events they do host and visit a few to see who attends. People who go to church singles groups are usually very pleasant, so this can be a way for you to ease into singles activities again. If you want to find out the sex and age range of people who tend to come to an event, just ask the organizers. They can usually tell you.

If you're a senior, check into seniors groups in your community. Many senior clubs get great discounts on trips, theater tickets and other activities. I once attended an Octoberfest with my mother's senior group, and I had a lot of fun! Seniors range in age from 50 years old and up, and many groups tend to attract lively, active people. It's often easy to meet people in such circumstances because there's no pressure to date.

As you develop new activities, interests and friends, you will come into contact with compatible members of the opposite sex. When you do, try to relax and be warm, upbeat, confident, and of course, fun to be with. In time, you should be ready to date again and able to find someone who is compatible.

Whatever you do, however, do not do fill your calendar with so many activities that you wear yourself out. The idea is to relax back into society, not go charging into it. Remember that this is only a transition stage, a time for you to explore new interests and begin building a new life.

There are usually a wealth of activities going on in any area. See **Chapter 2—Flirting & Dating** for more ideas about singles groups, dances and other activities specifically for singles that may be of interest to you, as well as tips on how to find such events.

So when should I start dating?

Dating before you file for divorce is premature, but it's fine to start dating after that—*provided* you can go on a date without crying and without talking about your estranged or deceased spouse.

If you can't, then you are not ready. Remember that your date is not your therapist. A date is a place to have fun with someone new. It is not a place to rehash your marriage, your breakup or your sadness about being widowed.

Nevertheless, you can start dating before you are fully over your divorce, breakup or death of your spouse. Although it will take two years or more to recover (less for a less traumatic breakup), you can make steady progress while you're dating. Getting out may even speed your recovery because it's difficult to fully heal from a divorce, serious breakup or death when you feel you have no other opportunities. Dating reminds you that life goes on and there are other options. It gives you opportunities and represents a positive step toward moving on with your life.

Reentering the dating game

When you begin dating, keep it casual. Don't sleep with anyone for awhile. Give yourself time to get to know different people on a relaxed, friendly basis. Get to know them as individuals, and learn more about what you need in a partner. See *Chapter 2—Flirting & Dating* to learn more about dating in general. Reading that chapter is particularly important if you have been married for a long time, since the dating world has probably changed a great deal from the way you remember it.

Ease yourself slowly into dating, just as you eased yourself slowly back into the world. It's a good idea to date two people casually at the same time, so that you can avoid getting too serious too soon. The last thing you want to do is quickly tie yourself down with someone and end up in a rebound relationship. If you feel a strong urge to become involved quickly, it's more likely to be driven by your dependency and a fear of being alone, rather than a true desire to be with that person. Continue to spend time with same-sex friends, pursue your own hobbies and adjust to being single.

When you find someone you like, enjoy the moment, but don't assume that the relationship's going to work out. Monitor your mood and your behavior frequently (the time right before you fall asleep is usually a good time), and be suspicious of any extreme feelings. Don't make any major decisions or jump into any relationships without talking them through in detail with your psychologist. Remember that your judgment may not be entirely back to normal yet.

Avoid the rebound relationship

There is no official definition of "rebound relationship." I use the term to describe an intense relationship that follows shortly after traumatic loss of a partner, before the person has had time to heal. What happens in that new relationship is greatly affected by the person's fragile, hurt state and needs at the moment, which will change as she continues to heal from the first relationship.

If you start a serious relationship too soon after you are divorced or widowed, you won't have a chance to resolve what happened in your last relationship before you begin the new one. That means you are more likely to choose someone problematic, either someone exactly like your ex or someone exactly the opposite. You may get involved with one of the first people you meet because you want the positive reinforcement and emotional support of having someone in your life again. It helps you feel better about yourself and life, and that is the overriding priority at the moment. But the relationship gets intense very quickly because you feel so needy. You're ready to push a square block into a round hole—just so you don't have to be alone anymore. You may then confuse the intense neediness with love, making the relationship progress very quickly.

If you then marry that person, you may find you are no longer compatible a few years down the road when you are feeling better about yourself and more independent. Now that your original needs, reassuring yourself that you're desirable and having someone around for companionship, have been filled, you notice incompatible traits in your partner that previously seemed unimportant. The man who seemed like a breath of fresh air after your husband's boring stodginess now seems flighty and immature. The take-charge man who originally gave you stability and emotional support now feels like he's trying to control you. The woman whose desire for nightly sex initially made you feel desired again now seems sexually demanding and tiring.

It's usually best not to marry anyone before you are at least two years past your divorce or spouse's death. During that time, you will change a great deal, and anyone you pick as your mate during this time may not be compatible when you finally stop changing. You may find yourself weathering the trauma of another divorce, prolonging the stress for you and your children.

When you're ready for another relationship

When you feel that you have healed sufficiently, are comfortable mixing with people, and are ready for serious dating with the objective of eventually finding a new partner, then you might want to consider meeting people through two direct methods: a quality introduction service and the personal ads.

These methods are the most efficient ways to meet people of the opposite sex who are looking for a serious relationship. They are a much more direct way of targeting available singles than any of the activities I've suggested in this chapter. You can join an introduction service or use the personal ads before you are totally ready to get married again, as it may take another year or two before you meet someone compatible. Be sure to read about these methods in Chapter 2, and also read *How To Choose A Dating Service* and *How To Date Through The Personal Ads* in the Appendix.

Keep your expectations realistic

Understanding what you're up against to find a mate is very important. Given the difference in mortality between men and women, the pool of available men slowly and gradually diminishes and the woman usually begins to feel the man shortage in her 40's and 50's. If you are an older woman, it's important to understand this age issue so you can have realistic expectations and use your opportunities wisely. The dating scene has changed quite a bit since you were younger; there simply aren't as many available men and you have to look harder.

I don't mean to imply that you have to settle for someone out of desperation, but for an older woman, it's important to recognize a diamond in the rough. Being understanding and working with such a man can produce good results and many more years of satisfying companionship, as Colleen discovered with Kevin.

Colleen & Kevin's Story

Kevin came to The Relationship Center™ six months after his wife died; he felt like he was ready to start dating and wanted to meet quality women. Being a social worker by profession, he was very much in touch with his feelings. I asked him several times if he felt ready to date, and he reassured me that he was. He also talked about his wife and her death without crying, and seemed to have a healthy attitude about dating, relationships and starting over.

We put Kevin into the introduction service and he began meeting single women. I soon received feedback from a few women who told me that Kevin had talked about his wife on their dates, and they felt he was still too consumed by his loss to be dating. They didn't want to fall in love with someone who was not ready to love back. Six months later, after meeting six women, Kevin asked to take a break. He'd decided that he wasn't as ready to meet people as he had thought. He needed time to get centered again, so we gave him the break he requested. Two years later, when I was matching an older woman, I thought about Kevin and gave him a call.

To my surprise and delight, Kevin had recently gotten married—to one of the women I had introduced him to! Colleen, his new wife, was one smart cookie. While she realized that Kevin was not completely ready to move on just yet when she first met him, she also saw that he had very good potential. She was willing to give him time and let the relationship grow. Colleen's tolerance and good judgment proved fortuitous. Kevin did progress and in time, fell in love and married her.

So the women who passed Kevin up had not acted in their best interest. They could have continued to date Kevin while seeing others as well. Instead, by being too impatient and critical, they passed up a truly remarkable man.

I don't mean to imply that a woman should date one man and pin all her hopes on him. Just as younger women should keep their options open, older women should definitely do the same. However, it's perfectly acceptable to occasionally date a man who may not be ready now, provided you also see others and pursue other options.

Recognize what's important

Our skill at reading people and our ability to see their negative characteristics tend to grow over time. Unfortunately, if you use this information incorrectly, in a judgmental way, it can greatly reduce your chances of finding a compatible mate. Now, with women who have a history of getting involved with controlling, negative or abusive men, getting pickier is a good thing.

However, for other women, being too selective can be a problem. It's important to remember that no one is perfect. You're not perfect, he's not perfect, and no two people are ever perfectly compatible. Emphasize the qualities that really matter and don't sweat the small stuff. Recognize the difference between workable qualities and incompatibilities.

So if you meet an honest, loyal, kind, and intellectually compatible man who wants to marry, don't give up on him if he dresses poorly or has different interests. You can help him dress once you get to know him better. You can expand your interests to include his, and he may be willing to participate in some of the activities you enjoy. Similarly, if the man has wonderful qualities, but is not yet over the recent death of his spouse, he may recover quite well in time. After all, you don't really want to marry a man who could be married for 30 years and then not feel anything when his wife dies, do you?

In contrast, if you want to get married, and you meet a man who is incredibly charming and witty, dresses beautifully, shares most of your interests, seems to be well past his divorce or the death of his spouse, but he doesn't *ever* want to get married again, he's a poor match. Similarly, a man who can't talk about his feelings or who lies to you is a poor candidate, no matter how charming, wealthy or well-dressed he is. On the other hand, a man who is a bit shy, but who tries to communicate and really reaches out to negotiate and compromise when you have differences may be a much better companion and mate, even if he is less charming and a little less fun.

To check your level of compatibility and communication with a significant someone, take *The Dr. Kate Compatibility Quiz* and *The Dr. Kate Communication Quiz* in the Appendix. In addition, read over *Chapter 3—Compatibility* to learn more about what's important and what isn't.

Help the kids through your transition

But what about the children? Many divorced and widowed people have an additional complication when they find themselves in the Starting Over Stage: their children. It is possible to date after your divorce or spouse's death without hurting your children or causing them to rebel. The key is to compartmentalize your life, keeping your dates out of your children's lives until you're fairly sure he's going to become your spouse.

The situation is similar to when you were young and brought your boyfriend or girlfriend home to meet your parents. Your parents automatically assumed the person was important and started their evaluation. When you're an adult with children and you bring a date home, the kids are going to think he's important. They may completely reject or quickly attach to your friend. If your children become attached to your new love, they will be upset if you break up. If you have several long-term relationships, when you finally do find the person you want to marry, your kids may not be able to attach at all. That's what happened to Paul and Allison.

Paul & Allison's Story

Paul married young and after 12 years, he and his wife divorced; their children were then 4 and 6. The kids lived with their mother during the week and saw their father on weekends and during the summers. Paul had several long-term (2 to 5-year) relationships that were fairly monogamous for as long as they lasted, and Paul included his girlfriends in activities with the kids. In addition, Paul lived with some of his girlfriends, and the kids stayed over with them during their visitations. As a result, the kids got to know each girlfriend pretty well.

However, as Paul broke up with each girlfriend, the kids had to readjust to someone new. Four girlfriends later, when Paul finally established a permanent relationship with Allison, the kids were not as loving or accepting as they had initially been. For the most part, they treated Allison as if she was nonexistent, and she found their disregard difficult to accept. Allison had always wanted a family and Paul didn't want to have more children. And now, because of their history with previous girlfriends, Paul's kids would never treat Allison like a real member of the family. The situation was unfortunate.

Keep your personal life separate until it's serious

In general, it's best to avoid introducing your kids to a significant love interest until you have set a date to be married. While this strategy may cause some inconvenience along the way, it shields your children from repeated episodes of attachment and loss. When you finally introduce the children to the person who is going to be your next spouse, they are free to get to know and love the person without having to worry about losing him. Although there's always the chance that the marriage could end, it's a much better bet than a dating or live-in situation.

Of course, the children can know you are dating, and you can introduce them to a *friend* on occasion if you've been dating for awhile and consider the relationship serious. You may want to have your friend over for holiday dinners, for example. But keep the contact brief and light. Do not interact on a regular basis or allow the children to participate in activities that will cause them to become attached. Don't allow your friend to sleep over. And never let your children see a succession of dates staying overnight at your house. If you do have a mix of sex partners over, don't be surprised if your children start acting out or hanging with a loose crowd. Remember, kids are very quick to hone in on any hypocrisy, and you teach more by your behavior than you words.

Even if your follow my advice to separate your love life from your children, you may experience a problem with a jealous child. He may fear losing your love, his status in the home or something else. Or he may be worried that the new person will disrupt the household in some other way.

Give your child lots of emotional support

One of the ways to make this situation better is to cultivate a healthy, thriving relationship with your children. Tell them often how much you love them and always will. Give hugs and kisses and listen to their problems with a loving, open mind. If you have more than one child, look for ways to spend time with each child separately, as well as all of them together. If your children react adversely to your divorce, waste no time in consulting a psychologist. Participate in family therapy sessions to strengthen your relationship with them and help them be happy.

Talk positively or neutrally about your ex in front of your children

Another way to help your children is to either say nothing or speak positively about your ex. Never badmouth him. Try to maintain a friendly enough relationship so you can confer amicably on issues concerning the children. You will have to discuss education, summers, holidays, health and a variety of issues over the years. The better you can get along, the better for your children.

Be the parent and an adult

Never rely on a child to be your therapist or best friend. Your child needs to be a child and you need to be the adult. See a psychologist for therapy and have an adult best friend. Similarly, don't live through your children or sacrifice your personal life for them. It's a burden your children should not have to bear.

Set a good example

Show a good example for your children. Model a balanced lifestyle for them. Taking some time for yourself is part of that good modeling.

What about your ex?

At *Love@AOL*, I receive many letters from people whose ex-spouses come around after the divorce and want to be involved in their lives again. Sometimes this situation occurs after an ex has had an affair, divorced, and then found that he made a mistake. Sometimes the ex is torn between the two people. Sometimes the ex realizes that he acted immaturely and the relationship you had was worth saving. Sometimes a spouse who was sick gets help and wants to return.

Should you consider becoming re-involved with your ex? The answer is: It depends on many factors.

If your spouse is contrite for something he did, such as cheating, you may want to consider forgiving and reuniting. If you have strong feelings for one another and want to reunite, you probably love one another very much and are highly compatible in many ways. If so, your problems are definitely worth fixing. However, I strongly recommend that you make seeing a psychologist a prerequisite to the reconciliation. Any couple that disagrees to the point that they divorce should never try to get back together without help. While the situation may be better for awhile simply because you miss one another, the old problems are still there. If you don't learn how to negotiate, compromise and fix the problems, you aren't likely to keep the relationship going very long this time around either.

If the spouse has a history of cheating, he has to make extensive behavioral changes, perhaps seeing a psychologist regularly for several years, going away with you to the country every other weekend, becoming more involved in the children's lives and becoming involved in church activities. The changes will be different for each person, but the bottom line is that for a cheating spouse to stay faithful, he has to show many behavioral changes over a period of time and establish a series of checks and balances to keep from acting on temptation.

If alcohol or drug abuse contributed to the divorce, the person must resolve the addiction problems for the relationship to work. Most addicted people need to go through at least one organized (usually inpatient) treatment program, then attend AA meetings, see a psychologist for ongoing therapy and have some kind of checks and balances in place to stay sober. While it takes considerable effort, cheating and addiction problems can be fixed if you and your spouse are committed to their resolution.

In contrast, some disorders are so severe that I do not recommend risking another try at marriage: physical abuse, especially over a period of time, and sexual abuse of a child. If a woman who has separated from her abusive husband reunites with him and he has a relapse, the violence could escalate to an even more serious level—and could even be fatal. See *Chapter 11—Letting Go* for more on physical and sexual abuse.

Sex with your ex

Sometimes ex-spouses want to have sex because they are both sexually frustrated and feel that they pose no risk of disease to one another. But before you consent to a sexual relationship with your ex, you need to consider several factors.

First, you don't really know that your ex-spouse is disease-free. While the risk may be lower because he's had fewer sexual partners over the past 10 years while married to you, if he has slept with anyone else before or since the divorce, there is still some risk.

You also need to be honest with yourself about the reason the two of you are sleeping together. For example, if he is sleeping with you because he's sexually needy and currently doesn't have anyone else to have sex with, and you are sleeping with him because you're secretly hoping he'll come back, you're setting yourself up for a lot of disappointment and hurt feelings. When he eventually finds someone else and feels strong enough to move on, you will have to go through the breakup all over again.

If both of you have reached the stage of being just friends and are sleeping together until you find other mates, that arrangement could work for a time. However, it's rare for a woman to be able to separate love and sex in that fashion. That difference between men and women and how they view sex could lead to problems; see *Chapter 4—Sex!* for more on this.

If you have children, they will be very confused, and probably very happy, when Dad comes back to the house and sleeps over. Then if the two of you split up, the kids may feel traumatized all over again. Similarly, it's best not to inform your relatives and extended family. By the time you're divorced, they generally feel animosity toward your ex or at least concern for your welfare. So, if you're thinking of reuniting with your spouse, keep it between the two of you and your psychologist, and work through your issues without the outside pressure of having to answer to your children, your parents or your extended family.

Finally, keep in mind that staying involved with your ex may cause you to delay looking for a more suitable partner. If your relationship with your ex is progressing well in therapy, fine. However, if your ex just drops by periodically and messes with your mind every time, it's not healthy to continue allowing it. He should either work on the relationship problems with you through regular, ongoing couples' therapy, or you should decide to keep the separation in place and not see one another.

It's important that you see people who are healthy for you. If you can see your spouse and still give other possible mates consideration, fine. If you can't, then know your limitations. Either work intensely on your relationship or break it off and pursue other options.

Real-life Love@AOL letters about starting over

AOL members write me frequently on the topic of starting over. Here are some of my favorites.

Trying-to-date dad

MY AGE: 44 MY GENDER: MALE

Dear Dr. Kate,
I've been divorced almost four years, and am now ready to get back into the flow of things. I have full custody of my two children. My 13-year-old girl is fine with me dating. She gave me a shirt that says, "Trust me, I'm single," as a way of telling me "OK, Dad, I'm ready for you to start going out." However, my 10-year-old boy says he's OK with it, but acts up really badly whenever a female he thinks I'm interested in is around. Help!

Dear Divorced, Trying-to-Date Dad,
It's one thing for kids to conceptually agree that it's OK for you to date, but it's entirely another for them to emotionally accept it. Sometimes girls accept such a situation faster because they are more interested in romance themselves and can identify with the need to be loved by the opposite sex. Your boy is younger and may not be able to empathize as much. He may also feel disloyal to his mother when he interacts with one of your dates.

In general, it's just much better not to introduce the kids to your dates. Don't lie about what you are doing, but don't tell them any details either. You can tell them you have plans for the evening and the time you will be back. Get a pager, give them the number, and be prepared to be interrupted the first few times you go out. Try going out with male friends first and intermittently, so that *having plans* could mean seeing friends, having a business meeting, visiting a relative, having a date—basically, anything that isn't any of their business.

You could also allow your kids to visit their friends for sleepovers on certain nights, and take turns having those friends over to allow their parents to date each other as well. This makes it more fun for the teens and you.

Be sure to give your son and daughter quality time on the same weekend you have your first dates, so they don't feel neglected. Expect that it may take some time for your son to accept that you are going out without him. You should only introduce the woman as a *friend* to your kids when you have been seeing her a few times per week for at least three to five months, and are serious about her. Even then, limit the contact you all have together until you are quite sure that you will marry. Then gradually increase the time you spend together, so that your kids can learn to love your fiancée and vice versa.

Best Wishes, and please let me know how you're doing from time to time,

Dr. Kate

Widow wants nice man... MY AGE: 44 MY GENDER: FEMALE

Dear Dr. Kate,
I lost my husband three years ago. I never dated much before my husband because my father was ill. My husband was not very nice to me, except on rare occasions. I stayed with him because we had four children and because he became ill, and I just could not leave him that way. Where can I find someone who is really nice in today's world?

Dear Someone Who's Not Been Around!,
There are at least three issues of importance here:

1. It sounds like you may have some hook from your past that causes you to choose difficult men. The fact that you didn't date because your dad was ill and then you sacrificed again because your husband was ill just tells me that you need to be careful that the next man you choose doesn't require another sacrifice. It's time to enjoy your life. You have a responsibility to choose someone who is healthy, but that may be emotionally difficult for you when the time comes.

2. You need to know where to look for a nice man.

3. You need to know how to recognize one when you find him.

Take The **Dr. Kate Compatibility Quiz** for your husband to explore the ways you and he were and were not compatible. Also take **The Dr. Kate Communication Quiz** to learn more about how you communicated and ways it could have been better.

Then run a **Love@AOL** Photo Personal and specify that you are looking for a man who is interested in a healthy marriage. Skim those in your geographic area for men who seem compatible, but stick with single, emotionally available men who also desire marriage. Even though you may not be ready for marriage just yet, you don't want to date men who don't desire marriage.

Also, interview several introduction services and choose the one that feels most comfortable to you. Pick a smaller, more personal matchmaking service that caters to people who want marriage, and where you will have frequent interaction (and a lot of input into the process) with the person who matches you.

For each man you meet, take **The Dr. Kate Compatibility Quiz** and compare them. Before long, you should be able to tell the differences between men. Don't get sexually involved with anyone until you have dated him several times weekly for at least three to four months, are in love with him and he with you, and he is willing to say so outside the bedroom.

Take it slowly. If you become confused, pick men who seem fine and later aren't, or if you feel that you are following the same pattern you had with your father and husband, then consult a psychologist to explore those issues further.

Best Wishes! And please keep me posted on your progress,

Dr. Kate

Exercises to help you start over

1. **Re-Examine Your Relationship History.** Review your notes from *Chapter 1— Getting Grounded* and *Chapter 3—Compatibility.* If you've been attracted to a particular kind of partner that hasn't worked out for you, how will you identify and avoid this type of person in the future? What were the early signs? How can you recognize those signs more quickly in the future? Now that you will be out and about and meeting new people, what are the most important things for you to remember so that those experiences will be positive and healthy for you? Write your answers in your Relationship Notebook.

   Don't blame yourself for anything. Just tell yourself what you will do *differently* in the future: *"Okay, now in the future, I will do _____ instead."* Be sure to write down your solutions and memorize them.

   Once you begin meeting people, do a quick mental check of the people you're dating to be sure they're really healthy choices for you.

2. **Change Negative Self-Talk To Positive Affirmations.** When you find yourself thinking negatively about yourself, write down the thoughts. Next to each irrational thought, write a rational thought. For example, if you write, "I'm lousy at relationships, I'll never find a decent guy," a rational replacement would be, *"I'm learning about my relationships. In the future, I will make better choices."* Each time you get a self-denigrating thought, say, *"Stop it!"* and tell yourself a rational thought, along with one of your positive qualities from your Chapter 11 list.

3. **Keep An Activity File.** How far along are you in the recovery process? What kinds of activities are you ready for? Research those in your area and keep information on any you want to attend.

Appendices

P.S.

Now use what you've learned!

Remember, *life is a series of relationship stages.* No matter what relationship stage you find yourself in at the moment, always look at the big picture. If you don't like the stage you're in now, do the work and progress to the stage you'd like to be in. If you do like where you are now, do the work to make it last as long as possible. You can be happy, no matter what relationship stage you find yourself in. And remembering that fact can make your life far more joyous and fun. Take a few moments now and maximize what you've learned by doing a few more exercises:

Exercises to maximize what you've learned in this book

1. **Review, Summarize And Remember.** Given everything you've learned from reading this book, what behaviors are most important for you to remember? List these in your Relationship Notebook. Every month, review your list and see how well you're doing. If something is falling through the cracks, review that chapter again. If you continue to have problems, see a psychologist to explore why—and how to fix it.

2. **Make A Plan.** Write your relationship, life and personal goals in your notebook, with realistic time frames. Where do you want to be in 5, 10 and 20 years? Review your list monthly to stay on track. It's perfectly OK to change your mind about some of your goals. But be *proactive* and *choose* the changes, rather than just reacting as life happens to you.

3. **Keep Reading And Learning.** If you have America Online, go to *AOL Keyword: Dr. Kate* and read more about any of the topics in this book, as well as many others. The site includes thousands of letters I have answered from AOL members on the topics of dating, sex, marriage, relationship problems, cheating, breaking up, divorce, losing a spouse and online/offline considerations. There's even a separate file for problems that don't fit into any of the above! You can browse through files of letters or use the search function to find letters about specific topics.

You can write me a letter there (use the form on that site), asking me about your individual problem. I post responses to select letters at the site and if yours is chosen, also send one to your individual email address. You can take *The Dr. Kate Compatibility Quiz* and *The Dr. Kate Communication Quiz* interactively as well. There's a link to my web page (http://www.therelationshipcenter.com), where you can learn about The Relationship Center™, take our most recent poll and see results of previous polls. There are also links to *Love@AOL* (Keyword: Love@AOL), where you can interact with other people through chats, games and the *Love@AOL* Photo Personals (Keyword: Photo Personals), the largest collection of personals online.

If you don't have AOL, you can still access my web page at ***http://www.therelationshipcenter.com*** and ***Love@AOL*** Photo Personals at http://www.love.com. But why not get AOL instead, and be able to use all the functions and activities of the Dr. Kate site and ***Love@AOL?***

If you're in the Chicago area and would like a private appointment for therapy or the introduction service, call *The Relationship Center™ at 312-337-3377.* To inquire about upcoming *Dr. Kate Seminars in your area, call 1-800-460-8604.*

If you find that my words have benefited you and would like to tell me your story, write to me at ***relationshipctr@aol.com*** or in care of my publisher, Paper Chase Press. I probably won't be able to answer any letters sent there personally, but if I think others might benefit from your experience, I might just publish your letter in an upcoming book!

I had a great time being with you, and hope you'll be able to use what I've written to enrich your life.

Best Wishes Always,
Dr. Kate

DR. KATE'S LOVE WORKSHOPS

Dr. Kate's informative and inspiring workshops are presented nationwide in select cities.

Explore The Love Cycle and your stage in it with Love@AOL's Love Doctor. Each workshop will provide the opportunity to join in open question and answer sessions, break out groups, and personal one-on-one attention with Dr. Kate Wachs.

To find out when Dr. Kate will arrive in your city to conduct a workshop, call **800.460.8604.**

To have Dr. Kate speak at your upcoming function, call **800.460.8604.**

Check out Dr. Kate on the Internet!

AOL or Love@AOL.com — *Keyword:* Dr. Kate
therelationshipcenter.com

Discover your Date IQ Quiz

What kind of dater are you? Pick the best answer to the following questions. When asked about your behavior, choose the answer that comes *closest* to accurately describing your *usual* behavior, even if you know that another answer would be more appropriate. For #9-11, answer the question corresponding to your sex. When you're finished, turn the page to score yourself.

1. When I first meet someone I'm interested in, I *usually*: (Choose 1.)
   a. Wait until he asks me out first.
   b. Take the bull by the horns and ask him out.
   c. Wait until we get to know one another as friends before even thinking about dating this person.
   d. Ask something like, "If I were to ask you out, would you say, 'Yes?'"

2. On a *first* date, I *usually:* (Choose 1.)
   a. Keep it casual and light.
   b. Hate small talk, so I tend to get the details of his personal life.
   c. Just talk about whatever I feel like at the moment. After all, that's honesty.
   d. Try to make sure my date is having a good time.

3. The purpose of the *first* date is: (Choose 1.)
   a. For me and my date to have fun.
   b. To get a second date.
   c. To explore each other and see if we're compatible.
   d. To take a break from my boring life.

4. In general, which of the following are most appropriate for the *first* date? (Choose 1.)
   a. Working out at the gym.
   b. Dancing at a trendy nightclub.
   c. A quiet dinner where we can hear each other talk.
   d. A strip joint.

5. In general, which of the following topics are INappropriate for a *first* date? (Choose 1.)
   a. Money.
   b. Why you or your date is still single.
   c. Details of your recent surgery.
   d. Your divorce.
   e. Your date's divorce.
   f. Dating services and personal ads.
   g. All of the above.
   h. None of the above.
   i. A and C.

6. When on a date, I *typically*: (Choose 1.)
    a. Ask penetrating questions to stimulate conversation.
    b. Talk only about things I wouldn't mind seeing in 4"-high letters on the cover of the *New York Times* the next day.
    c. Talk about myself, and allow my date to share whatever he wants about himself.
    d. Refrain from asking questions, in case I might accidentally touch on a sensitive subject.

7. Who *usually* pays for the date? (Choose 1.)
    a. The man always pays.
    b. Whoever asked the other person out.
    c. Whoever makes the most money.
    d. They split the tab.
    e. The woman pays her own tab if she doesn't want another date with the man, so he won't feel badly when she tells him.

8. What do you *usually* wear on a date? (Choose 1.)
    a. Something that fits my mood that day.
    b. Something that fits the activity and weather.
    c. Something that looks good, feels good and smells good.
    d. Something that is in sync with what my date will be wearing.
    e. Nothing too revealing or seductive.
    f. B and C.
    g. All of the above.

9M. (FOR MEN) When do you *usually* arrive to pick up your date? (Choose 1.)
    a. On time.
    b. A little (less than 5-10 minutes) early.
    c. A little (less than 5-10 minutes) late.
    d. She usually picks me up or meets me there.
    e. More than 10 minutes early.
    f. More than 10 minutes late.

9W. (FOR WOMEN) What best describes your *usual* behavior? (Choose 1.)
    a. I'm ready on time.
    b. I'm ready 5-10 minutes early.
    c. I'm dressing or busy when he arrives, so I invite him to sit down and relax while I finish.
    d. I'm running late, so I telephone and rearrange the time.
    e. I'm ready at least 15-30 minutes early.

10M. (FOR MEN) What best describes your *typical* behavior on a date? (Choose all that apply.)

a. I offer to pick her up.
b. I open most doors for her, and let her walk in first.
c. I bring flowers or a gift to the first date.
d. I help her off with her coat before taking mine off; I help her on with her coat before putting mine on.
e. I pull out her chair and push it in under her.
f. When we are dining in a more expensive restaurant and she goes to the Ladies Room, I stand up when she comes back to the table and readjust her chair.
g. I let her order dinner first.
h. I stay with her when crossing a street, and walk near her down the sidewalk.
i. I make friends with the doorman while waiting for her to come down.
j. I take her hand when in a crowd so we don't get separated.
k. I ask her if she wants to order a drink or appetizer.
l. I ask her if she likes the table, and if not, offer to summon the waiter to change it. If I see that the table is not conducive for conversation, I summon the waiter and politely ask for another.
m. I like to people watch.
n. If it's raining or snowing, I drop her off at the restaurant door before I go park the car.
o. I walk on the side of the sidewalk closest to the street.
p. I offer to carry any packages she has.
q. I pick up the tab.
r. I give good eye contact.
s. I answer my cellular phone or pager during dinner.
t. I listen carefully to her conversation, and try to compliment her when it's appropriate.
u. I sometimes ogle other women when they walk by.
v. I try to show her a fun time.
w. I try to tell her my worst qualities, to make sure she'll accept me.
x. I try to engage in challenging conversation that demonstrates my strengths.
y. I comb my hair in such a way as to cover my bald spot.
z. I drive her home and wait for her to get in the door before leaving.

10W. (FOR WOMEN) What best describes your *typical* behavior on a date?
(Choose all that apply.)
  a. I introduce the man to my family when he comes to pick me up for the first date.
  b. I try to make myself look as attractive and pleasing as possible.
  c. I don't like when a man opens doors or helps me on and off with my coat,
     so I hurry up and do it myself before he gets the chance.
  d. I thank him when he performs any helpful gestures (e.g., opening the car door,
     helping me on and off with my coat, offering to carry packages).
  e. I usually laugh nervously or say, 'What are you doing?" when a man tries to
     perform chivalrous gestures.
  f. If we are going through two doors and my date has opened the first one for me,
     I open the next one, walk through it and hold it for him.
  g. I invite the man into my apartment for a drink before going out to our first date.
  h. I give good eye contact.
  i. I concentrate on what's right about him, rather than dwelling on what I don't like.
  j. If he's treating me, I try to order food that's more intermediate in price.
  k. I invite the man into my apartment for a drink after our first date.
  l. I offer to pay the tip or parking charge.
  m. I offer to split the tab.
  n. I pick up the tab if I invited him out.
  o. I compare him to my favorite ex-boyfriend in my mind.
  p. I jump if he tries to touch my hand or arm.
  q. I try to show him a fun time.
  r. I thank him for inviting me.
  s. I listen carefully to his conversation, and try to compliment him when it's appropriate.
  t. I try not to spend too much time in the Ladies Room when I know he's waiting for me.
  u. I try to put my best foot forward.
  v. I ask about his relationship goals, e.g., if he wants to get married or have
     kids someday, so I'll know if he's husband material.
  w. If I don't like him, I try to say things I know he won't like, so he won't try
     to ask me out again and then I won't have to hurt his feelings.
  x. I smile at him frequently, and try to make him feel comfortable.
  y. I try to switch places with him in my mind, and be understanding and supportive.
  z. I tend to talk about my past relationships and ask him about his.

11M. (FOR MEN) At the end of the first date, I *usually*: (Choose all that apply.)
  a. Tell my date if I enjoyed her and ask if I can call again.
  b. Tell her I'll call her, even if I have no intentions of doing so.
  c. Say, "Thank you," and make no mention of future plans if I didn't enjoy
     her company and don't intend to call her again.
  d. If I really enjoyed the date, try to extend it for as long as possible by
     suggesting other activities.
  e. Try to have sex or at least some heavy necking and petting.

11W. (FOR WOMEN) At the end of the first date, I *usually*: (Choose all that apply.)
   a. Thank him for taking me to dinner (or whatever the activity was).
   b. If he asks me out and I don't want to go, I accept anyway, but ask him to call back to confirm on a certain night. Then I don't pick up my phone that night.
   c. If he asks me out again, and I don't want to go, I say, "No," and tell him why he's not compatible with me.
   d. Drive myself home.
   e. Have sex or at least some heavy necking and petting.

12. With regard to touching and other physical signs of affection on the first date, I *usually:* (Choose 1.)
   a. Touch hands occasionally during dinner when speaking and gesturing, and shake hands at the end of the night, but do not kiss.
   b. Sit close, hold hands, get into some heavy petting at the end of the first date.
   c. Often have sex on the first date, especially if I like my date and intend to see him again.
   d. Often have sex on the first date, regardless of whether I like the person or not.
   e. Try to pace any touching, kissing, etc., with the length of the relationship and depth of my feelings for the person and vice versa.
   f. Just go with the flow.

13. On subsequent dates, I *usually:* (Choose all that apply.)
   a. Drop the façade and let myself just be me.
   b. Continue to try to show him a good time.
   c. Open up very quickly once I know I've gotten past the first hurdle.
   d. Stay positive.
   e. Pace my self-disclosures based on the length of our relationship and the level of mutual trust.

14. On subsequent dates, I *usually:* (Choose 1.)
   a. Try to vary our activities, so we don't do the same things all the time.
   b. Rely on him to plan the activities.
   c. Am a creature of habit. I like doing the same things most of the time.
   d. Go with the flow.
   e. Am pretty spontaneous, and dislike planning dates in advance.

15. As our relationship progresses, I *usually:* (Choose 1.)
   a. Go to his house or vice versa, rather than going out on dates.
   b. Visit friends with him or double-date.
   c. Include my kids, rather than going out alone.
   d. Continue to plan special dates for the two of us.
   e. Don't really pay much attention to our dates.

Congratulations! You have finished the questionnaire. Now, turn to the next page to score your answers.

Scoring for Discover Your Date IQ Quiz

Score your responses by drawing a circle around the answer you chose.

1		a -1; b +2; c -1; d -1
2		a +1; b 0; c -1; d +1
3		a +1; b 0; c -1; d -2
4		a 0; b +1; c +2; d -4
5		a +1; b +1; c +1; d +1; e +1; f +1; g +6; h -6; i +2
6		a -1; b +1; c 0; d -1
7	M	a +1; b +1; c -1; d -4; e -1
	W	a -2; b +1; c +1; d -4; e -1
8		a +1; b +1; c +1; d +1; e +1; f +2; g +5
9	M	a +1; b +1; c +1; d -2; e -2; f -2
	W	a +1; b +1; c -2; d -2; e +2
10	M	a +1; b +1; c -1; d +1; e +1; f +1; g +1; h +1; i -1; j +1; k +1; l +1; m -1; n +1; o +1; p +1; q +1; r +1; s -3; t +5; u -5; v +5; w -5; x -3; y -4; z +1
	W	a -1; b +3; c -1; d +1; e -1; f +1; g +1; h -1; i +1; j +3; k +1; l -3; m +1; n -1; o +2; p -3; q -2; r +2; s +1; t +3; u +1; v +1; w -4; x -2; y +3; z -4
11	M	a +1; b -5; c +1; d -1; e -5
	W	a +1; b -4; c -2; d -1; e -4
12		a +1; b 0; c -2; d -5; e +2; f -2
13		a -1; b +1; c -1; d +1-2; e +2
14		a +2; b -2; c -2; d -2; e -2
15		a -2; b -2; c -2; d +5; e -2
Write your total plus points here		
Write your total minus points here		
Subtract (Plus Points – Minus Points)		
Add 50		+50
Total Date IQ score		

Now, see the following pages to Discover Your Date IQ!

Results for Discover Your Date IQ Quiz
If you scored:

+100 to +111 POINTS = Dater with finesse

Congratulations! You have pretty much mastered the fine art of dating. (Or else you haven't been completely honest in the way you've answered the questions!) You usually conduct yourself with social skills and grace when dating, at least in the early days. If you are experiencing difficulty in your relationships, the problem is likely to stem from other problems, not your dating acumen.

If you are not succeeding with your relationships, you may be picking incompatible people (see *Chapter 3—Compatibility).* Or you may be experiencing difficulty in keeping the communication going (see *Chapter 7—Communication),* or in moving the relationship to the next level (see *Chapter 5—Making A Commitment).* Or you may be taking your partner for granted and cheating on him, ruining a good relationship (see *Chapter 10—Tough Times).* But whatever the case, the problem is not due to your dating acumen per se.

Perhaps you are just not dating enough people to be able to find a compatible partner. If so, do Exercises 3 and 4 in *Chapter 2—Flirting & Dating,* and read *How To Choose A Dating Service* and *Dating Through The Personal Ads* in the Appendix. If you're not ready to find a relationship because you're recently divorced or widowed, read *Chapter 12—Starting Over,* for more tips.

+80 to +99 POINTS = A good dater, but still fine-tuning

You usually conduct yourself fairly well on a date, but need a little fine-tuning to present yourself at your best. You may have acquired some bad dating habits along the way, or perhaps it's been a long time since you've dated. Be sure to read Chapter 2 thoroughly, and try Exercise 1 at the end. If there's any behavior (e.g., talking positively) that you find especially difficult, you can roleplay it first with a friend, as described in Exercise 2. Or if you think just bringing it to your attention and remembering to do it on dates will help, try practicing one or two each time on a real date. Write a note to yourself before the date reminding yourself which behaviors you'll work on this time, and after your date, review your behavior mentally to see how you did. Keep doing this until you are able to retake the *Discover Your Date IQ Quiz* and score in the category above.

If you need more dating candidates, do Exercises 3 and 4, and read *How To Choose A Dating Service* and *Dating Through The Personal Ads* in the Appendix.

+46 to +79 POINTS = An average dater, but still learning

Some of your dating behaviors are probably appreciated, but others probably are not. Read *Chapter 2—Flirting & Dating,* and then practice the exercises at the end. Do Exercise 1 first, using this quiz to make a list of the behaviors you need to improve. Then rank order each behavior depending on how hard you think it will be to learn. Do Exercise 2 to roleplay these behaviors. If you find the behaviors lower on the list easier to do, you can try roleplaying several at a time until you master them together. Then add one new behavior and try again. If you find any behavior especially difficult to remember (e.g., remaining positive), be sure to practice that behavior in a concentrated fashion before trying to join it with others in your roleplays or on real dates.

Once you feel comfortable that you can do the behaviors in private, try Exercises 3 and 4, and practice the behaviors on real dates. You may want to list the behaviors on a small card you carry to the date in your wallet or purse, and look at it when you visit the restroom. Doing so can help remind you to alter your date behavior accordingly.

Wait a few months, then try taking the **Discover Your Date IQ Quiz** again. If you realize that you have forgotten to do any of the behaviors, it should be much easier to relearn them again!

+10 to +45 POINTS = A fair dater

You probably feel like you have a lot to learn about dating, but don't worry, Rome wasn't built in a day. It takes time to learn any new skill, and as long as you are reading this book, you are going in the right direction! Perhaps it's been a long time since you've dated, or maybe you've never really dated. Whatever the case, read **Chapter 2—Flirting & Dating,** then do the exercises at the end. Start with Exercise 1, making a list of the behaviors you need to improve, and rank ordering them in terms of how difficult you think they will be to learn. Then practice the roleplays in Exercise 2 until you have mastered all these behaviors during roleplay. Try using videotape (preferably) or audiotape, so that you can see what you are doing after you roleplay with your friend. Be sure to keep a copy of your first roleplay and review it periodically, so that you can see how much progress you're making. (A little positive reinforcement does wonders for motivation!)

Once you have mastered all the behaviors together, try Exercises 3 and 4 and practice doing those same behaviors on dates.

Wait a few months and then take the **Discover Your Date IQ Quiz** again. See how you score this time. If there is still anything you have forgotten, try making another list, and keep practicing on each date until you have mastered all of them and your dates are going well. If anyone refuses to date you again, ask why and use that information to improve your next dating experience.

BELOW 0 (-15) to +9 POINTS = A struggling dater

You've got a ways to go to be a good date. However, you've already bought this book, so you are on your way! Read **Chapter 2—Flirting & Dating,** then practice Exercises 1 at the end. Use this quiz to make a list of all the behaviors you need to improve. Then choose one behavior to work on each time you do the roleplays described in Exercise 2 with a trusted, confidential friend. Have your friend read this chapter as well, so that she'll know how to roleplay and what to look for in your behavior.

Keep practicing each new behavior until you have mastered it. Then try another. At the same time, remember to do the other behavior you have just mastered. Keep doing this until you can do all the behaviors well during roleplays. Then try practicing those behaviors on real dates.

If possible, try videotaping or audiotaping your roleplays. Replay the tape to learn how to improve your behavior. You'll probably notice things you didn't think you were doing! Keep a copy of the first videotape you make, and review it from time to time as you progress, so you can see your progress and be encouraged!

Don't be discouraged if it takes awhile to learn all the behaviors. In order to improve, you'll need to practice regularly. So, after you have mastered the roleplays with a friend, try to use the personal ads or a dating service as described in Exercises 3 and 4, so you can locate enough dating candidates.

If possible, join a dating service that gives its members feedback. That way, you can also find out how you have been doing on your dates. When someone doesn't want to see you again, ask why. Try to use that feedback, if you feel it's helpful, on your next date.

Try to imagine yourself from your date's perspective as well. Imagine that you are him and he is you. How would you want to be treated in that situation? Doing this exercise frequently should help you consider others' feelings in most situations, including dating. You should find that as you continue to change places with others in your mind, you become better and better at it.

Just take it slow, don't be discouraged, think positive and keep plugging!!! Once you've done what you can, take a break for a few months, then take the *Discover Your Date IQ Quiz* again. See how you do! Any behaviors you have forgotten should be easier to relearn this time. Keep working on your dating skills in this fashion until you are able to score in one of the top two categories on this quiz.

How to date through the personal ads

1. I recommend running an ad rather than answering them, since the response is generally better. ***Online:*** If you have Internet access and would like to meet through Internet personals, I recommend the ***Love@AOL*** Photo Personals, the largest collection of online personal ads. It's fast and free and offers some back-up against people who might harass you. If you have AOL, go to Keyword: Personals; if not, go to http://www.love.com.

    Offline: If you don't have Internet access or just prefer using offline personal ads, I recommend a newspaper that will allow you to receive both written and voice responses. Read the ads there first to see if opposite-sex people similar to those you'd like to meet actually place ads there. Newspapers are usually cheaper and faster than magazines.

2. ***Online:*** Set up a separate screen name that you won't mind changing if you want to avoid someone in the future. Do ***NOT*** use a name that includes your real name or your master account name, which cannot be changed. ***Both Online & Offline:*** Identify which phone number you're going to use. If it's listed, get a new number, pager or cell phone that is ***NOT*** listed. Do ***NOT*** use a listed phone number.

3. Read some ads to learn what goes in them. Then write your ad. Include some adjectives that describe your personality (playful, fun, intelligent) and adjectives that describe the kind of person you seek (responsible, monogamous). Or just describe yourself and note that you want someone similar. ***Online:*** The ***Love@AOL*** Photo Personals form will take you step-by-step through the ad-writing process.

4. Be sure to include your relationship goal. If you're looking for marriage and kids, say so. Do not give out your income, any information that could be used to identify you, a female weight over 120 or a male weight under 170. Do not talk about sex.

5. Try to make your ad stand out. If you're funny, use your humor. If you're not, try to say something in a more poignant or romantic way. Be friendly and upbeat. ***Offline:*** Include, "All written responses will be answered," and you should receive more responses.

6. Have a single, opposite-sex platonic friend review the ad and make suggestions.

7. Place your ad. ***Offline:*** If you will be retrieving phoned-in responses, get an answering machine that allows for 2-way conversation recording. Then record the voice message responses as you retrieve them so you can review them later and take notes.

8. **Online:** Use a photo for your AOL Photo Personal and you'll probably get a lot more responses. Choose a recent color photo that shows you smiling and at your best.

9. **Offline:** Respond to all written responses if you said you would. If you're not interested, just drop a friendly note, thanking the person for writing (do not include your return address).

10. **Online:** Chat with interesting respondents online for awhile. **Both Online & Offline:** Don't give out your last name or phone number right away. The woman should get the man's number first. If your city has a "name and address service" number, call the number, dial in his number and find out what name and address are listed to his phone number. If he seems legitimate, call him. But press *67 first, so that your number will not show on his caller ID. **Offline:** Women should stay on the phone for at least an hour to get to know him better before deciding to meet in person. **Online:** If you've already been chatting, it doesn't have to be that long, but do get to know him better before meeting him. **Both Online & Offline:** Don't give him your identifying data (last name, address, where you work) until/unless you do feel more comfortable. Remember, once he has the information, you can't take it back. If you do decide to give him a phone number, use an unlisted number, pager or cell phone, so he can't find your address the same way you found his. Men don't need to be as cautious, but do take some care, or someone may show up unexpectedly at your front door— or at work!

11. **Both Online & Offline:** If you decide to meet, get together in daylight in a public place where there are many people around, and where you can easily leave if you so desire (e.g., a busy restaurant for Sunday brunch). Be sure you have transportation there and back and plenty of money. Keep the first meeting short (a few hours), not all day or all weekend. You can take a friend with you or meet in a group setting. If you go alone, tell a girlfriend where you'll be. Arrange to call in once from your date and when you're finished. Give her your date's name, address, phone and any other information you have; tell her about when to expect your call at the end of the date to say that everything went fine. Be sure to do this as extra security if you meet in another city.

12. Get yourself home after your date. Listen to your gut when you are out. If you don't feel comfortable about your date in any way, excuse yourself and leave earlier.

13. Keep in mind you don't really know this person yet. You can meet honest and dishonest people online and off. You are meeting a stranger, and you need to trust gradually and slowly, as you see that he is worthy of your trust. See the circles of relationship stages in **Chapter 2.** Remember to start on the outermost ring of **Strangers,** and only move inward slowly as you learn that he is worthy of your trust. If you have good people sense, listen to your intuition. (If you don't have at least fairly good people sense, common sense and judgment, or if you

tend to have bad luck with people using you, don't use the personals of any kind, online or off!) If something doesn't seem to fit the story or if you become uneasy, don't continue. At least figure out if the uneasiness is because there is something about this person that doesn't jive, or if you're uneasy because you're new at meeting this way.

14. If you meet someone in a different city, book and pay for your own hotel and flight arrangements. Do not stay with your new date. Bring plenty of money, so you aren't dependent on him in any way. You can certainly see each other more than once a weekend if you travel to meet each other, but don't spend every moment of every day together. It's just too much too soon, and that can kill any budding relationship. For the same reason, don't sleep together or invite him to your place or hotel room the first time you meet.

15. Don't be too invested in pleasing him, and keep your expectations in check. Remember, if it doesn't work, it just means the two of you aren't compatible. Also, don't see so many people that you burn out on dating. It takes time to meet this way, so be sure to pace yourself!

16. Finally, a few cautions from *Love@AOL*:

"DON'T believe everything you read...Remember that the person at the other end may not be who they say they are. DON'T respond to any correspondence that's lewd or crude or in any way makes you feel uncomfortable. AOL offers you the option of Mail Controls, which allow you to block unwanted mail and attached files, among other options." They also add that you should forward any obscene emails and IMs (Instant Messages) by using Keyword: Notify AOL," and they will take appropriate action.

See *Chapter 2—Flirting & Dating,* for more on using the personal ads to meet people.

How to choose a dating service

Questions to ask before you sign

1. To find services in your area, check the Internet, *Yellow Pages* and any singles publications and city magazines. Ask services you call where they advertise, and then check those publications for more services. Choose four to call and visit.

2. Before you visit the service, call on the phone: *"What kind of programs do you have? How much do they cost? What age range, profession, education, religion, etc., are your members? Please describe the range of your members."* Avoid services that will not give you a price or price range over the phone before you come in for an interview, or before asking what your income is. They should be willing to describe their programs over the phone, and be able to tell you the parameters of their membership (age range, education, professions, religions, races, relationship goals, what members are looking for, why they use service). If they won't answer these questions, don't visit.

3. *"How many members do you have? Percentage male vs. females? What steps do you take to make sure you have enough men and women at different ages to accommodate your members?"* I suggest 1000-2000 members with equal males-females at all levels. More than 2000 members is not personal; less than 1000 is too small for much compatibility. If they quote you a very large number, it's either bogus or they're quoting national figures, not how many members are available as potential matches for you.

4. *"Who does the matching? His credentials? What makes that person competent to match me?"* If not the interviewer: *"How can that person match me when he's not interviewing me?"* The person interviewing you should be matching you. It's almost impossible to match anyone without interviewing them first. Look for someone who seems interested in you personally, not just for the money you bring in.

5. *"On what variables will I be matched?"* Beware those promising to match you within "X amount of points" on some test (see #7 re: tests), "on X number of variables," or according to some type of very specific system. None really exists, and their claims are probably unjustified. Conversely, avoid those who show no ability to determine or match personality or intelligence and those who give superficial interview.

6. *"How will I be informed re: my matches?"* Look for service that calls you on the phone, describes match and asks your consent before exchanging identifying data with another client. Avoid those that mail phone numbers or your videotape to clients!

7. *"What are the relationship goals of the membership—do most people seek a compatible marriage partner, or are they dating for fun?"* Make sure it fits your goals!

8. *"What steps do you take to ensure that I fit your membership? Who do you turn down?"* Interviewer should describe exactly what kinds of people they accept/don't accept and in what ways you fit the accepted group. Acceptance should NOT be based only on ability to pay, but on psychological variables and compatibility with other members.

9. *"What steps are taken to ensure the confidentiality of my information?"* All data should stay on premises under lock and key, not mailed to clients or to another city. Staff must be trained in confidentiality procedures, including how to answer people pretending to know you. Avoid services where staff dates the members or where staff is not professional.

10. If psychological tests are administered: *"What happens to this data? How it is used to match me? Who interprets it? His credentials? What steps are taken to ensure my confidentiality?"* Any test administered without a Ph.D. psychologist's supervision is either not a valid psychological test, or it's been stolen. They are sold only to Ph.D. psychologists qualified to interpret them in an ethical manner. Also see #9 on confidentiality.

11. *"What programs do you have? Prices? Does everyone pay the same price?"* Beware those refusing to quote prices over the phone or those bartering different prices for the same program. A person paying less is often less sincere and less motivated to find a mate than a person paying more. Prices should not vary with your income.

12. *"What makes your service better than your competitors?"* THINK and make sure the answer makes sense!

13. *"Who owns this company? How long have you been in business? How often does the staff turn over? How long have you been working here?"* You should be able to meet the owner. If that person is matching you, see #4. Avoid franchises and silent owners unless you desire impersonal "mass quantity" approach. Beware new companies; they often go under in less than 5 years. They also have much fewer members, and hence, less compatible matches. Staff turnover is very high in this industry. Beware those who have sales people interviewing you, as they don't stay long. If you call a week after joining, you want the same person who knows you to be there! If she's not, ask for a re-interview.

14. *"What steps do you take to help me once I become a member? Do members give feedback? Will I be told about it if I ask? What do I do if I'm dissatisfied? When people are unhappy with this program, why are they dissatisfied?"* They must get feedback from the members, and it's best if they are willing to pass it on to you. Company should regard their #1 priority as service, not making money. Beware those who tell you everyone is satisfied; there is no such

thing. Interviewer should be able to describe procedures and support services available to help clients resolve problems.

15. *"Why (in what way) do you think the program you're offering me fits me?"* Answer should be personal, detailed and make sense. Avoid companies with canned responses, hard sells, or "I'm not sure you're right for this program" (take away) sales maneuvers. Ask you gut if the answers given are honest, and act accordingly!

16. *"Do women and men receive the same amount of matches?"* If you're asking for something more unusual (e.g., a certain religion, men over 40): *"How many members do you have who _____ (have that characteristic) and would also be willing to meet me?"* Beware services loaded with young men and older women, and those who give younger women and older men more matches.

Don't worry if they won't let you talk to former members. A truly confidential service would not encourage this. Forget 900 numbers, services charging less than $500 a year, and those run part-time on someone's dining room table. The service should have a professional office and caring staff who treat you with respect. Be very wary of services who come to your home or meet you in a hotel lobby. Avoid any hard sells or anyone who implies there's something wrong with you for wanting to sleep on your decision. Visit at least four services, ask these questions, take notes and review them at home. Wait 2 days before making any decisions. Read a copy of the contract over carefully before you sign it; ask questions. Take a copy home with you. Make sure you understand how the program works. They should give you a handout detailing their procedure. If not, take lots of notes. Trust your gut and join only a service where you feel comfortable.

Thought-stopping

*T*hought-stopping is a simple technique that has many beneficial uses. Use it whenever you need to replace bothersome, non-productive thought (worry, obsessions, internal monologues that blame you or someone else) with healthy, productive thoughts.

To identify whether a particular thought is productive or not, keep this in mind: If you run a past event through your mind once to learn what you can from it and apply that knowledge to make your future relationships better, that's productive. However, if you then continue to run that same scene through your mind over the over and over again, it's very nonproductive. You won't learn anything else from it; you're just making yourself sick. The same holds for events in the future. You can rehearse a scene once or twice in your mind to practice what you're going to do in a particular situation. But any further thought wears you out.

1. Start by identifying the type of thought you need to change. For example, if you are obsessed with your ex, stop all thoughts about your ex. If you have low self-esteem, stop all denigrating thoughts about yourself. If you worry too much, stop your anxious thoughts.

2. When you get one of those thoughts, say, *"Stop it!"* to yourself. (Not out loud, unless you want to get arrested! ;-) Then say the opposite of whatever is bothering you. Phrase it in the most positive, uplifting terms you can. For example, if you're widowed and get a thought like, "I miss my ex so much, I'll never be happy again," say, *"Stop it! I loved him, but I can be happy without him. And when I am ready, I will find a new partner and companion."* If you're divorced and get a thought like, "He didn't love me, and no one will ever love me again," say, *"Stop it! I am lovable, and I will find someone more compatible who will love and cherish me."* Be careful that the replacement thought is positive and uplifting, and remember to say it after saying, *"Stop it!"* In other words, don't just stop the thought—**replace it** with that positive, uplifting thought. Otherwise, you're just thinking negatively.

3. Then turn your attention to what you are doing—if you are working on a task that requires thought, such as writing checks or reading. If you aren't doing anything that requires focused concentration (if you're washing dishes or driving a car, for example), have a positive fantasy that does not remind you of what you are trying to forget. For example, you can plan your day, or have a fantasy about floating down the river on a raft.

4. Calmly repeat this process every time you get an unhealthy thought.

5. In the beginning, you'll find yourself thinking the unhealthy thought for awhile before you catch yourself. You'll also find that after you stop the thought, it quickly returns. You'll be in the middle of your fantasy, and there it will be! However, the more you practice this technique, the quicker you will catch your-

self and the longer you'll be able to keep the thought away—until one day, you'll suddenly remember that you have forgotten your bothersome thoughts altogether! That is the nature of the technique. In order to realize that it has worked, you have to remember that you once had this problem!

6. One caution: Every psychological technique can be used in an inappropriate way or at an inappropriate time—making it unhealthy, rather than healthy. For example, if you use this technique to forget about paying your bills, it's not healthy! If you use it to avoid feeling guilty about having an affair or deserting your mate, that's not good either. Basically, use the technique to end thoughts that are really hurting you, not uncomfortable thoughts that you need to remember—at least long enough to take action and resolve the problem.

7. So don't use thought-stopping to avoid taking positive behavioral action. For example, besides stopping thoughts about your ex, pursue activities that can help you find someone compatible in the future. And if you're constantly worrying about bills, make up a workable budget. In other words, brainstorm and execute solutions that will solve the problem that is triggering the worry thoughts.

8. Sometimes you can use thought-stopping to temporarily stop a thought that you can't do anything about at the moment. If it's midnight, for example, and you're in bed worrying about something you can't take care of tonight, get up and write it down, and put the note where you'll see it in the morning. Then go to bed and use thought-stopping to fall asleep, so you can wake up the next day, well-rested and able to take care of whatever it is you wrote down. If you are obsessing about your ex, write down the thought that's bothering you, put it in your purse and explore it with your psychologist at your next session. In the meantime, however, use thought-stopping to stop worrying about it in between.

9. If you're trying to get over the loss of a love, be sure to put away everything you can that reminds you of him. Otherwise, you'll think about him every time you look at the object, and it will take far longer for the thought-stopping to work. You don't have to throw the object out. Just put it where you won't see it unless you deliberately look for it. Then forget it for awhile—until you are able to look at it again without becoming sad or upset.

10. Sometimes people say, "Doctor, the technique didn't work." That's impossible. Every time you use it to stop a thought, it's working. Just keep using it each time—until it becomes automatic. And then all of a sudden, one day, you'll say, *"Wow! I remember when I used to think about my ex every day and cry myself to sleep. But I haven't thought about him in months now!"* And that's when you'll realize the technique worked—even when you forgot to notice it.

That's it! By learning and using this simple technique, you can control your thoughts and make them productive and happy. You can make them work for you, rather than the other way around!

The Dr. Kate Communication Quiz

*H*ow are your communication skills? Would your partner agree? Answer these questions as they relate to your opinion of your communication skills. Then follow the instructions at the end to improve your relationship with your partner. Of course, this is a fun quiz, not a psychological test. But what do you have to lose? You'll have fun taking it, and you just might learn something valuable!

1. When I was growing up:
   a. My parents communicated with each other very well, and I learned a lot from them.
   b. My parents really didn't communicate well; I learned a lot of bad habits from them.
   c. Everyone yelled one minute, then forgot it the next.
   d. No one really talked about problems.
   e. I learned a lot of bad communication habits, but have since improved/corrected them through reading, classes or psychotherapy.

2. In regards to my feelings, I usually:
   a. Have a hard time telling my loved one what I think or feel.
   b. Tell it like it is, and let the chips fall where they may.
   c. Believe that my loved one should know what I'm feeling without my telling him.
   d. Express myself in a way that is direct and straightforward, but also shows respect for my partner.
   e. Believe that what my partner doesn't know won't hurt him. After all, you have to keep some things to yourself.

3. When my partner expresses feelings, I usually:
   a. Try to paraphrase what he says ("Oh, that must have been hard for you") to show understanding.
   b. Show emotional support by saying things like, "I'm sorry you had a rough day."
   c. Show support by telling him why he shouldn't feel badly.
   d. Think about how his feelings might affect my future, and choose my response accordingly.
   e. My partner never listens to me, so why should I listen to him?

4. In general, when I talk to my partner, I:
   a. Try to take responsibility for my feelings by starting sentences with, "I feel __ when you __."
   b. Usually phrase remarks, "You (or it) made me ____."
   c. Let's not split hairs. I have no idea how I phrase things; I just TALK.
   d. Am frequently not sure how I should feel about anything, so I just don't bring it up.
   e. Try to be subtle. So I say, "We/they feel ____," or, "In this situation, most people would __."

5. When we disagree, I generally:
   a. Try to help my partner by telling him what he should and shouldn't do, i.e., how to do things the right way.
   b. Share my feelings in a direct, calm way, and allow my partner to do the same. Then I suggest compromises.
   c. Give in. I don't speak up well, and I HATE fighting.
   d. Let my partner think I'm agreeing with him, then do what I want.
   e. Am very indirect about my feelings. But if I don't get my way, I later show my displeasure (e.g., by sulking, coming home late, withholding sex).

6. Usually, when our argument escalates, I:
   a. Raise my voice, talk faster and faster, cut off (interrupt) my partner, and end up yelling. I may also pound my fist, gesture emphatically, point my finger, throw something or punch the wall.
   b. Try to have the last word, even if I have to stomp out of the house to get it.
   c. Use words like: *right/wrong, good/bad, always/never, everyone/no one, have to/can't, you've always been* _____ (negative adjective: *stupid, ridiculous, pathetic,* etc.).
   d. Keep my voice calm and modulated, and suggest tabling the discussion for now and agreeing to disagree.
   e. Can hardly speak; I just give in. I can't stand it when my partner is mad at me.

7. When I don't like something my partner is doing, I usually:
   a. Just cry and feel useless.
   b. Give him the "silent treatment," but complain to anyone else who will listen.
   c. Pick and choose my battles carefully, and praise him often before requesting any behavioral change.
   d. Let him know about it, in no uncertain terms. I say, "*You* _____ (always do that wrong)," or, "*You are* _____ (the worst housekeeper I've ever seen)."
   e. Describe the behavior I find objectionable, rather than attacking my partner.

8. When I am offended by something my partner has done, I usually:
   a. Tell my partner right away, no matter where we are or who is around.
   b. Make time to discuss it when we are both rested, calm and alone, turning off the TV and any other distractions.
   c. Suffer in silence. Life is too short to disagree about things.
   d. Tease about it when he can't really fight back (e.g., in front of a business client), or ask my in-laws or others to pressure him into giving me what I want.
   e. Only bring it up if/when I think it's in my best interest to do so.

9. In terms of praise, I usually:
   a. Reward my mate generously and often with praise and physical affection (hugs, kisses).
   b. Don't praise my partner. He never praises me, so why should I?
   c. Praise my partner to get something I want. When I want something really big, I can be extremely charming.
   d. Show my mate I care by doing nice things, rather than saying anything.
   e. In my opinion, he gets way too much praise as it is.

10. When it comes to apologies, I usually:
    a. Don't apologize; it's a sign of weakness.
    b. Apologize, whether or not it's my fault; I can't stand conflict.
    c. Apologize if I think it will get me what I want. After all, all that matters is the final outcome.
    d. Apologize if I have done something inappropriate or hurtful, even unintentionally.
    e. Pretend like the incident never occurred, rather than apologizing; that really gets him!

11. When it comes to saying, "I love you," I:
    a. Don't tell my partner, "I love you," because he never says it to me.
    b. Don't say, "I love you," because I find it hard to talk about feelings in general.
    c. Don't say, "I love you," because I find it easier to say what I don't like than what I do like.
    d. Say, "I love you," when I want something or if I'm in the mood, but behave differently later.
    e. Say, "I love you," when I feel that way, and demonstrate behavior consistent with that message.

12. In terms of honesty, I generally:
    a. Tell my partner the truth, even when it's difficult.
    b. Tell little white lies that won't matter down the road if I think it will serve my purpose.
    c. Lie whenever I feel like it. My partner is too stupid to know the difference, and besides, I really don't care if he finds out.
    d. Lie (or just imply an untruth through my silence) to make my partner feel better, or just because it's easier.
    e. Lie whenever I feel like it. After all, he lies to me, so why shouldn't I?

13. I usually feel that I:
    a. Love talking with my partner about all kinds of things. I can't wait to share things with him.
    b. Get tired of constantly having to set my partner straight about his priorities.
    c. Prefer the company of my friends, and love to make my partner jealous by talking about them.
    d. Think talking is overrated. My partner can tell how I feel just by watching my actions.
    e. Talk whenever necessary to achieve my needs. Communication is a great tool.

14. When it comes to asking for help:
    a. I ask for too much help. Sometimes I solicit so many opinions, I get totally confused as to what I should do.
    b. I don't really have a problem. My mate is the one with the problem. If he would only change....
    c. I don't really need therapy. Normal people solve their own problems.
    d. I try to solve my problems with my partner, but would consider therapy before the situation got out of hand.
    e. Why should I go to therapy? He won't go anyway, and he's the one who needs the shrink!

15. You want me to ask my partner to complete this questionnaire and discuss it with me?
    a. I would feel comfortable asking my partner; I believe in self-help.
    b. I am apprehensive about asking my partner. He might do it, but I wouldn't want him to find out about all my insecurities and faults.
    c. I wouldn't want to admit I actually took this questionnaire. There are a lot of crazies out there, but I'm not one of them!
    d. I wouldn't want to share such personal information with my partner. He might use it against me later.
    e. I would not feel comfortable, because I wouldn't want to reveal my hand. It might ruin a future plan.

Scoring for The Dr. Kate Communication Quiz

Score your responses to the quiz by drawing a circle around the appropriate number of points for the answer you chose as indicated below. Note the behavior or attitude assessed by each item to the right of the scoring.

	A	B	C	D	E	Behavior or Attitude Assessed
1	10	0	0	0	10	Early Learning
2	0	0	0	10	0	General Pattern Of Communication
3	10	10	0	0	0	Reflective/Supportive Listening
4	10	0	0	0	0	Taking Responsibility For Feelings
5	0	10	0	0	0	Handling Disagreement
6	0	0	0	10	0	Choice Of Words, Tone Of Voice
7	0	0	10	0	10	Asking For Behavioral Change
8	0	10	0	0	0	Choosing Time And Location To Talk
9	10	0	0	0	0	Ratio Of Positive Reinforcement
10	0	0	0	10	0	Willingness To Apologize
11	0	0	0	0	10	Saying, "I Love You!"
12	10	0	0	0	0	Honesty, Respect And Maturity
13	10	0	0	0	0	Attitude Toward Communication
14	0	0	0	10	0	Willingness To Seek Help/Therapy
15	10	0	0	0	0	Openness And Trust
Total:						

Now, see the following pages to discover how well you communicate!

Results for The Dr. Kate Communication Quiz

GREAT COMMUNICATOR—if you scored 120-150:

("I love communicating!")

Congratulations! You scored in the range of great communicators. Now you weren't just picking the ones that sounded right, were you?

If you were objective: You enjoy expressing yourself in a direct, straightforward, honest manner that also shows respect for your partner. You are able to say, *"I love you,"* and show it through praise and affectionate gestures. You respect your partner's right to hold an opinion that is different from yours. You are able to take responsibility for your own feelings and behavior, rather than blaming your partner for your problems. You pick and choose your battles wisely, and give lots of reinforcement before asking for a behavioral change. When you and your partner have a conflict, you remain calm, discuss your feelings, listen attentively to your partner's feelings, make supportive statements, then look for ways to compromise. If an argument escalates and you are unable to reach an agreement, you calmly suggest tabling the discussion for another time. You are able to apologize and ask for help when you need it.

If your mate is also assertive, you are likely to share good communication and a good relationship together. However, whether or not your relationship is successful is not completely dependent on you; it's an ***INTER*action. So, if your relationship doesn't seem to be going that well, *discuss your relationship with your partner, and work together to improve it.***

Ask your partner to complete this questionnaire. Then both of you can retake it as if you were each other. Make time to calmly discuss your answers to each question, using them as jumping-off points to discuss both your helpful and problematic behaviors. Talk about the answers you gave as yourself and as each other. You may be surprised to find that your partner holds a different view of your behavior and vice versa.

Your ability to communicate will serve you well. Keep up the good work!

GOOD COMMUNICATOR—if you scored 90-110:

("I'm good and getting better!")

Congratulations! While you did not score in the top category, you did very well. You selected many answers which suggest that you frequently behave assertively. You tend to express your feelings, both pleasant and unpleasant, in a direct, honest, straightforward way, while also showing respect for your partner's rights.

At times, however, you do make mistakes. You may sometimes act aggressively (i.e., taking advantage of the other person's rights when expressing your feelings) or passively (i.e., not standing up for your feelings at all). You may also act out in passive-aggressive ways (indicating displeasure by doing something indirectly aggressive), or you may act politically (using communication to manipulate your partner into doing something you desire).

However, practice makes perfect! To learn to communicate even better:

1. Read ***Chapter 7—Communication*** with your partner to learn more about communication skills, assertiveness, reflective listening, supportive statements, negotiation and compromise.

2. If your partner tends to be respectful of your feelings, ask him to complete this questionnaire. Then both of you can retake it as if you were each other. Make time to calmly discuss your answers to each question, using them as jumping-off points to discuss both your helpful and problematic behaviors. Talk about the answers you gave as yourself and as each other. You may be surprised to find that your partner holds a different view of your behavior and vice versa.

3. You may also benefit from assertiveness classes held at a local college, or from reading books on assertiveness and communication skills (see the recommended reading list in the back of this book). If you have AOL, you can also access the Dr. Kate site (***AOL Keyword: Dr. Kate)*** and use the search function to locate many advice letters and articles I have written on the topic of communication.

You are well on your way to becoming a great communicator. Now, keep up the good work!

AVERAGE COMMUNICATOR—if you scored 60-80:
("Doing OK, but lots of room for improvement!")

You selected many answers which suggest that sometimes you behave assertively. That is, you sometimes express your feelings, both pleasant and unpleasant, in a direct, honest, straightforward manner, while also showing respect for your partner's rights.

Often, however, you make a number of mistakes. You may sometimes act aggressively (i.e., taking advantage of the other person's rights when expressing your feelings) or passively (i.e., not standing up for your feelings at all). You may also act out in passive-aggressive ways (indicating displeasure by doing something indirectly aggressive), or you may act politically (using communication to manipulate your partner into doing something you desire).

However, practice makes perfect! So, my advice for improvement would be:

1. Read ***Chapter 7—Communication*** with your partner to learn more about communication skills, assertiveness, reflective listening, supportive statements, negotiation and compromise.

2. If your partner tends to be respectful of your feelings, ask him to complete this questionnaire. Then both of you can retake it as if you were each other. Make time to calmly discuss your answers to each question, using them as jumping-off points to discuss both your helpful and problematic behaviors. Talk about the answers you gave as yourself and as each other. You may be surprised to find that your partner holds a different view of your behavior and vice versa.

3. You may also benefit from assertiveness classes held at a local college, or from reading books on assertiveness and communication skills (see the recommended reading list in the back of this book). If you have AOL, you can also access the Dr. Kate site *(AOL Keyword: Dr. Kate)* and use the search function to locate many advice letters and articles I have written on the topic of communication. Put energy into improving your communication, so you can thoroughly enjoy your romantic relationships, as well as those with close family and friends.

You're on your way to becoming a great communicator. Now, keep up the good work!

MEDIOCRE COMMUNICATOR—if you scored 30-50:
("Well, at least my mother loves me!")

Your answers suggest that once in awhile, you behave assertively. That is, you occasionally express your feelings, both pleasant and unpleasant, in a direct, honest, straightforward manner, while also showing respect for your partner's rights.

However, you are not acting assertively in the majority of situations. You may sometimes act aggressively (i.e., taking advantage of the other person's rights when expressing your feelings), or passively (i.e., not standing up for your feelings at all). You may also act out in passive-aggressive ways (indicating displeasure by doing something indirectly aggressive), or you may act politically (using communication to manipulate your partner).

However, the good news is by learning and practicing, you can significantly improve your communication style, and along with it, your intimate relationship. To become a better communicator, I would suggest:

1. Read *Chapter 7—Communication* with your partner to learn more about communication skills, assertiveness, reflective listening, supportive statements, negotiation and compromise.

2. If your partner tends to be respectful of your feelings, and you feel that the two of you can discuss the questionnaire productively, ask your partner to complete the quiz and discuss it with you.

3. Remember not to take any remarks personally; focus on the behaviors being discussed, and just try to understand how your partner views your behavior. Be sure to thank him for the help. You may also be surprised to find that your partner holds a different view of your behavior, and vice versa.

4. You may also benefit from assertiveness classes held at a local college, or from reading books on assertiveness and communication skills (see the recommended reading list in the back of this book). If you have AOL, you can also access the Dr. Kate site *(AOL Keyword: Dr. Kate)* and use the search function to locate many advice letters and articles I have written on the topic of communication.

5. Finally, I would encourage you to consult a psychologist for individual sessions or couples counseling, so you can receive personal instruction on how to apply what you have learned. The psychologist will teach you whatever else you need to know so you can be assertive and practice good communication skills. If you follow these suggestions, you should eventually be able to enjoy your romantic relationships (as well as those with close family and friends), more than you ever thought possible!)

You've already begun by taking this quiz. Now, keep the momentum going!

POOR COMMUNICATOR—if you scored 0-20:

("Help me quick! No one will talk to me any more!")

Cheer Up! You have lots of room for improvement! Your answers suggest that you very rarely behave assertively. That is, you rarely express your feelings, both pleasant and unpleasant, in a direct, honest, straightforward manner, while also showing respect for your partner's rights.

Instead, you may act aggressively (i.e., taking advantage of the other person's rights when expressing your feelings), or passively (i.e., not standing up for your feelings at all). You may also act out in passive-aggressive ways (indicating displeasure by doing something indirectly aggressive), or you may act politically (using communication to manipulate your partner into doing something you desire).

However, the good news is that by learning and practicing, you can significantly improve your communication style, and along with it, your intimate relationship. Here are my suggestions:

1. Read *Chapter 7—Communication* with your partner to learn more about communication skills, assertiveness, reflective listening, supportive statements, negotiation and compromise.

2. You may also benefit from assertiveness classes held at a local college, or from reading books on assertiveness and communication skills (see the recommended reading list in the back of this book). If you have AOL, you can also access the Dr. Kate site *(AOL Keyword: Dr. Kate)* and use the search function to locate many advice letters and articles I have written on the topic of communication.

3. Finally, I would encourage you to consult a psychologist for individual sessions or couples counseling as soon as possible, so that you can learn better communication skills. Discuss your responses to this quiz in therapy, and learn to be more assertive. By working hard, you should eventually be able to enjoy your romantic relationships (as well as those with close family and friends), more than you even imagined!

You've already started by taking this quiz. Now, keep the momentum going!

The Dr. Kate Compatibility Quiz

*A*re you compatible with your partner? Take this questionnaire and find out. As with the other quizzes in this book, this is a FUN questionnaire, not a psychological test. But what have you got to lose? You just might learn something and have fun in the process. *Choose the answer that comes closest to describing your situation.*

1. When I am around my partner:
    a. It doesn't matter what we do; everything is just more fun, and the time just flies.
    b. It's really fun sometimes, but at other times, we just don't seem to connect.
    c. I find myself thinking of other people and what might have been.
    d. I can't stand it. I try to get away as soon as possible.
    e. Most of the time, we don't connect.

2. I have been with my partner:
    a. Less than 3 months
    b. 4 - 12 months
    c. 2 Years
    d. 3 - 7 years
    e. 8 or more years

3. If I relax and allow my partner to do anything he wants:
    a. He would walk all over me. I really have to protect myself.
    b. He would go out of his way to look out for my interests. I don't have to ever worry about that.
    c. Sometimes he would manipulate and use me. Other times, he's selfless.
    d. I haven't caught him yet, but I just sense that he wouldn't be faithful for long.

4. With regard to intellectual stimulation:
    a. We are intellectually on the same wavelength. We enjoy talking about all kinds of things, and it excites me.
    b. He takes off on issues I know nothing about and don't really follow.
    c. I don't expect my partner to stimulate me intellectually. I get that from my coworkers.
    d. He's fun, but not as intellectually stimulating as I would like.
    e. We are very different intellectually.

5. Physically:
    a. I am extremely attracted to my partner.
    b. I am mostly attracted to my partner.
    c. I am somewhat attracted to my partner. If she would just have that plastic surgery...
    d. I'm kind of turned off by his looks, but I find other things more important, so it's OK.
    e. I'm really turned off by his looks and it bothers me.

6. Sexually:
   a. I enjoy him completely. It's always great.
   b. Sometimes sex is great, sometimes it's good, and sometimes it's just maintenance sex, but I always enjoy it because it's with the one I love.
   c. We don't really get into sex much, but it's OK.
   d. I abhor sex with my partner, but I do it to please him.
   e. I try to go to bed before my partner does, so I can sneak out of sex. When I have to make love, I try to get it over with as soon as possible.

7. When it comes to money:
   a. My mate and I always disagree on how to spend it. It's the cause of many of our fights.
   b. We sometimes disagree, but we talk it through and make compromises.
   c. My partner and I almost always agree on how to spend our money.
   d. My mate and I have separate bank accounts. We divide up any joint activities (and if living together), our expenses.
   e. My partner hides bills and checks from me. I never know what's going on.

8. With regard to the future:
   a. We talk about our goals and plans, and they seem to fit well together.
   b. We sometimes talk about our goals and plans, but I sense that we're not in sync there.
   c. We sometimes talk about our goals and plans, and I'm hopeful that we can make a future together.
   d. We never talk about goals and plans. We just live day to day.
   e. My partner is a planner and I'm a day-to-day person (or vice versa), but we negotiate on things, and even each other out in the end.
   f. My partner and I vary greatly on how we approach things, so we don't talk about it unless we have to.

9. With regard to our future together:
   a. My partner and I are in agreement that we are going to get married and have children (or get married without children). We are both sincere about this.
   b. My partner and I can't agree on our relationship goals. We fight about them often.
   c. My partner and I can't agree on our relationship goals, so we focus on the present and don't discuss them.
   d. My partner and I are both single, but agree that our relationship is just temporary. We're not ready for anything permanent.

10. My partner and I:
   a. Share a lot of cultural, ethnic and religious similarities. Our families and friends would (or do) like each other, and are usually supportive of what we do.
   b. Are very different with regard to culture, ethnicity and/or religion. However, our family and friends have met and are supportive, and they usually pull through with support in times like this.
   c. Are very different with regard to culture, ethnicity and/or religion. We're afraid to tell our family and friends, so we keep our relationship our little secret.
   d. Are very different with regard to culture, ethnicity and/or religion. Our family and friends have met and they are most definitely against our union.
   e. One or both of us come from a dysfunctional family who are constantly fighting with people and/or cutting them off.

11. My partner and I:
    a. Never have any problems. We never disagree on anything.
    b. Communicate regularly, with great success. We have conflicts sometimes, but we calmly work them out through negotiation and compromise. I love talking to my partner.
    c. We limp along. Sometimes we communicate well, sometimes not.
    d. Try to keep things light. But if we have disagreements, we may not talk to each other for days. Then we just pretend that it never happened.
    e. Communication? What's communication?
    f. We try to talk, but always end up yelling and screaming at each other.

12. My partner and I:
    a. Love to do the same things. We enjoy doing them together.
    b. Love to do some of the same things. But we also take time alone to do separate activities with others.
    c. Really don't share many of the same interests, but we go along with each other anyway, so we can be together.
    d. Really don't share many of the same interests, so we spend quite a bit of time apart.

13. My partner and I:
    a. Are ordinarily very honest, trustworthy and loyal.
    b. Try to be honest, trustworthy and loyal, but sometimes are not as honest, trustworthy or loyal as we would like.
    c. Make a lot of mistakes.
    d. Have had a lot of affairs on each other.
    e. Are not very honest with one another; we keep a lot hidden.

14. Once my partner and I commit to something:
    a. We don't give up easily. We work very hard to accomplish our goals.
    b. We give everything a good shot, but we don't try to excess.
    c. We figure relationships should be fairly easy. Otherwise, it just isn't compatible.
    d. We don't really try very much at anything. Life is too short to work too hard.

15. My partner is:
    a. My best friend.
    b. We haven't been friends for a long time.
    c. We have our ups and downs, but we're still closer to each other than to anyone else.
    d. I feel my mate tries to please other people (e.g., family, other friends) more than me.
    e. I don't believe mates have to be friends.

Scoring for the Dr. Kate Compatibility Quiz

Score your responses by drawing a circle around the appropriate number of points for the answer you chose. Note the relationship characteristic/quality and component of compatibility measured by each item to the right of the scoring.

	A	B	C	D	E	F	Quality Measured
1	10	7	2	0	0		Overall Fun And Chemistry
2	0	1	2	6	10		Length Of Time
3	0	10	5	2			Trust, Loyalty
4	10	2	7	3	0		Intelligence/Intellectual Interests
5	10	7	2	4	0		Physical Attraction
6	10	10	4	1	0		Sexual Attraction
7	1	10	10	3	0		Financial Disagreements
8	10	2	4	0	8	0	Shared Goals And Plans
9	10	0	2	2			Shared Relationship Goals
10	10	8	1	0	0		Culture/Religion/Ethnicity; Support
11	5	10	4	1	0	0	Communication
12	10	8	6	0			Similar Interests
13	10	6	2	0	0		Honesty, Loyalty, Monogamy, Trust
14	10	6	2	0			Perseverance
15	10	0	7	2	0		Friendship, Solidarity
Total:							

Now, see the following pages to discover how compatible you are!

Results for the Dr. Kate Compatibility Quiz

PLEASE NOTE: This questionnaire ONLY applies if you and your partner are not married to anyone else, and are not involved in any affairs with other people. It also only applies if neither of you is physically abusive. If one or both of you are having affairs (with each other or other people), or if one or both of you are physically abusive, see the appropriate sections (first two answers) below instead.

IF YOU OR YOUR PARTNER ARE PHYSICALLY ABUSIVE:

This relationship has very little potential for success. The abuser does not respect the abused partner, and both of you probably have long-standing psychological problems.

IF YOU ARE THE ABUSER: You have a host of characterological problems that require urgent treatment by a psychologist. You may also have drug or alcohol problems. You have trouble with control and self-esteem, and you blame your mate for things she is not responsible for. You have a distorted vision of reality and a double standard of behavior for you and your partner. Seek treatment immediately from a psychologist, and let him know that this is an emergency.

IF YOU ARE THE ABUSED: You also need to see a psychologist immediately to get help. Check into services for abused people in your area, and take measures to save yourself. Your relationship isn't worth saving, but you are. Act now to change your present and your future. To read more about physical abuse, see *Chapter 10—Tough Times.* You can also find a wealth of advice on the topic at the AOL Dr. Kate site *(AOL Keyword: Dr. Kate).* Use the search function there to locate many advice letters I have written to abused people.

IF YOU OR YOUR PARTNER ARE HAVING AFFAIRS:

You're not being realistic with yourself about this relationship. You are involved in an affair, and are romanticizing about your current situation. If your partner is married and you are fantasizing about your future together, there is little likelihood that he will suddenly change and be "perfect" for you. If both of you are married, it is probably just a matter of time before the situation blows up in your faces. You probably feel attracted to one another on a variety of levels, but the bottom line is that because one or both of you are married, the relationship will probably not grow into anything permanent or fully satisfying.

IF YOU AND YOUR PARTNER ARE NOT BEING ABUSIVE/ABUSED AND ARE NOT MARRIED AND HAVING AN AFFAIR, THEN LOOK UP YOUR SCORE BELOW:

HIGHLY COMPATIBLE—if you scored 130-150:

You have a really compatible relationship. You share many levels of compatibility with your partner. You probably feel close intellectually, physically, sexually, and with regard to shared goals and interests, including the goal of this relationship. You probably believe in communication, and try to work resolve your problems together. You tend to work hard at most things, including this relationship, and you probably have support from your family and friends. You probably view each other as best friends and feel a strong bond to one another. You enjoy each other's company, and you have lots of fun together. You trust each other; you believe in monogamy, honesty and loyalty, and you practice them with each other. Congratulations! You're very fortunate! Keep that in mind and live every day intimately connected, no matter what stresses befall you in the future. Never take your relationship for granted. Many people never even experience a relationship like this. Value what you have and make your relationship a priority, so that it will continue to thrive.

WORKING RELATIONSHIP—if you scored 100-129:

You and your partner are somewhat less than ideally compatible, but then most things in life aren't perfect. You have a working relationship. You probably feel that many features of your relationship could be more in sync, but many could also be a lot worse. You usually value what you have, although you may take each other for granted from time to time. Some aspects of your relationship feel really good and others don't. You may get along on a number of variables, but fall flat regarding your goals, your sex life or some area of your life together that causes conflict.

However, with hard work and tenacity, you can probably keep this a workable and satisfying relationship and even improve it. You both could benefit from a psychologist's help from time to time, e.g., when you are unable to reach compromises together, or when you occasionally need to jump-start your relationship. But therapy does not need to last long to produce benefits and overall, your prognosis is good.

If your goals for your relationship together vary a great deal and you are unable to work them out in successful compromise, even through therapy, then you might want to seek another relationship. This is particularly true if you have been together awhile and cannot reach a compromise regarding your future (marriage or marriage and kids vs. living together). However, you do find many parts of this relationship satisfying, so such a decision would be difficult to make. If you're not sure whether or not your relationship has enough positives that you should compromise, see a psychologist for direction and support, and to help you figure out how you feel and where you want to go with this relationship.

MEDIOCRE COMPATIBILITY—if you scored 60-100:

There's quite a bit lacking in this relationship. You may be compatible in some ways, but very incompatible in others. Or you may just have a lower level of compatibility across the board. You realize that there are a lot of differences between you and your partner. These differences may be physical, sexual, intellectual and/or with regard to goals and shared interests. You may lack the social support of family and friends. You may also disagree greatly with regard to your relationship goals. If you have known each other less than 2 years, you may just not have enough in common to make a relationship work. If you have known each other for many years, you may be drifting apart. See the suggestions below as well, and use those that seem appropriate for you.

NEED A PSYCHOLOGIST—to learn to be a better partner and avoid psychological hook. Issues of honestry, cheating and trust if you scored 0-60:

You may have a lot of disagreements about money, and/or doubt your partner's faithfulness or honesty. Or you may often be dishonest with your partner. You and your partner don't communicate well, and there are probably many things festering beneath the surface. You really aren't enjoying this relationship very much. It will take a lot of effort to fix what ails you. And you'll probably need the help of a psychologist to do it. You both have a lot of learning to do, and without help, there's little hope that the relationship can be satisfying for you.

IF YOU AND YOUR PARTNER ARE MARRIED: See a psychologist together to jumpstart your relationship. Try to work out your differences in therapy, while you also learn to communicate better with one another. Give therapy a good try before throwing in the towel.

IF YOU ARE MARRIED, BUT YOUNG OR NEWLY WED: You and your spouse may have a lot to learn regarding how to communicate with each other and what constitutes reasonable expectations for your marriage. Communication skills are not inbred, but therapy can help you learn skills necessary to continuing your relationship.

IF YOU HAVE BEEN TOGETHER MANY YEARS, MARRIED OR NOT, AND HAVE A LOT OF HISTORY (INCLUDING GOOD HISTORY) TOGETHER: There's no way that either of you could have behaved perfectly toward each other all this time. Couples who have been together a long time need to learn to forgive and "re-birth" the relationship. They also need to learn to communicate better so that they can negotiate and compromise regarding any present and future disagreements. Stay in therapy until you have made significant progress and can retake this questionnaire and score in the top 1-2 categories. If you don't see improvement with one psychologist within 6 months, try another. Don't throw in the towel until you have tried your best in therapy for several years.

IF YOU AND YOUR PARTNER HAVE JUST RECENTLY MET, ARE LONG-DISTANCE, ARE NOT MARRIED OR HAVE LESS SHARED HISTORY TOGETHER FOR ANY REASON: You may be better off just looking for another partner. Why not try a quality introduction service or the *Love@AOL* Photo Personals? It is unlikely that your current relationship will be saved, and in the long run, it will probably be less frustrating if you look elsewhere. You may want to consult a psychologist to learn more about what you need in a relationship and for encouragement to keep looking. Review your current and past relationships with your psychologist. Why are you staying with your current partner when you don't enjoy him very much? Perhaps you're with him because he's a hook from your dysfunctional past. Apply what you learn in therapy to your future relationships, so that you can make them better. That way, the time spent and experience gained through your current unfulfilling relationship will be put to good use.

Exercises to make your sex life sPaRk! ZiNg!! SiZzLe!!! ;)

*I*t's time to examine your sex life in the daylight! Put aside your defenses, inhibitions and insecurities for a few minutes and take some time to review this important area of your life and how much fun you're having.

1. In your Relationship Notebook, write the following words in a column on the left side. Leave 10 blank lines in between the words:

   WITH WHOM:
   WHEN:
   HOW MUCH:
   WHERE:
   HOW:

2. Now, go through each category and ask yourself the questions listed below. (We're basically going out of the usual order, because it will be easier to answer the questions in that manner.) Write the answers to the questions below after the corresponding word.

   WITH WHOM: With whom are you having sex? Are you happy that you are having sex with this person? Or would it be healthier if you didn't sleep with him? If there is more than one person, are you making the best decision for your psychological health when you choose to sleep with both/all of them? Are you conducting yourself in a way that is likely to lead you to your relationship goal? If you're married, but having sex with someone other than your spouse, how is your affair affecting your life? Your husband's? Your children and extended family? Your lover's life? If you are married, but NOT having sex with your spouse, how did this happen? What precipitated your drifting apart? How has this rift maintained itself? What is the effect on you, your husband and your children?

   WHEN: When are you having sex—in the morning? evening? Is that satisfactory? Are you rushing to fit lovemaking into your schedule between work, kids, relatives and other responsibilities? What would you like to see changed, if anything?

   Also, if you are single, when (how soon) in the relationship are you having sex? Are you having it during the first 3 months? If so, what effect does getting sexually intimate that soon have on your relationships? How is your self-esteem? Does having sex the way you've been having it seem to strengthen your relationship? Or does it encourage your partner to devalue you and not take you seriously? What is your relationship goal? Is your behavior likely to lead you to this goal?

   HOW MUCH: How much are you and your partner making love? Are you satisfied with the frequency? Is your partner?

   Also, if you are single and having too much sex: When did this problem start? What was going on in your life at the time? Why do you think this happened?

How are you feeling about yourself as a result? Why do you continue this behavior? Are you sleeping around because you want someone to love you? If so, do you really think it's helping?

WHERE: Where are you having sex? Is that satisfactory to you and your partner? Do you want to have sex anywhere else?

HOW: How are you having sex? Are you making love? Just having first-date sex (one-night stands) or just maintenance sex? If you have a significant other, are you having maintenance sex, good sex and great sex in levels acceptable to you? Are you satisfied with the quality, romance and intimacy (basically the mood) of your love life and lovemaking?

Are you satisfied with the mechanics of your sex life? Are you having fun and enjoying your lovemaking? Are you satisfied with the quality of your interaction? If not, what seems to be the problem?

If you're not married, are you having sex responsibly and always using two forms of birth control, with one being a latex condom? If not, why not? What do you think the outcome of this will be? What will you do then? If you've been having unprotected sex: How is your self-esteem? Do you like yourself? Or are you feeling suicidal? If your partner doesn't want to use birth control and condoms: What does that say about his concern for your welfare?

3. Now, go through the items above again, and ask yourself the same questions as if you were your partner. Try to switch places with him, and respond to each question as he would. For example, perhaps you are satisfied with the frequency of your sex life, but your husband is not. Note that in your answer.

4. For each item where you or your partner were not satisfied, write down what steps you will take to fix the problem. Of course, sex is an interaction between two people, so depending on what is causing the difficulty, you may need your partner's cooperation to resolve it. But don't shove the responsibility off on your partner and delay working on it. Instead, one of the steps you may need to take is talking with your partner about the problem and enlisting his cooperation and support.

5. If you find that your sex life has been decreasing because you and your partner have been drifting apart, or because you tend to stay angry and carry that into the bedroom, then be sure to read *Chapter 7—Communication, Chapter 5—Making A Commitment* and *Chapter 9—Marriage.* If the problem lies in your communication, then you can expect your love life to improve as soon as you improve your interaction with your partner.

6. If you have AOL, go to *Keyword: Dr. Kate* and use the search function to find hundreds of letters I've written about sex. Learn what you can.

7. Finally, if you continue to have considerable sexual problems, consider seeing a psychologist who has an expertise in sex therapy.

How to invite your mate to counseling

1. Use the techniques for discussing difficult topics (see **Chapter 7—Communication**). Pick an appropriate time and place. Get him ready. *"I've been wanting to talk to you about something for awhile..."* When you have his attention: *"I've been thinking about seeing a psychologist to try to make our marriage the best it can be. How would you feel about that?"*

2. Let your mate talk about his feelings, agree with whatever you can agree with, use reflective listening and supportive statements. When he's done, present your position in a gentle, but assertive manner. *"I'd like you to come because I love you, and I'd like the psychologist to understand your point of view. If you don't want to come, I respect your choice, and I'll try to tell your side fairly. But it would be better if you went yourself since you know exactly how you feel, and I don't. I think it's important that you tell your perspective."*

3. If he refuses to go, don't make it a power struggle. Just say, *"OK, well, then I guess I'll go by myself, but remember, you're always welcome if you change your mind."* Pick a regular appointment time that he could make if he decided to come. Wait a month. Then let him know that the appointments are *"every week on ____ (Saturday) at ____(11 a.m.). I just wanted to let you know, in case you ever want to come. You're always welcome."*

4. Be sure you don't tell him what is happening in the sessions. If/when he asks, tell him, *"We had a good session—it was helpful,"* but don't go into detail. If he asks what you said about him, tell him you tried to represent his point of view. Don't give any more details.

5. He may eventually go out of curiosity, or to make sure his side is fairly represented. People get a little concerned wondering what you're telling the psychologist when they're not there to defend themselves. If he does go, it's up to the psychologist to make rapport, peak his interest, and gently motivate him to keep coming.

6. Just keep the door open, and allow your mate to change his mind without losing face. It's even OK if he thinks he's going as a favor to you, or because you have a problem. Even if he doesn't go, therapy can still be helpful by helping you live with him better.

Counseling options

There are usually therapy options for everyone, even people without much money:

Community Mental Health Centers (CMHC)—Funded by the federal government, they use a sliding scale, basing your fee on your income and debts. Intake interview usually by a social worker, who then assigns you to a therapist. The plus is the cost;

the liability is you don't get to choose your therapist, who is often a mental health worker with less training.

Church-Affiliated Mental Health Centers—Same pros and cons as CMHC above.

Campus Counseling Centers—Free to students and sometimes at reduced rates for others. Supervised by professors, clinical/counseling psych grad students often see clients.

Veterans Administration Hospital Outpatient Mental Health Clinic—Free to veterans. Many fine Ph.D. psychologists work for the VA, so treatment is usually excellent.

Psychologists In Private Practice—Most private; standard of care is usually excellent. Psychologist generally has 21-22 years of education, as well as many years of hands-on training/practice prior to being licensed. Many insurance policies cover 50-80% of therapy cost when administered by a Ph.D. psychologist. Check your insurance book for coverage.

The Dr. Kate Quick and Dirty Crying/Grieving Technique

When you experience a major loss, use thought-stopping to replace your irrational thoughts with more rational ones. See a psychologist to talk about your loss and any fears or strong feelings bothering you. Review your relationship in a productive fashion and get closure.

But let's say you're doing all that, and one day, the irrational thoughts seem to be winning. The lump in your throat is so big, it's difficult to swallow; it feels like someone is sitting on your chest; the cat spills her milk and you get teary; or you're so irritable, you almost start screaming at your coworker for no reason.

That's when it's time for ***The Dr. Kate Quick & Dirty Crying/Grieving Technique.*** This technique allows you to get irrational for an evening, so you can get your emotions out, then go back to being rational and feeling better the next day. Here's how to do it:

1. Ask a friend to take your kids for the evening. Or wait until they're asleep, then put some music on and shut the bedroom door, so no one will hear you or interrupt you.

2. Then give yourself permission to think about every irrational thought you've been trying to stop, and magnify the thought as much as possible: "No one will ever love me again. My life is over. I'll never meet anyone as nice as my husband. I'm so ugly! It was all my fault he left! I was a horrible wife!" Sob for as long and as hard as you can. Spread his pictures across the bed and take a long look. Remember how much you loved him, how happy you were with him and how much you wanted your marriage to work. "I was so happy, I'll never be that happy again! He was the best thing that ever happened to me!" Whatever those nagging fears in the back of your head, think about them and sob.

3. Now we're not talking a little crying here; we're talking mega-buckets. Cry for at least a half-hour—or for two or three. Don't be afraid. If you've had problems with psychosis (losing touch with reality) or suicidal attempts, don't use this technique. However, if you're a relatively normal person with no such history, then don't worry—you won't go crazy. You're still in control; you're just allowing yourself to vent for an evening to get the pain out.

4. Go through a whole box of tissue. Just keep crying and crying until you finally find yourself saying, "No one will ever love me again" (or one of your most irrational thoughts), and this little voice in your head answers, "I don't give a damn!"

5. By this time, your eyes should be puffed up and your lips swollen, you'll look a little like Godzilla, and you'll probably have a whopping headache. So take some aspirin, Tylenol or Advil and go to bed. Then when you get up the next morning, resume the thought-stopping. Once again, replace all your irrational ideas with more positive, realistic thoughts.

6. Use this technique as needed to work through your grief and speed your recovery.

7. If you don't know why any of your thoughts are irrational or you find yourself somewhat believing them, ask your psychologist to teach you why the self-denigrating, blaming or otherwise catastrophic thoughts that are bothering you are not realistic.

This technique is not a substitute for therapy. It's an adjunct to help you get the stress out in a controlled fashion, so you can heal faster. Confronting your fears head-on in this manner can greatly reduce the time you suffer—and allow you to live the days in between with as much dignity, grace and comfort as possible.

May your days be brighter and brighter...

Recommended reading

The books below are classics, so many of them are older. But they're my favorites, and I highly recommend them. If you try to find a book and it's not currently in print, you may be able to buy it used from the Barnes and Noble or Amazon.com out-of-print books online site. You should also be able to rent it through your local library.

Your Perfect Right, by Alberti, Robert, and Emmons, Michael, San Luis Obispo, CA: Impact Publishers, 1995. Classic book on assertiveness.

Understanding Human Sexual Inadequacy, by Belliveau, Fred, and Richter, Lin, NYC: Bantam Books, 1970. Summary of the Masters and Johnson 1969 landmark work, Human Sexual Inadequacy, for the layman.

The Love Test, by Bessell, Harold, NYC: Warner Books, 1984. This book is currently out-of-print, but you may be able to rent it from your library. Please note that the author is Harold Bessell, Ph.D. There is a different book with the same name (different authors) that is in print now, but my favorite is this older one by Dr. Bessell. Excellent book for understanding love.

People Skills, by Bolton, Robert, NYC: Simon & Schuster, 1979. Communication skills.

An Analysis Of Human Sexual Response, by Brecher, Ruth, and Brecher, Edward. NYC: New American Library, 1966. Summary of the Masters and Johnson 1966 landmark work, Human Sexual Response, for the layman.

A Guide To Rational Living, 3rd revised edition, by Ellis, Albert, NYC: Wilshire Book Co., 1998. A classic work on how to change your thoughts to feel better, by the pioneer in cognitive-behavioral psychotherapy. Dr. Albert Ellis was one of the most influential people in 20th century psychology and psychotherapy and is still alive (and kicking!) and prolific today. This book has been in print for many years, and past editions have been titled New Guide To Rational Living.

Men Are From Mars, Women Are From Venus: A Practical Guide For Improving Communication And Getting What You Want In Your Relationships, by Gray, John, NYC: Harper Collins, 1992. Easy-to-understand book about differences in male-female communication and how to get along better.

Human Sexual Response, by Masters, William H., and Johnson, Virginia E., NYC: Little, Brown & Co., 1996. Reprint of their 1966 landmark work.

Loving Styles: A Guide For Increasing Intimacy, by Rosenman, Martin F., NYC: Prentice-Hall, 1979. Excellent book for understanding love.

Talking From 9 To 5: How Women's And Men's Conversational Styles Affect Who Gets Heard, Who Gets Credit, And What Gets Done At Work, by Tannen, Deborah, NYC: Avon Books, 1995. Excellent book by a pioneer in the field of male-female conversational differences.

Index

abuse
  drug 144, 202
  emotional 89, 97, 157, 167, 168
  physical 46, 50, 53, 97, 106, 157, 167, 168, 202
  sexual 56, 62, 167, 168, 202

abusive men 18, 19, 48, 50, 53-54, 172, 199, 202

accusations 66, 122, 173

actions 5, 7, 26, 34, 49, 65, 70, 83, 87, 111, 146, 150, 158

after-dinner drink 39

age 11, 26, 27, 28, 29, 30, 36, 44, 46, 48, 55, 62, 78, 84, 90, 91, 98, 133, 142-143, 151, 164, 184, 195, 198

agreement 46, 47, 86, 103, 110, 114, 115, 118, 119, 121, 122, 123, 124, 129, 145, 164, 168, 174, 177, 181, 203

alcohol 63, 64, 70, 132, 181, 182, 193, 202

Alcoholics Anonymous (AA) 202

alcoholism 21, 56, 89, 144, 166, 167

America Online 2, 3, 6, 27, 28, 40, 56, 62, 69, 123, 129, 137, 209, 210

AOL Keyword 3, 27, 42, 210

apologize 39, 66, 69, 70, 107, 108, 109, 118, 119

appropriate 36
  behavior 36, 37, 39, 40, 52, 57, 58, 108, 111, 121, 136, 143, 149, 171
  language 38, 114, 125, 165
  people 28, 91, 142
  time 120, 148, 149

assertiveness 105, 108, 110, 111, 112, 115-117

attention 19, 36, 37, 38, 44, 69, 83, 95, 99, 112, 121, 127, 129, 130, 134, 147, 161, 175, 193

attention deficit hyperactive disorder (ADHD) 165

attitude 15, 31, 45, 49, 61, 106, 110-113, 139, 159, 182, 198

balancing act 144

bars, dance clubs 21, 30, 37, 88, 167

bedtime 147, 148

being in love myth 15-16

biophysical 64, 65

birth control 34, 62, 67, 68, 71, 192
  condom 34, 67, 68, 71, 72, 192
  diaphragm 67
  IUD 67, 71
  morning-after pill 68
  the Pill 67

blame 65, 113, 116, 117, 150, 152, 158, 159, 160, 166, 167, 173, 175, 176, 177, 178, 179, 184, 205

breaking up 3, 4, 5, 12, 13, 171, 176, 177, 184, 209

career 12, 79-80, 84, 142, 143, 145, 149, 150, 151, 169, 174, 181

chance encounters 30

Chase's Calendar of Events 29

cheating 3, 5, 11, 12, 13, 41, 46, 50, 80, 98, 101, 132, 144, 157, 159, 161, 172, 179, 201, 202, 209
  sexual 136

chemistry 49, 50, 70

child abuse 56, 62, 136

childhood 85, 87, 109, 110

children 11, 14, 27, 37, 54, 79, 80, 83, 84, 95, 105, 112, 122, 126, 130, 134, 135, 142, 143, 149, 151, 152, 159, 164, 168, 171, 172, 173, 174, 175-176, 177, 179, 180, 182, 191, 194, 197, 199-201, 202

church 29, 195, 201

closure 123, 181-182, 184

commitment 2, 12, 51, 56, 70, 77-91

Other books from Paper Chase Press

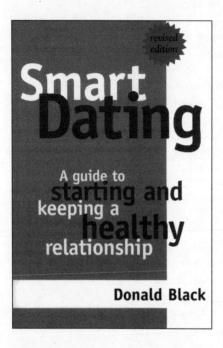

Smart Dating: Starting and Keeping a Healthy Relationship
Donald Black
paperback, 256 pages

Donald Black, bestselling author and creator of the successful Smart Dating workshops, has guided thousands through the sometimes challenging world of dating and relationships.

> *"Black doesn't believe games, tricks, or formulas lead to perfect relationships...*
> *He gives you the principles that work and points in the right direction."*
> – Tucson Citizen

> *"Smart Dating is a book every single person should keep on their night stand."*
> – The Norman Transcript

> *"Smart Dating is straightforward and easy-to-read...definitely will work*
> *to your advantage."*
> – Hugh B. Jones, President, Southeast Singles Assoc.

$14.95